THE ORIGIN OF THE FAMILY, PRIVATE PROPERTY AND THE STATE

THE ORIGIN OF THE FAMILY, PRIVATE PROPERTY AND THE STATE

In the Light of the Researches of Lewis H. Morgan

by FREDERICK ENGELS

With an Introduction and Notes by
ELEANOR BURKE LEACOCK
Professor of Anthroplogy, Polytechnic Institute of Brooklyn

INTERNATIONAL PUBLISHERS
New York

PUBLISHER'S NOTE

The text of *The Origin of the Family* is essentially the English translation by Alec West as published in 1942, but it has been revised against the German text as it appears in Karl Marx, Friedrich Engels *Werke,* Vol. 21 (Dietz Verlag, Berlin, 1962) and the spelling of names and other terms has been modernized. The text of "The Part Played by Labor in the Transition from Ape to Man" is based on the English translation as it appears in Marx and Engels, *Selected Works,* International Publishers, New York, 1968.

Library of Congress Catalog Card Number: 79-184309

ISBN: (cloth) 0-7178-0338-4; (paperback) 0-7178-0359-7

Printed in the United States of America

CONTENTS

METHOD OF ANNOTATION

All footnotes by Engels are indicated by the asterisk system; footnotes by the Editor are indicated by superior numbers. When both appear on the same page, Engels' notes are given first.

Bibliographical references are given in abbreviated form: the last name of the author, year of publication, and page number; the full data can be found in the Bibliography in back of the book. Bibliographical references within square brackets in the text have been added by the Editor; all other editorial inserts are also within square brackets.

Page numbers to quotations from *Origin of the Family* refer to the text in the present volume.

INTRODUCTION

by Eleanor Burke Leacock

IN THE *Origin of the Family, Private Property and the State,* Engels outlines the successive social and economic forms which underlay the broad sweep of early human history, as mankind gained increasing mastery over the sources of subsistence. The book was written after Marx's death, but was drawn from Marx's as well as Engels' own notes. It was based on the work, *Ancient Society,* which appeared in 1877 and was written by the anthropologist Lewis Henry Morgan, who, as Engels wrote in 1884, "in his own way . . . discovered afresh in America the materialistic conception of history discovered by Marx 40 years ago." The contribution Marx and Engels made to Morgan's work was to sharpen its theoretical implications, particularly with regard to the emergence of classes and the state. Although Engels' book was written well before most of the now available material on primitive and early urban society had been amassed, the fundamentals of his outline for history have remained valid. Moreover, many issues raised by Morgan's and then Engels' work are still the subjects of lively debate among anthropologists, while the theoretical implications of these issues are still matters of concern to Marxist scholars generally.

Morgan described the evolution of society in some 560 pages. Engels' book is far shorter, summarizing Morgan's material and focusing sharply on the major differences between primitive society and "civilization" with its fully developed classes and political organization. The questions Engels deals with pertain to three major topics: (a) developmental stages in mankind's history, (b) the nature of primitive society with regard to property, rank, family forms and descent systems, and (c) the emergence of commodity production, economically based classes and the state. A fourth subject of importance to contemporary anthropological research and but briefly referred to by Engels involves primate social organization and its relevance for an insight into early man. Engels' separate but incomplete paper on the subject, "The Part Played by Labor in the Transition from Ape to Man," has been included in this volume as an appendix.

MORGAN'S ANCIENT SOCIETY

THE IDEA central to Morgan's *Ancient Society,* that human history could be defined in terms of successive "stages," was an old one hinted at in classical Greek and Chinese writings, and well established in 19th century thought. However, theorists have not always separated stages in the evolution of culture as a whole—the background for historical events—from historical sequences specific to a single area. The early 18th century Italian historian, Giovanni Battista Vico, proposed a theory of historical cycles which were cultural in nature in that they comprised both institutional and ideological components of society. However they were tied too closely to European history to qualify as "evolutionary." According to Vico's proposal, the "divine" stage represented by early Greece gave way to the "heroic" of classical times, which was superseded by the "stage of man" in later Greece and in the Mediterranean world. The cycle was repeated in northern Europe, with the "divine" Dark Ages and the "heroic" Medieval, leading to the 18th century "stage of man." In content, Vico's periods were suggestive of Comte's later sequence in the development of knowledge from "theological," through "metaphysical," to "scientific."

The first four stages of human history proposed by Condorcet at the end of the 18th century were fully cultural. The first was characterized by hunting and fishing, the second by herding, the third by tilling of the soil, and the fourth by commerce, science and philosophy. Condorcet's later periods, however, were more specific to European history. They were marked by the decline of Rome, the Crusades, the invention of printing, the Protestant Revolt, and the establishment of the French Republic. In the 1850s, the pioneer anthropologist Gustave Klemm, who collated ethnographic materials on societies around the world, projected an outline of man's development from nomadic, egalitarian hunting society ("savagery"), through settled agricultural society organized politically and in great part dominated by religious institutions ("tameness"), to the civilizations of the classical Arabic, Greek, Persian and Roman worlds ("freedom").

The extent to which Morgan was directly acquainted with writings such as these is not clear, but in any case, his initial interest was not in tracing the major periods of cultural development. Instead, the theory of history embodied in *Ancient Society* grew out of questions raised by his empirical researches. Morgan's discovery of what seemed to be an unusual system of naming kinsmen used by the Iroquois Indians in his native state of New York led him to unearth the fact that similar systems existed independently thousands of miles away. This set him to collecting information on kinship systems among other American Indians, to which he added material from around the world by writing to missionaries, traders and government agents.

The result was data on a bewildering variety of terminologies used for naming relatives in many different societies. Morgan's first attempt to reduce his material to some order was beset with difficulties and was declared unsatisfactory by the publisher to whom he presented his manuscript. As a result, Morgan worked through to a theory of sequential stages in marriage represented by differing terminological systems, a theory he propounded in his *Systems of Consanguinity and Affinity of the Human Family,* published in 1871. The assumption upon which his theory was based, that kin terms represent actual or possible *biological* relationships, has been superseded by the understanding that the literal biological meaning of terms are often secondary to their *social* implications. However, Morgan's work was of tremendous importance not only to the formulation of problems in the comparative study of social institutions, but also in setting Morgan on the track that was to result, near the end of his life, in the publication of *Ancient Society*. The question posed by his study of kinship systems stayed with him. What had been the sequence of institutional forms in man's early history? For Morgan, this problem raised a more fundamental issue. What was the basis for the emergence of new and successive social forms?

Morgan found the answer to this question in the Darwinian interpretation of biological evolution. Morgan was familiar with and very much interested in Herbert Spencer's writings on social evolution in which Spencer spoke about the growing complexity and increasing specialization and differentiation of function in social institutions. However, it was not until Darwin seized upon the Spencerian concept of functional *adaptation* and interpreted it as the pivotal mechanism whereby successively "higher" biological forms had evolved that Morgan found the clue he had been seeking.

Morgan had remained dubious about the hypothesis of human evolution until he met and talked with Darwin when on a European tour. After this meeting, he wrote that he was compelled to accept the "conclusion that man commenced at the bottom of the scale and worked himself up to his present status," and that the "struggle for existence" was involved. (Like Darwin, Morgan understood the term to connote a process of active adaptation, rather than the "aggressiveness" emphasized by so-called "social Darwinism.") Morgan stated in a letter at that time, "I think that the real epochs of progress are connected with the arts of subsistence which includes the Darwinian idea of the 'struggle for existence'" (Resek, 1960: 99, 136-37). In his opening sentence to *Ancient Society,* he wrote that the process whereby man "worked himself up" was "through the slow accumulations of experimental knowledge," that is, through inventions and discoveries—the human counterpart to the physical adaptations of the lower species.

"As it is undeniable that portions of the human family have existed in a state of savagery," Morgan continued, "other portions in a state of barbarism, and still other portions in a state of civilization, it seems equally so that these three distinct conditions are connected with each other in a natural as well as a necessary sequence of progress." He stated that it was the "successive arts of subsistence which arose at long intervals" which were responsible for the development of the three major stages. He proposed parallel sequences in the history of social, economic and political institutions. By implication, they were closely related to the economic sequence, although Morgan achieves this integration only in relation to the transition from "barbarism" to "civilization."

Here, then, was the discussion of early social and economic forms which Marx and Engels needed to supplement their own historical inquiries. In the first full joint statement of their dialectical materialist theory of history presented in *The German Ideology* in 1846, Marx and Engels had outlined "various stages of development in the division of labor." Since "the existing stage in the division of labor determines also the relations of individuals to one another with reference to the material, instrument, and product of labor," these stages are "just so many different forms of ownership." Early "tribal" ownership gave way to "ancient, communal and State ownership," which in turn was superseded by the third major form of pre-capitalist ownership, "feudal or estate-property" (Marx and Engels, 1970: 43-45). In another manuscript, completed some 11 or 12 years later, Marx speculated about the various kinds of relationships which obtained in societies in which "the labourer is an owner and the owner labours," and about the processes whereby these relations were later dissolved or transformed (Marx, 1965: 96). His emphasis, however, was on the classical societies of the Mediterranean and Oriental worlds, and on early societies of northern Europe. What Morgan supplied was data which opened up to view developments within the enormously long period represented by "tribal" ownership, as well as material that illuminated the steps whereby private property emerged.

And a wealth of data there was. Morgan always stayed close to the details of specific institutional forms and events. He avoided a common 19th century practice of documenting a theory with items pulled out of their cultural context. Instead he built his exposition on detailed analyses of whole cultures: Australian, Iroquois, Aztec, Greek and Roman. The commonly echoed accusation that Morgan projected a grand but mechanical scheme into which he pigeonholed different cultures could only be made by those who have read no further than the first few pages of *Ancient Society.* Morgan's focus was on the details of social arrangements in specific societies, on the implications of historical events, on problems raised by new inventions, and on steps whereby new relations emerge. Indeed, his shortcomings lay where it came to carrying through his theoretical hunches and formulating them with consistency. His major discovery was profound and the wealth of insights gained by reading his book is enormous. But he was, and remained essentially, the pragmatic scholar, insightful, but not committed to theory. He was certainly no dialectician and was not consistent in his materialism. It fell to Engels in *Origin* to pinpoint the critical issues raised by Morgan's work, to define sharply the distinguishing features of the three major stages in early history, to clarify the relations between the subsistence base and socio-political organization in primitive and "civilized" societies, and to focus on the critical steps in the emergence of class relations and the state.

THE CONCEPT OF STAGES

THE CATEGORIZATION of successive levels in the integration of matter, as a step toward understanding, is taken more for granted in the natural than in the social sciences. To a greater extent than the social sciences, the natural sciences have been able to disentangle themselves from a metaphysical attempt to put the "things" of this world in their rightful places and the disillusionment that follows when this does not work. For example, it is taken for granted that the existence of forms intermediate between plants and animals does not invalidate the categories "plant" and "animal" but illuminates the mechanisms that were operative in the development of the latter from the former. Discovering that a whale is not a fish deepens the understanding of mammalian processes. Rather than calling into question the category of "fish," the discovery indicates the functional level more basic to the category than living in the sea. The fact that some hunting, gathering and fishing societies have achieved institutional forms generally found only with the development of agriculture does not invalidate the significance of distinguishing between food gathering and food production. Instead an examination of such societies deepens the understanding of why the distinction is significant and clarifies some of the reasons why on the whole there are rather marked differences in social organization between hunter-gatherers and simple agriculturists.

It used to be commonplace in American anthropology, following the anti-evolutionary empiricism associated with the name of Franz Boas, to question Morgan's sequence of stages since many groups, including some Morgan gave as instances, do not really "fit" into a particular stage. However, Morgan himself knew the limits of his scheme, which he offered as "convenient and useful," but "provisional." He wrote that he would have liked to base his major divisions on the "successive arts of subsistence," which he saw as: (1) subsistence on available fruits and roots; (2) addition of fish with the use of fire, and slow addition of meat as a permanent part of the diet, particularly after the invention of the bow and arrow; (3) dependence on cultivated cereals and plants; (4) dependence on meat and milk of domesticated animals; and (5) "unlimited subsistence" through the improvement of agricultural techniques, notably through harnessing the plow to domesticated animals. However, he found himself unable to relate each new technique satisfactorily to a social stage. His aim was perhaps for too precise a fit, and he was, after all, working with limited data. "Investigation has not been carried far enough in this direction to yield the necessary information," he wrote, so that he had to fall back on "such other inventions or discoveries as will afford sufficient tests of progress to characterize the commencement of successive ethnical periods." These were: fish subsistence and the knowledge of fire (marking the transition from the primeval period of lower savagery to that of middle savagery), the bow and arrow (initiating upper savagery), pottery (lower barbarism), domestication of animals and the use of irrigation in agriculture (middle barbarism), iron (upper barbarism), and the alphabet and writing (civilization).[1]

Engels accepted Morgan's criteria, but he clarified and emphasized the major distinction between the periods of so-called "savagery" and "barbarism," each taken as a whole. The former, he wrote, was "the period in which man's appropriation of products in their natural stage predominates," and the latter was "the period during which man learns to breed domestic animals and to practice agriculture, and acquires methods of increasing the supply of natural products by human activity." This distinction is now commonly phrased by anthropologists as that between food *gathering* and food *production*. With civilization, Engels wrote, "man learns a more advanced application of work to the products of nature." It is "the period of industry proper and of art." After elaborating

---

1. The accumulation of evidence indicates that fishing was in fact not that early in the history of man (*see* chapter by Washburn and Lancaster in Lee and DeVore, 1968: 294). Morgan discusses his stages and the criteria for them in Chapters 1 and 2 of *Ancient Society*. I have elsewhere discussed in some detail the problems which they involve (Morgan, 1963: I: xi-xv).

on Morgan's interpretation and adding material on early Germanic and Celtic society in his discussion on the emergence of classes, private property and the state, Engels stated: "civilization is, therefore . . . the stage of development in society at which the division of labor, the exchange between individuals arising from it, and the commodity production which combines them both come to their full growth and revolutionize the whole of previous society" (233).

A rather simple but often overlooked confusion has plagued subsequent discussions of historical "stages." There is a common failure to distinguish between the definition of stages as a necessary preliminary step to asking meaningful questions about a given period, institution or event, and stages seen as themselves the answers. "Stages" define major alternatives in the structure of productive relations; they afford a conceptual framework for the study of historical process. To place a society in a central or transitional position in relation to one or more stages is a necessary preliminary step to inquiry, not a straitjacket that limits it.[2]

POLITICAL IMPLICATIONS OF EVOLUTIONARY THEORY

THE SOLUTION of theoretical problems basic to the science of society does not, of course, follow smoothly from the accumulation of scholarly time and effort. Social science has always been vexed by the political implications of one or another theory, and evolutionary assumptions have always aroused subjective and ambivalent

2. For discussions of the relation between technological innovations and the emergence of new economic relations that inaugurate new "stages" of historical development, see Childe, 1944, and Semenov, 1965. Semenov writes: "The major shortcoming of Morgan's periodization lies in the fact that it was not a periodization of the history of society itself. The development of productive forces is certainly the basis for the development of society, but does not coincide with it. Even major turning points in the evolution of productive forces do not lead automatically or at once to a change in the relationships of production and, consequently, in all other social relationships. As for less significant changes, they may, by merely accumulating, lead to changes in social relationships, first in the economic and then in the ideological field. Therefore it is impossible to create a true periodization of the history of society if we take as the criterion for the onset of the new state in its evolution the appearance of some one change, even a major one, in the development of the productive forces."

responses. Morgan himself was no radical, but neither was he among those who used inferences drawn from past history merely to justify the social institutions of his day. He did share the belief of 19th century liberal Americans that the United States had left the class system behind in Europe and was capable of rational and continued improvement, but he did not see such progress as inevitable. He was concerned about the "property career" upon which society seemed bent, and the threat it represented. Property had become an unmanageable power, he stated, which could destroy society unless checked. The powerful passage in which he projected his view of the future as "a revival, in a higher form, of the liberty, equality and fraternity of the ancient *gentes,*" is quoted by Engels as the closure to *Origin.*

Engels sharpened the implications of the comparison Morgan drew between primitive communal and class society, using it as an argument for socialism. Therefore, both Morgan's and Engels' work have had checkered careers, and opinions about them have shifted as the political atmosphere has changed. Only in recent years has renewed critical review and debate on some problems of evolutionary theory been seriously engaged in by Soviet scholars (*Soviet Studies in History,* 1966). In western academic circles second-hand knowledge of (or assumptions about) Marxist ideas are legion, but Marx's and Engels' works are all too seldom read. The usual practice is to set up as Marxist theory the straw man of economic determinism and then to knock it down. When more inquisitive students read some of Marx's and Engels' works, they commonly end up distorting the ideas they have gleaned therefrom, as they search for modes of discourse acceptable for the publications which are the means of successful entry into the academic brotherhood. Morgan's *Ancient Society* too is seldom read, and when mentioned in college classes is often distorted and rejected out-of-hand. Further confusions arise when well-meaning scholars employ the slightly more acceptable name of Morgan as a euphemism for Marx (or Engels), and the assumption grows that their thinking was identical.

After the Russian revolution lent support to Marx's assumption of an impending socialist "stage" of history, a plethora of studies anxiously attempted to demonstrate that the institutions of class, private property, the monogamous family as the economic unit, and even the state itself could be found in all levels of human society, and that there was basically no predictable "order" to human history. In the United States such studies were carried out in the tradition of the "historical" school associated with the name of Franz Boas that emphasized the uniqueness of each people's individual history. In England they were conducted under the rubric of "functionalism" that decried what was considered to be a hopeless attempt to trace institutional origins and turned to "synchronic" analyses of how the various institutions in any given society interrelated.

Battles among adherents of the "historical" and "functionalist" schools, and between them and the remaining champions of "evolutionism," often waged hot and heavy. Among the majority of anthropologists, however, a scarcely formulated, pragmatic eclecticism prevailed. Rapidly accumulating material on primitive societies raised unending detailed problems that absorbed people's interests and enabled them to avoid many broader theoretical questions and their troublesome implications. In the long run, the eclecticism was perhaps not such a serious drawback. The fact of the matter is that only through a narrow approach can "evolutionism," "functionalism," and "historicism" be placed in opposition. Functional concerns are essential to a fully conceived evolutionary theory. The hypothesis of the basic relation between economic and other institutions is itself "functional." "Evolutionary" theory assumes economic factors to be primary, but it certainly does not deny the continual internal adjustments that take place among the various parts of a social system. Further, "evolution" cannot be studied apart from specific histories, of which it is the theoretical or explanatory element. Historical events can be recounted, but they cannot be *understood* without recourse to a broader theory such as that supplied by "evolutionism."

Criticisms of evolutionary theory have characteristically emphasized the infinite variability of specific lifeways found around the world, each the historical end product of unique events and influences. Yet the accumulation of data has not merely documented diversity. Archaeological researches have yielded an undeniable picture of mankind's development from "savage" hunters to "barbarian" agriculturalists and finally to the "civilizations" of the Ancient East, as made explicit by the British scholar V. Gordon Childe.[3] Meanwhile, ethnographic data have made it increasingly clear that fundamental distinctions among societies at different productive levels underlie the variations among individual cultures. Leslie White (1945, 1947) long the foremost voice of the "evolutionist" minority, argued this point in a series of debates with Robert Lowie (1946), his most prolific antagonist.[4]

At the same time as archaeological and ethnological materials were contributing to an evolutionary view of world history, the push of world events was forcing a changed intellectual climate. In the West, the floundering of social science in the face of pressing social issues and the growing disenchantment with positivist or purely pragmatic inquiry has caused a renewed interest in theory in general, and in Marxist theory in particular. In the socialist world, the tremendous theoretical and practical problems posed by the transition from socialism to communism, which had often been seen as too automatic a process of planned change, has shown how serious an obstacle a doctrinaire approach to Marxist theory can be, and how pressing is the need for its growth and expansion. Meanwhile, the former "primitive peoples" studied by anthropologists are emerging as new nations that are seeking social and economic forms in keeping with both industrial technology and

3. Childe (1935, 1969) summarizes the results of archaeological research with regard to the prehistory of Europe and the Middle East, and traces the initial development of urban civilization in the latter area in the late fifth millenium B.C., as well as the much later developments in the Mediterranean world that are discussed by Morgan and Engels. Childe retains the terms "savagery" and "barbarism" that have fallen out of use on the whole, due to their pejorative connotations. Contemporary terminologies generally refer instead to major productive techniques, such as "food gathering" ("savagery") and "food producing" ("barbarism"). Food gatherers are usually referred to as "hunters and gatherers" (although they also fish). Food producers are divided into an initial "horticultural" phase, also called "hoe agriculture," "slash and burn agriculture," or "swidden agriculture," and a more developed agricultural phase involving the use of the plow and/or systematic fertilization and/or irrigation. For a recent discussion of archaeological levels, see Robert J. Braidwood, "Levels in Prehistory: A Model for the Consideration of the Evidence," in Tax, 1960.

4. For Robert Lowie's discussion of Morgan, see *The History of Ethnological Theory*, 1939. Leslie A. White's major works are *The Science of Culture*, 1949 and *The Evolution of Culture*, 1959

their own traditions. This development renders it ridiculous to treat such societies as isolated self-contained enclaves that can be described without a theory of economic effects on social and political structures.

All of this has contributed to the growth of an active and influential "neo-evolutionary" wing of American anthropology, and a wide acceptance of the fact that broad evolutionary trends have given form to mankind's history.[5] The result, however, has not been entirely salutary. "Evolution" has been and continues to be many things to many people. The conscious application of dialectics to a materialistic view of history is a far cry from the strong current of economic determinism characteristic of contemporary evolutionism in the United States.[6] Nor have issues been clarified by the popular but theoretically flabby formula of "multilinear" evolution, a supposed correction to the straw man of "unilinear evolution" ascribed to Morgan (and by implication Marx and Engels). However, the stage has at least been set for the redefinition and reexamination of issues. Some scholars have given serious consideration to arguments against Marxist hypotheses, and, rather than simply reasserting earlier arguments, they have contributed new data and insights to the interpretation of history.

PRIMITIVE COMMUNISM

MAJOR SUBJECTS for debate raised by the Boasian school of anthropology have pertained to the nature and existence of a primitive collective. Morgan had referred to the "liberty, equality and fraternity of the ancient *gentes*" and had written that the "passion" for the possession of property did not exist in the early stages of society. In defining the relations of production that obtained in such societies, Engels wrote that they were "essentially collective," and that "consumption proceeded by direct distribution of the products within larger or smaller communistic communities" (233).

5. General statements of contemporary evolutionary theory from somewhat different points of view, in addition to the works of Childe and White already cited, are those of Steward, 1955, and Sahlins and Service, 1960.

6. This view has been put forth most explicitly by Harris, 1968a. Harris writes (1968b: 519) that "Hegel's notion of dialectics" was a "crippling heritage" from which "Marxism has never recovered."

The sole division of labor was by sex, and society was not as yet divided into classes of exploiters and exploited. Lands were held in common and tools and utensils were owned directly by those who used them. Political organization, continued Engels, did not exist apart from the social group. By comparison with the political leader who poses "as something outside and above" the society, the gentile chief "stands in the midst of society" (230). The participation of all adults in public affairs was taken for granted; to ask an American Indian whether it was his "right" or his "duty" to take on social responsibilities would seem as absurd, Engels wrote, as to question "whether it was a right or a duty to sleep, eat, or hunt" (217).

As supposedly definitive proof that a stage of primitive communism could not in fact be demonstrated, the work of Frank G. Speck posited that the Montagnais Indians, hunters of the Labrador Peninsula, divided their lands into tracts or "hunting grounds," which Speck stated were individually owned and were passed down from father to son. Early records for the area, Speck argued, (1926; and Eiseley, 1939) indicate that this had been the case prior to the penetration of Europeans into the New World, and a review of literature on other hunting peoples suggested to him that similar forms of land ownership were worldwide and ancient. This supposed finding became a standard reference to be found in anthropological texts and journals. Speck and Eiseley wrote that such discoveries "must inevitably be troubling to those who, like Morgan, and many present-day Russians, would see the culture of the lower hunters as representing a stage prior to the development of the institution of individualized property" (1942: 238).

However, the assumption that privately held hunting tracts were aboriginal was questioned by the Canadian anthropologist Diamond Jenness (1935: 4-41; 1937:44) on the basis of his work among the Ojibwa and the Sekani Indians, and by Julian Steward (1941: 501), who found evidence of their late development among the Carrier. Detailed archival and field research by the present author (Leacock, 1954) among the same Indians with whom Speck had worked showed that the hunting-ground system had indeed developed as a result of the fur trade, and further, that it did not involve true land ownership. One could not trap near another's line, but anyone could hunt game animals, could fish, or could gather wood, berries or birchbark on another's grounds *as long as these products of the land were for use, and not for sale*. A man in need of food when in another's trapping area could even kill beaver, a most important fur-bearing animal, but he could not kill one in order to sell the fur. An account by Father Le Jeune, a Jesuit missionary who wintered with a group of Montagnais during the year 1632-33, reveals the aboriginal practices of the Indians with regard to land. In the summer relatively large groups would come together at lake shores and river mouths, and each fall they would break up into small family bands which would ascend the rivers into the interior and scatter widely over the countryside so as not to starve each other by overcrowding any one area. However, they would remain sufficiently in touch to be able to turn to one another for help should it be necessary (Leacock, 1954: 14-15).[7]

Another argument against the existence of a primitive communal stage in human history arose from the fact that various rank and status differentiations are found in societies loosely designated as "primitive." In some cases there are divisions into social groupings the names of which were translated by early observers as "nobles," "commoners," and "slaves." Two points need clarification here. First, a distinction must be made between social ranking of various sorts and a system of classes based on differential relations to the basic sources of subsistence and production; rank *per se* does not indicate the existence of classes. As Fried puts it, in "rank societies" marks of prestige are not "used to acquire food or productive resources." They do not "convey any privileged claim to the strategic resources on which a society is based. Ranking can and does exist in the absence of stratification" (1967:110).[8]

Second, the term "primitive" has been applied very loosely.

7. The full argument and related issues are summarized by Julia Averkieva in "Problems of Property in Contemporary American Ethnography," 1962; and by Harold Hickerson in "Some Implications of the Theory of Particularity, or 'Atomism,' of Northern Algonkians," 1967.
8. This point is elaborated upon and documented in detail by Fried, 1967. See also: Service, 1962, although I differ with Service on the relative roles of men and women in hunting society (Leacock, 1969); Sahlins, "Political Power and the Economy in Primitive Society," in Dole and Carneiro, 1960; and Leacock, 1958a.

Many societies in West Africa, Mexico and the Andean area, and Polynesia that are often designated as "primitive" are far away indeed from hunting-gathering peoples and horticulturalists. Although it is difficult to define with certainty the precise extent to which there had emerged in these areas a sizeable class that was "non-free" in the sense of being alienated from traditional rights to land and to the products of their labor, yet it is clear that in many cases peoples were close to or beyond the threshold of class organization and political statehood. In pointing out the fact that Montezuma was not the emperor he had been called by the Spanish, Morgan overstated the case for Aztec egalitarianism (1876). He also grossly underestimated the complexity of Hawaiian society. Since the Hawaiians lacked pottery, they fell into his stage of "savagery" although wooden bowls and coconut shells served very well in this highly productive agricultural economy. Finally, Morgan dismissed African society as "in an ethnical chaos of savagery and barbarism" in an inexcusably offhand manner, and accorded Africa no further attention. Engels drew on original sources in his chapters on the German state, and was familiar with material on classical Mediterranean and Asian societies, but with few exceptions (Australia was one) he was not familiar with primary sources on non-Eurasian peoples and did not question Morgan's evaluation of them. Thus any implication that Engels' characterization of primitive communism should apply to all non-Eurasian peoples is erroneous; it simply does not. In fact, the attempt to reconstruct the complex socio-economic and political forms that obtained in parts of West Africa, Polynesia, Mexico, and the Andes prior to European expansion has absorbed the attention of quite a few scholars who have been influenced by Marxist theory.[9]

A third challenge to the understanding that a pre-class stage in human history was characterized by an unquestioned cooperative-

9. For recent books synthesizing some of the materials on the areas, see: Adams, 1966; Davidson, 1959; Sahlins, 1958; Service, 1963; and Wolf, 1959. For articles, see Klein, 1969 and Murra, 1967. Murra's unpublished doctoral dissertation, 1956, was on *The Economic Organization of the Inca State.* In another unpublished doctoral dissertation, Armstrong, 1950, examines the relations between the economy and political organization in five African societies.

ness was posed by the "culture and personality" school of anthropology associated with the names of Ruth Benedict and Margaret Mead. (A third pioneer in this area, Edward Sapir, was less prolific a writer and not popularly known). The establishment, during the 1920s and 1930s, of a subfield within anthropology devoted to interpreting the relation between the individual and his culture was in keeping with general intellectual developments. Emile Durkheim had emphasized the influence of the group on the shaping of individual goals; and the founders of social psychology, Charles Horton Cooley and George Herbert Mead, had pinpointed as an important area for study the socialization process whereby growing infants develop a sense of identity and purpose in interaction with their social milieu. Soon Sigmund Freud's insight into the role of symbolism in human action and into the sources of irrationality in man's interpretation of reality afforded a clue to processes whereby people, in trying to "make sense" out of their experiences, project rationales or explanations that may become incorporated into institutionalized ideologies. However, these various endeavors developed implicitly, if not explicitly, not as extensions of Marxist materialism, but as alternatives. Therefore, the direction of their elaboration was toward a psychobiological determination of social forms, or a closed-circle functionalist type of description that stressed the intermeshing of individual behavior and social forms and avoided problems having to do with fundamental determinates and sources of change.

Ruth Benedict was interested in the way institutional forms and individually held goals mesh in different configurations or "patterns" from one culture to another. In her influential book, *Patterns of Culture,* she stressed the variability of man's cultures and the fact that each unique way of life had to be understood in its own terms, free from the biases of a Western viewpoint. However, she emphasized the psychological patterning of motivations to the exclusion of the socio-economic structure of interaction, and she stressed and exaggerated the unique and often the bizarre, thereby underplaying cross-cultural commonalities and overriding the theory that the relations obtaining among a people as they produced and distributed the means of their livelihood would ramify through all other aspects of their life. The assumption that the forces and relations of production would be of no greater relevance to culture patterns than other social dimensions was shared to a greater or lesser extent by other students of the "ethos" or "value-attitude system" of various cultures, and of the "basic or social personality" or "national character" supposedly common to all members of a culture.[10]

The extreme relativism which characterized the culture and personality school is exemplified by the book, *Cooperation and Competition Among Primitive Peoples,* a collection of papers on different peoples edited by Margaret Mead (1937). One might expect from the title an exploration of ways in which cooperative and competitive themes can be interwoven in hunting-gathering and horticultural societies where the underlying structure necessitates a fundamental cooperation, and how these begin to change when improvements in agricultural techniques lay the basis for economic inequalities. Instead, as the organizer of the book, Mead assumed a random distribution of cooperation or competition throughout early society, which is precisely what most (not all) of the authors found, working as they did with limited materials, limited theoretical orientations, and societies long adapted to the effects of European expansion.

One chapter in particular, that by Jeanette Mirsky on the Eskimo of Greenland, ties in with a line of argument parallel to that of Frank Speck on individually owned land among the Northeast Algonkians. The Eskimo come through as a highly competitive people, a picture thoroughly demolished in a critical response by Hughes (1958). Another chapter in Mead's book, "The Ojibwa"

10. For a full discussion of Benedict, and the "culture and personality" school generally, from a materialistic (albeit anti-dialectical) viewpoint, see Harris, 1968a: Chapters 15-17. Kardiner (1939, 1945), a Freudian analyst who worked with Linton and other anthropologists, sought commonalities in relations between "primary institutions" or "maintenance systems" and aspects of personality and ideology. The implications of this work have been carried further and subjected to statistical analysis by Whiting, 1953, and his co-workers. However, these scholars make no clear distinction between the more determinate aspects of socio-economic structure and its other dimensions; essentially they do not break out of a "psychological reductionist" framework whereby child-training practices to do with weaning, toilet training and the like become the major determinants of institutional forms through their effects on adult personality. For further discussion of limitations in "culture and personality" theory see Leacock, 1971: Introduction.

by Ruth Landes presents a similarly competitive picture of these Algonkian peoples who live in the area north of the Great Lakes. The influence of fur-trapping and trading upon life in the north woods has already been mentioned, but there are additional issues involved in the interpretations of Mirsky, Landes, and others who share the same views. Too often, the physical separation of hunting people who may scatter widely over an area in certain seasons is equated with "separatism" or "social atomism," without recognition of the mutual interdependence that is nonetheless maintained. Furthermore, and particularly in the case of the Eskimo, there is an implied equation of "individualism" with "competition" and little awareness of the way in which a fully cooperative society can enable the expression of individuality. Something of a Freudian assumption is commonly made, that man innately possesses some essential measure of aggression that must be expressed through competition, and that cooperativeness demands a bland, muted type of personality (as is often the case, apparently, in religious communities that adhere to a communal ethic in conflict with the competitive mores of the surrounding society). However, from my own field work experience among the Naskapi hunters of Labrador, it was beautiful to see the latitude allowed for personal idiosyncracies.[11]

11. More than I myself expected, I realized, when distributing the molasses I had been asked to buy for everyone in camp to make some beer. It was illegal to sell it to an Indian, but one of the men in the band was mildly alcoholic and often managed to get some and have his private drunk on home brew. At these times he would immobilize the camp, for he had to be watched constantly to keep him from hurting himself, or from such things as bumping into a tent and accidentally setting it afire against the stove. He was such a nuisance when drunk that I assumed there would be tacit agreement that he should not have any of the molasses. But no, "Where's Charlie's?" was asked although he was not there at the time. Charlie was not even an old-timer in the band, but had come from western Labrador. For further discussion of these points in relation to Labrador hunters, see Leacock, 1958 and 1964. For an excellent autobiographical account of an Eskimo woman who left her traditional Eskimo culture to become involved in our own, see Washburne, 1959. For full accounts of life among hunting peoples of Africa, see Thomas, 1959, and Turnbull, 1968. For a further illustration of the "atomistic" view of Canadian hunters, see Barnouw, 1961. The alternative view is presented by Hickerson, 1962, as well as in review articles by Averkieva, 1962, and Hickerson, 1967. The assumption that cooperativeness automatically entails a muting of individu-

The fact that communism preceded the emergence of classes in human history should not be taken to mean, in some Rousseauesque fashion, that man has lost a utopia. The limited technology available to hunter-gatherers of "upper savagery" (the category which would include all mankind after Homo sapiens emerged in the late Pleistocene), and to the horticulturalists of "lower barbarism" meant that life was rigorous and relatively restricted. Yet the glimpses into the quality of interpersonal relations that we are afforded from accounts of North American Indians and peoples in the rest of the world before they had experienced the alienation from the produce of their labor, and the divisiveness of being placed in fundamental competition with their fellow men (whether as exploiters, exploited, or "hangers-on,") do indeed make us somewhat envious. Behind the enormous variety of environmental adaptations and cultural embroideries which can be observed among these peoples, there did seem to be an underlying sense of self-respect and an ability to draw great satisfaction from work and personal relations. Perhaps most bitter to industrial man is the divisiveness which permeates relationships with those most dear, and the enmity between husbands and wives, parents and children. It is to the subject of the family in the primitive collective by comparison with that of class-based industrial society that we turn next.

KINSHIP AND MARRIAGE IN PRIMITIVE SOCIETY

THE GROUPING of fellow tribesmen into kin of various categories, some of whom one can marry and some of whom one cannot, is central to the social organization of most primitive peoples. Morgan assumed that the terms used for designating these different categories of kin represented possible biological relationships that derived from different forms of marriage. For instance, he argued

---

ality is seemingly illustrated by the much studied Pueblo Indians of the American Southwest, where someone who is too ambitious or becomes too successful is liable to be accused of witchcraft. Assumptions such as this ignore history. The Pueblo Indians have fought for over four centuries to maintain their autonomy and their cooperative society; this has not been without its toll. Moreover, in the 16th century, the Spanish introduced the practice of killing rebellious Indians as witches. For an overview of changing Indian society, see Leacock and Lurie, 1971: Introduction.

that the not uncommon use of one term for one's father, his brothers and certain male cousins stemmed from a time when any of the men called father could have cohabited with one's mother (or any of her sisters and certain female cousins designated by a "mother" term). On the basis of such reasoning, and after examining some 80 systems of kin terminology from around the world, Morgan inferred that four successive forms of the family had followed an original promiscuity.

The first form of the family postulated by Morgan was the "consanguine family," or the marriage of brothers, sisters and cousins that resulted from the prohibition of intercourse between fathers and daughters, and between mothers and sons. As evidence of this form, Morgan cited the Hawaiian system of kin nomenclature, whereby all the children of brothers and sisters call one another brother and sister. The second form, the "punaluan family," followed from the prohibition of intercourse between siblings. The third, the "pairing family," resulted from the extension of the incest group to include collateral brothers and sisters, and finally, with civilization, monogamy arose.

The problem with Morgan's formulation is not so much his sequence of progressive limitations in marriageable partners (although generational difference is seldom an issue among contemporary hunter-gatherers), as the assumptions he makes about both the function of kinship terminologies and the nature of incest taboos. Discussions about primeval forms of society will doubtless remain in large part conjectural, although the study of primatology is suggestive in revealing a wide variety of mating patterns among those closest relatives of man who were in the line that did *not* become human; and archaeology is beginning to yield clues to the nature of man's early societies, albeit highly scattered and indirect. It is quite another question, however, to assume that kinship terminologies of contemporary peoples afford direct evidence of formerly existing biological relations. To take Morgan's case of Hawaii, his reference to occasional brother-sister marriage, in conjunction with the grouping of siblings with cousins of several degrees, reveals nothing about early institutions. Polynesia, as has been pointed out, does not represent a "savage" level, but is comprised of complex "barbarian" societies. Brother-sister marriages occur only among the highest ranks in Hawaii, and their purpose is to preserve the purity of the royal line as did brother-sister marriages among the Pharaohs of Egypt. In the rest of Polynesia such marriages were prohibited, although Linton cites cousin marriage to be "favored as a means of keeping property in the family"—an indication of the advanced state of Polynesian economy (1926: 152).

Morgan attributed the limitation of the marriage group to the more or less instinctive restriction of inbreeding, which he saw as operating, according to the principle of natural selection, to the advantage of the tribes practicing it. Engels realized that incest was an "invention," and that primitive conceptions of incest are "totally different from ours and frequently in direct contradiction to them." However, he did not follow through on the implications of this point and explore possible factors which might explain such differences, but referred instead to an "obscure impulse" or "urge" against inbreeding that "asserts" itself "instinctively" (108, 109, 111). The fact is that the widespread custom of "exogamy," or marrying *out* of one's kin group, often resulted in a specialized form of *inbreeding*. When kin is counted on one side only, certain cousins are outside one's kin group and are not only eligible as marriage partners, but are often preferred. To marry one's "cross-cousin," the child of one's father's sister or of one's mother's brother, both cements already close ties and binds a person to another kin group. The cementing of such ties may be perceived as more important than avoidance of incest *per se*. When Margaret Mead asked her Arapesh informants why they disapproved of sexual relations with a sister, she received the reply: "What is the matter with you? Sleep with your sister? But don't you want a brother-in-law? With whom will you garden, with whom will you hunt, with whom will you visit" (1937:34)?

Rather than categorizing people one formerly might have married, kinship systems reveal presently or but recently past social and economic relationships. Engels recognized this to some extent when he stated that "The names of father, child, brother, sister are no mere complimentary forms of address; they involve quite definite and very serious mutual obligations which make up an essential part of the social constitution of the peoples in question" (95).

However, his acceptance of Morgan's hypothesis on the limitation of inbreeding as the dynamic factor behind successive family forms led him to make some important mis-statements. "Natural selection," he wrote, "with its progressive exclusions from the marriage community, had accomplished its task; . . . Unless new, *social* forces came into play, there was no reason why a new form of family should arise from the single pair" (117; italics are his). In the Preface to the First Edition of *Origin,* he explicitly assumes an independent development of the family:

According to the materialistic conception, the determining factor in history is, in the final instance, the production and reproduction of the immediate essentials of life. This, again, is of a twofold character: on the one side, the production of the means of existence . . . on the other side, the propagation of the species. The social organization under which the people of a particular historical epoch and a particular country live is determined by both kinds of production; by the stage of development of labor on the one hand and of the family on the other (71).

The fact is, of course, that social forces were never new to mankind, as Engels points out in "The Part Played by Labor in the Transition From Ape to Man" when he develops the theme "that labor created man himself" (251). Moreover, the discovery of the enormously long period during which man was evolving, which the Australopithecine discoveries in South Africa have now stretched from a million years to twice that long (some estimates run even longer), has radically shifted perspectives on the relevance of near-contemporary peoples living at a simple technological level to an understanding of primeval man. The some two million years during which a lively, curious, sociable, chattering primate, endowed with an opposable thumb and stereoscopic vision, slowly learned to manipulate his environment and himself, and developed languages and cultural traditions as his own body developed, raise questions about social and sexual relationships that cannot be answered by simple reference to near-contemporary kinship terminologies. On the basis of hunting-gathering societies, we can draw conclusions about the character of fundamental relationships at a technological level which has its historical roots in the cultures of the Upper Paleolithic a few tens of thousands of years ago when Homo sapiens emerged. However, our evidence from physical anthropology, archaeology and primatology about the earlier societies of pre-Homo sapiens man is slim and indirect. We can be certain that he must have lived in relatively small communal groups, but around what specific nexus of relations these groups were organized, how they articulated with other groups or what the range of variablility was both over time and in different areas remain questions for further debate.[12]

THE EMERGENCE OF MONOGAMY AND THE SUBJUGATION OF WOMEN

THE PAGES in which Engels discusses early marriage forms are the most difficult in *Origin,* partly because kinship terminologies and practices are complicated and unfamiliar to the Western reader, and partly because confusions about biological and social forces obscure the significant parts of his discussion. However, Engels' fundamental theme is clear. He writes: "We ... have three principal forms of marriage which correspond broadly to the three principal stages of human development: for the period of savagery, group marriage; for barbarism, pairing marriage; for civilization, monogamy. ... " Monogamy arises from a transitional stage of polygyny, "when men have female slaves at their command;" coupled with male supremacy, it is "supplemented by adultery and prostitution," and is from the beginning monogamy for the women only (138). Marriage was frankly polygynous throughout classical times, and covertly so thereafter.

The significant characteristic of monogamous marriage was its transformation of the nuclear family into the basic economic unit of society, within which a woman and her children became dependent upon an individual man. Arising in conjunction with exploitative class relations, this transformation resulted in the oppression of women that has persisted to the present day. As corollary to, or symptomatic of this transformation, the reckoning of descent was changed from "mother right" (matrilineality) to "father right."

12. However, Soviet anthropologists take a more optimistic view of how justifiably one can come to conclusions about the transition from the society of early hominids to that of Homo sapiens on the basis of survivals into recent times of presumably ancient customs (*see* Semenov, 1964, and Averkieva, 1964).

In the field of anthropology, it is the last proposition, that matrilineality was prior to patrilineality in the history of mankind, which has received most attention. The rest of Engels' discussion has been virtually ignored, and it is unfortunate testimony to the status of women both within and without the field that detailed studies of women's status and role in primitive societies are so rare. Nonetheless, there is sufficient evidence at hand to support in its broad outlines Engels' argument that the position of women relative to men deteriorated with the advent of class society, as well as data to fill in many particulars of his thesis. Above all, however, there is crying need for further analysis of existing materials and for the collection of new data.

Let us first examine the point that marriage is essentially different in hunting-gathering ("savage") and horticultural ("barbarian") societies on the one hand, and class society ("civilization") on the other, and that there is a further distinction between the freer "group marriage" of hunter-gatherers and its successor, "pairing marriage." The term "group marriage" unfortunately conjures up an unrealistic image of mass weddings that are nowhere to be found. In fact, however, Engels' actual analysis of "group marriage" as it obtained in Australia concurs with what has come to be called "loose monogamy" in anthropological writings. "All that the superficial observer sees in group marriage," Engels pointed out, "is a loose form of monogamous marriage, here and there polygyny, and occasional infidelities." Through the "mass marriage of an entire section of men . . . with an equally widely distributed section of women . . . the Australian aborigine, wandering hundreds of miles from his home . . . often finds in every camp and every tribe women who give themselves to him without resistance and without resentment" (109). On a day-to-day basis, marriage takes the form of a "a loose pairing" among partners whose marriageability is defined at birth by their membership in one or another so-called "marriage class."

The Australian "marriage classes" are today conceived to be part of a system whereby various categories of kin are named so that a person can readily define his relationships within any group with

whom he comes into contact.[13] The system is far more elaborate
than anything found among other hunter-gatherers, but nonetheless, all of them share common features of family life. Divorce is
typically easy and at the desire of either partner, although it is not
particularly common. Death more frequently seems to break up
the marriage relationship; close and warm pairing relationships are
the rule. These are not based, however, on any assumption of
sexual exclusiveness for either partner among most hunter-gatherers
about whom we have information. Perhaps it is because they were
first contacted by whalers instead of missionaries that we have so
much data on this point for the Eskimo. According to custom, it is
hospitable for an unattached Eskimo woman, or else the host's
wife, to sleep with a visitor. The practice has at times been referred to as evidence of the low status of women where it obtains—
an ethnocentric reading which presumes that a woman does not
(since she should not) enjoy sex play with any but her "real" husband and which refuses to recognize that variety in sex relations is
entertaining to women (where not circumscribed by all manner of
taboos) as well as to men (a moralistic assumption from which
Engels himself was not wholly free).

"Pairing marriage" is more hedged around with restrictions.
Engels wrote: "the decisive considerations are the new ties of kinship which are to give the young pair a stronger position in the
gens and tribe" (142). Parents take a hand in the choice of marriage partners, and marriages are cemented through an exchange of
goods—cattle, foods, or luxury items—between the relatives of the
bride and those of the groom. The kin of the young partners now
have a vested interest in the permanence of the marriage. Engels
wrote, that although "still terminable at the desire of either
partner . . . among many tribes . . . public opinion has gradually
developed against such separations. When differences arise between
husband and wife, the gens relatives of both partners act as mediators, and only if these efforts prove fruitless does a separation take
place" (112).

13. A description of kinship among the Arunta of Australia can be found
in Service, 1963. These systems become unusually elaborate in parts of
Australia, although somewhat comparable elaborations are to be found in
nearby Melanesian tribes.

There is no lack of data on what Morgan called the "pairing family." It is intimately related to the clan organization of agricultural peoples, whereby communal relations in the production and distribution of goods are maintained in what have become relatively large and stable groups. Hunting-gathering bands of some 25 to 40 or so people can operate almost anarchistically, but with the development of agriculture more complex institutions are needed for ordering interpersonal relationships in villages of several hundred and more. Virtually everyone still stands in the same direct relation to production; at most a healer or priest-chief may receive gifts enough to release him or her from some agricultural and other labors. Therefore, economic, political, and social relations remain united; ties of kinship formalized as "gentes" or the term more commonly used today, "clans," form the framework of community life. With clan organization, kin are counted on one side only— you belong either to your mother's or your father's clan, not to both, and you marry "out" (clans are normally "exogamous"). The two practices, unilineality and exogamy, enable discrete groups to last over generations (which is difficult with "bilaterality" and overlapping lines of kinship), while at the same time the groups become linked through a network of marriage ties.[14]

The nuclear family of parents and children was embedded in the clan and village structures through a network of reciprocal relations.[15] Parties of relatives worked together in the fields and on

14. The social basis for incest taboos and exogamous marriage are discussed in White, 1949: Chapter 11; Slater, 1959; Aberle *et al.*, 1963; and in Washburn and Lancaster, "The Evolution of Hunting," in Lee and DeVore, 1968: especially 302. The ties of kinship and exogamous marriage were already practices in hunting-gathering societies, although they were more formally defined among the settled gatherers and fishermen than among nomadic hunters. This raises the question whether they were generally more well defined in early human society and lost under the harsh conditions endured by the Indians and Eskimo of the north and other hunters pushed into marginal areas. In any case, with agricultural society, they become highly defined and elaborated upon with endless variations from group to group. The Soviet anthropologist, Julia Averkieva, has suggested to me that in her view clan organization was primeval, and that its elaborate definition occurred when it was already beginning to decay. For further discussion of hunting-band organization, see Leacock, 1969.

15. These have seldom been described better than by one of the founders of the "functionalist" school of anthropology, Bronislaw Malinowski, in his writings on the Trobriand Islanders of Melanesia. Try, for example, his very readable *Crime and Custom in Savage Society,* 1926.

the hunt, and exchanged foodstuffs and manufactured goods on the many occasions that called for festivity, such as at births, baptisms, puberty rites, marriages, deaths, and seasonal and religious ceremonies. The acceptance by the clan and village community, as formally represented by its respected elders, of the ultimate responsibility for the welfare of any member, was so totally taken for granted that it went unstated. On a day-to-day basis, however, it was the immediate lineage of grandparent, parent, and children, with spouses, that functioned as a working unit.

The significant point for women's status is that the household was communal and the division of labor between the sexes reciprocal; the economy did not involve the dependence of the wife and children on the husband. All major food supplies, large game and produce from the fields, were shared among a group of families. These families lived together in large dwellings among most village agriculturalists, and in hunting-gathering societies either shared large tepees or other such shelters in adverse climates, or might simply group together in separate wickiups or lean-tos in tropical or desert areas. The children in a real sense belonged to the group as a whole; an orphaned child suffered a personal loss, but was never without a family. Women did not have to put up with personal injuries from men in outbursts of violent anger for fear of economic privation for themselves or their children. By comparison with more "advanced" societies where wife-beating became accepted, even to the point of death, a mistreated wife could call on her relatives for redress or leave if it was not forthcoming. Nor can "household management" be construed as it would be today. Whether a "public" industry or not, "managing the household" as the "task entrusted to the women" might be viewed dubiously as hardly very satisfactory. However, in primitive communal society, the distinction did not exist between a public world of men's work and a private world of women's household service. The large collective household *was* the community, and within it both sexes worked to produce the goods necessary for livelihood. Goods were as yet directly produced and consumed; they had not become transformed into "commodities" for exchange, the transformation upon which the exploitation of man by man, and the special oppression of women, was built.

In fact, women usually furnished a large share—often the major share—of the food. Many hunter-gatherers depended on the vegetable foods gathered by women as the staples to be augmented by meat (the Bushmen of the Kalahari Desert are a case in point), and in horticultural societies women, as the former gatherers of vegetable foods and in all likelihood, therefore, responsible for the domestication of crops, generally did most of the farming. Since in primitive communal society decisions were made by those who would be carrying them out, the participation of women in a major share of socially necessary labor did not reduce them to virtual slavery, as is the case in class society, but accorded them decision-making powers commensurate with their contribution.

There has been little understanding of this point in anthropological literature. Instead, the fact that men typically made decisions about hunting and warfare in primitive society is used to support the argument that they were the "rulers" in the Western sense. Men did indeed acquire power under the conditions of colonial rule within which the lifeways of hitherto primitive peoples have been recorded. Nonetheless, the literature again and again reveals the autonomy of women and their role in decision-making; albeit such data are as often as not sloughed off with supposedly humorous innuendos about "henpecked husbands" or the like, rather than treated seriously as illustrative of social structure and dynamics.

Unfortunately, the debate over women's status in primitive society has largely ignored the actual role of women in primitive society in favor of an almost exclusive focus on descent systems. The growing body of literature on the world's cultures in the latter 19th century showed the clans of horticultural peoples to be commonly matrilineal, and that women often participated formally in the making of "political" decisions. Morgan had described the power the elder women among the Iroquois held in the nomination and possible deposition of the sachems, and the importance of "queen mothers" in Africa had been described. There, a woman and her brother (or son or nephew) often shared chiefly or royal responsibilities somewhat analogous to those of a Department of the Interior and Department of State respectively. And the magnificent army of perhaps 5,000 volunteer women soldiers of Dahomey were the legendary Amazons incarnate. All of this caught the imagination of theoreticians in so male-dominated and property-conscious a culture as was Victorian society,[16] and scholars spoke of patriarchal society as historically preceded by the "matriarchy," where rule by women was based on the indisputability of legitimacy reckoned in the female line.

It soon became clear that matriarchy, in the sense of power held by women over men comparable to that later held by men over women, had never existed. However, questions about the significance that matrilineal descent held for the status of women in primitive society remained. It is impossible to review here the twists and turns of subsequent argument over the universal priority of matrilineal descent. Suffice it to say that it is clear that matrilineal systems give way to patrilineal systems with the development of exploitative class relations. In many cases a patrilineal (or patrilocal) system can be shown to have been matrilineal (or matrilocal), but in other cases ethnohistorical data sufficient for definitive proof are lacking. Hence statistical studies of descent and its correlates have yielded conflicting interpretations.[17]

16. Although one cannot help but note that the very age was named after a woman. This fact points to the priority of class considerations over sex in the socialization of women when it came to royalty. Princesses were, first of all, potential rulers. Thus we have the anomaly that in the history of Europe the only public area in which individual women were in every way the equal of men, both to the general view and in their own behavior and abilities, was that associated most deeply with stereotypes of masculinity— the area of leadership, power, and decision-making.

17. An early study by Hobhouse *et al.* (1965) found the matrilineal-matrilocal principle to be more common among "lower hunters" than the patrilineal-patrilocal principle. A later study of Murdock's finds that "simpler cultures tend to be matrilineal, more advanced ones patrilineal," although "the patrilineate coexists too frequently with the absence of traits ... (of more complex culture) and the matrilineate with their presence, to be consistent with the theory of universal matrilineal priority" (1937: 467). In a later work, Murdock writes: "While matrilineal societies appear, on the average, to be somewhat more archaic in culture than patrilineal societies the difference is relatively slight, the overlap is very great, and the disparity may well reflect principally the preponderant influence exerted throughout the world in recent centuries by the bilateral and patrilineal peoples of the Eurasiatic continent," (1949: 186). Using Murdock's figures, but without reference to Murdock's early study that involved a relatively sophisticated statistical analysis, Aberle comments on the greater patrilineality among hunter-gatherers than matrilineality, although bilaterality far exceeds them both (Schneider and Gough, 1961). Two distinctions between

A standard contemporary formulation, at least in the United
States, is that horticultural societies were generally structured
around matrilineally related groups since women were responsible
for the major share of the farming, but that hunting societies were
male-centered in their structure due to the importance of the men
as hunters. The fact that the produce gathered by the women in
many such societies was as important a source of food, or more so,
than the produce of the hunt, led Service, in a recent formulation
of this position (1966: 37-38) to point out that hunting required a
close collaboration that is not important in most gathering activities.
To Service, it was the need for the "delicate coordination of several
people" that led to the practice whereby closely related men stayed
together as the core of a hunting band while women married into
other bands. The case is, however, that some hunter-gatherers are
matrilineal, and others have been so in the recent past. My own
field work among the Naskapi hunters of the Labrador Peninsula
showed that patrilineal-patrilocal ties were strengthened at the expense of matrilineal-matrilocal ties after European contact, under
the influence of missionaries, government agents, and especially the
fur trade (Leacock, 1955, 1969). Despite the arduousness of hunting in the northern woods and tundra, there was no suggestion
whatever that men had to grow up together to work well as a unit.
Instead it was the norm for men in the past to marry away from the
band of their youth.

In a recent study Martin also questions the "patrilocal band" as
the primordial type of social organization. On the basis of reviewing
descent and residence patterns, interband relations, and the recent
histories of 33 predominantly matrilocal South American hunting-
gathering peoples, she points out that there is greater cohesiveness
with matrilocal rather than patrilocal organization. With matrilocal

---

Murdock's figures and those of Hobhouse *et al.* must be noted. First, one of
Murdock's criteria for selection of his sample was that each major rule of
descent should be represented for each culture area, a factor he took into
account in his own analysis, but which does not seem to have been considered by Aberle. The second consideration involves the passage of time.
For the people with whom I am most familiar, the Naskapi, Hobhouse *et al.*
use a 17th century Jesuit account that showed them to be matrilineal-matrilocal in orientation; Murdock uses 20th century accounts that describe
them as bilateral and bilocal with a paternal emphasis.

residence the men, who are responsible for defense and hence offense, are dispersed among related bands rather than forming localized clusters (1969: 256-57).

Works that deal directly with the role of women in primitive society are few and far between, and much of what has been done pertains to personality rather than socio-economic structure. Margaret Mead's early exposition of contrasting sex-role definitions in three primitive societies is a case in point (1950). Interestingly enough, Mead contradicts her own argument for the cultural definition of sex role by her later position which, in conformity with widely accepted Freudian thought, argues for a universal active-passive dichotomy differentiating male from female roles (1955). By contrast there is an early book by Mason, *Women's Share in Primitive Culture,* and the book, *The Mothers,* by Briffault, a surgeon, novelist, and amateur anthropologist. These draw together scattered ethnographic references to (1) women's role in decision-making and the administration of tribal affairs; (2) their importance as inventors of techniques for food production and the manufacture of baskets, leather goods, woven materials, etc.; and (3) their part in ritual and religious life. Impressive though the record of women's part in society appears, however, the data are lifted out of context and seem to be contradicted by the vast majority of extant ethnographic materials, for these seldom assess the impact of colonialism on the peoples described and generally focus on the activities and affairs of men. (This latter is not solely a problem of masculine bias, but also due to the greater ease of communicating with men who are far more commonly thrown into contact with Europeans and speak a European language.)

An unusually detailed study of women among a hunting-gathering people is afforded by Kaberry's work on the original inhabitants of Northwest Australia (1939). It is commonly stated that women's status is low among these people, as evidenced by their exclusion from the important ceremonies of the men and from participation in political affairs. Kaberry points out that the men in turn are kept out of the secret rituals held by the women; and that while warfare and the holding of formal meetings are the sole responsibility of the men, intragroup problems are handled by older women along with older men. Women are restricted as to whom they may marry;

but so are men, and young people are free to have premarital affairs which either sex may initiate. In daily life, these Australian women emerge as autonomous participants in the affairs of their people, acting with assurance upon their rights and responsibilities, a view reinforced by a newly published study of Tiwi women by Jane Goodale (1971).

Similarly, biographical materials on Eskimo women contradict common assumptions about their subservient role, even in spite of its deterioration in recent times. The biography of Anauta (Washburne and Anauta, 1940), an Eskimo woman of Baffin Land who migrated to the United States with her children after the death of her husband, reveals her independence of action and strong sense of personal autonomy. Short biographies of Nunivak Island Eskimo women, one of them a shaman (a person who can communicate with the supernatural powers, usually for healing and/or divination), likewise indicate considerable freedom of choice and leeway for women to take the initiative in the running of their own lives (Lantis, 1960).

The position of women among the Naskapi hunting people of the Labrador Peninsula was stronger in the past than it is today. Seventeenth century Jesuit missionaries writing of their experiences state that "the women have great power here" and that "the choice of plans, of undertakings, of journeys, of winterings, lies in nearly every instance in the hands of the housewife" (Thwaites, 1906: Vol. V, 181; Vol. LXVIII, 93). A Jesuit scolds a man for not being "the master," telling him "in France women do not rule their husbands" (Vol. V, 181). To make the women obey their husbands became one of the concerns of the missionaries, particularly in relation to the sexual freedom that obtained: "I told him that it was not honorable for a woman to love anyone else except her husband, and that, this evil being among them (women's sexual freedom) he himself was not sure that his son, who was there present, was his son." The Naskapi's reply is telling: "Thou hast no sense. You French people love only your own children; but we love all the children of our tribe" (Vol. VI, 255).

Women are no longer shamans, as they could be in the past, nor do they commonly hunt, nor join the men in the sweat bath, nor hold their own formal councils in case of emergency (Vol. II, 77;

Vol. VI, 191; Vol. VII, 61, 175; Vol. XIV, 183). However, traditions of individual autonomy, mutual support, and collective responsibility for the children still leave their mark on Naskapi life despite great changes. One of many incidents I observed must suffice to indicate what can lie behind the stereotyped ascription in monographic accounts of such people: the men hunt; the women gather berries and care for the children. For the greater part of one day a man sat patiently, lovingly crooning over his sickly and fretful infant of but a few weeks old. His wife was busy. Though worried for the baby's health, he appeared in no way inept or harassed by his responsibility, nor did he call on another woman around the camp for help. His unself-conscious assurance and patience set him quite apart from latter-day readers of Dr. Spock. This was his task while his wife tanned a caribou skin, a skilled and arduous job that demanded her complete attention. The men knew how to cook and tend the babies when called upon to do so, but did not really know how to tan leather.

There is a real need for studies that reconstruct from extant materials on primitive communal and transitional societies something of women's functioning before the development of the male dominance that accompanied European economic and colonial exploitation. For example, how were goods distributed in horticultural societies where garden produce still lay in the women's domain? How did older women function in the settling of disputes, a role often referred to but little documented? What were the paths of influence women held in relation to the men's sphere of war and the hunt? Conversely, what was the role of men in socializing young children? A recent analysis by Mintz (1971) of the entrepreneurial role played by Yoruba women traders exemplifies how published data can be used to begin answering such questions.

An interesting subject for reassessment is the mystique that surrounds the hunt and, in comparison, that surrounding childbirth. A common formulation of status among hunter-gatherers overlooks the latter and stresses the importance and excitement of the hunt. Albeit the primary staple foods may be the vegetable products supplied by the women, they afford no prestige, it is pointed out, so that while not precisely subservient women are still of lower status than men. However, women's power of child-bearing has been a focus for awe and even fear as long ago as the Upper Paleolithic, judging from the fertility figurines that date from that period. This point is easy to overlook, for the ability to bear children has led in our society not to respect but to women's oppressed status. Similarly, the mystique surrounding menstruation is underestimated. Attitudes of mystery and danger for men are interpreted in terms of our cultural judgment as "uncleanliness." Indeed, the semantic twists on this subject would be amusing to analyze. Women are spoken of as "isolated" in "menstrual huts" so that the men will not be contaminated. Where men's houses exist, however, they are written about respectfully; here the exclusion of women betokens men's high status. Doubtless this congeries of attitudes was first held by missionaries and traders, and from them subject peoples learned appropriate attitudes to express to whites.

However, a recent study by Hogbin (1970) on the religion of a New Guinea people reveals another side to the picture. Intriguingly titled "The Island of Menstruating Men," the study describes a practice also found among other peoples in this part of the world whereby the men simulate the phenomenon of menstruation. Blood is drawn from the penis (or some other part of the body among other groups) and men go through the ritual cycle of menstruation, retreating from the ordinary round of daily affairs, observing various taboos, then reentering, cleansed and renewed.

In some ways it is the ultimate alienation in our society that the ability to give birth has been transformed into a liability. The reason is not simply that, since women bear children, they are more limited in their movements and activities. As the foregoing discussion indicates, this was not a handicap even under the limited technology of hunting-gathering life; it certainly has no relevance today. Nor did women's low status simply follow their declining importance in food production when men moved into agriculture; nor automatically follow the growth in importance of domestic animals, the province of the men, although herding did relate to lowered status for women. However, what was basic was that these transitions occurred in the context of developing exploitative relations whereby communal ownership was being undermined, the communal kin group broken up, and the individual family separated out as an isolated and vulnerable unit, economically responsible for the maintenance of its members and for the rearing of the new generation. The subjugation of the female sex was based on the transformation of their socially necessary labor into a private service through the separation of the family from the clan. It was in this context that women's domestic and other work came to be performed under conditions of virtual slavery.

The separation of the family from the clan and the institution of monogamous marriage were the social expressions of developing private property; so-called monogamy afforded the means through which property could be individually inherited. And private property for some meant no property for others, or the emerging of differing relations to production on the part of different social groups. The core of Engels' formulation lies in the initimate connection between the emergence of the family as an economic unit dominated by the male and this development of classes.

The distinction of rich and poor appears beside that of freemen and slaves—with the new division of labor, a new cleavage of society into classes. . . . The transition to full private property is gradually accomplished, parallel with the transition of the pairing marriage into monogamy. The single family is becoming the economic unit of society (223).

Engels outlines for early Greece the way in which the division of labor and development of commodity production enabled new wealth in the form of slaves and herds to be accumulated by single individuals, thereby leading to a conflict between the family and the gens. Since men owned the "instruments of labor" (having largely displaced women in the fields, it is important to note, following the decline of hunting as an important activity), conflict between family and gens took the form of a conflict between the opposing principles of father right and mother right. "As wealth increased it made the man's position in the family more important than the woman's, and . . . created an impulse to exploit this strengthened position in order to overthrow, in favor of his children, the traditional order of inheritance" (119). Therefore, the formation of the family as the economic unit of society was affirmed by the overthrow of mother right, the *"world historical defeat of the female sex"* (120; italics Engels').

Far more empirical documentation than Engels offers is needed to clarify the process of women's subjugation, both in relation to the initial rise of class societies in the Old and New Worlds, and to the secondary diffusion of commodity production and class divisions that accompanied European expansion and colonial domination. Essentially Engels offers a paradigm, posing a sharp contrast between women's status in primitive communal society and in classical Greece and Rome. He then touches on Medieval Europe and jumps to industrialization. The many changes within the great span of history covered and the variations from place to place need analysis and, even more important, so do the variations in women's position in different classes: slave, free worker, peasant, serf, burgher, aristocrat.

Engels focuses on the emergence of the upper-class family as an instrument for the concentration of individual wealth. He does not clearly define the lower-class family as affording an important buttress for class society by making the individual acutely vulnerable to exploitation and control. The separation of the ordinary laborer from the communal security of the gens meant the worker was responsible as an individual not only for his own maintenance but also that of his wife and children. This to a large measure insured not only his labor, but also his docility; it rendered him— as he is to this day—fearful of fighting against the extremities of exploitation as endangering not only himself but also his wife and his dependent children. With wonderful wit and satire, and warm sympathy, Engels deals with the conjugal relations produced by monogamy, but largely in relation to the bourgeois family. He writes of the proletarian wife who moves into public industry under conditions of great difficulty for herself and her children, but does not elaborate on the enormous ambivalence the individual family creates in the working-class man and his wife as a result of their isolation.

The dehumanization of conjugal relationships, caught as men and women are in a network of fear and confusion; the brutalization and petty dominance of the man; the anger and bitterness of the woman; the nature of marriage, all too often as a constant battle—

all this is only too well known. Despite the fact that the pre-class societies which have been studied have already been undercut by European and American colonization, a quality of respectful ease, warmth, and assurance in interpersonal relations, including those between husband and wife, often persists as evidence that the tensions associated with conjugal relations in our society are based in our social structure, not in the natures of women and men.

POLITICAL RAMIFICATIONS OF ENGELS' ARGUMENT ON WOMEN'S SUBJUGATION

ENGELS WRITES, "the peculiar character of the supremacy of the husband over the wife in the modern family . . . will only be seen in the clear light of day when both possess legally complete equality of rights," although, in itself, legal equity affords no solution. Just as the legal equality of capitalist and proletarian makes visible "the specific character of the economic oppression burdening the proletariat," so also will legal equality reveal the fundamental change that is necessary for the liberation of women. Engels goes on to say: "Then it will be plain that the first condition for the liberation of the wife is to bring the whole female sex back into public industry, and that this in turn demands that the characteristic of the monogamous family as the economic unit of society be abolished" (137–38).

Such a change is dependent on the abolition of private ownership. "With the transfer of the means of production into common ownership, the single family ceases to be the economic unit of society. Private housekeeping is transformed into a social industry. The care and education of the children becomes a public affair; society looks after all children alike" (139). Only when this is accomplished will a new generation of women grow up, Engels writes, who have never known "what it is to give themselves to a man from any other considerations than real love or to refuse to give themselves to their lover from fear of the economic consequences." Then men and women "will care precious little what anybody today thinks they ought to do; they will make their own practice and their corresponding public opinion about the practice of each individual—and that will be the end of it" (145). To which must be added today that the destruction of the family as an economic unit does not *automatically* follow with the establishment of socialism, but rather is one of the goals to be fought for as central to the transition to communism.

There has recently been much discussion about the extent to which women can achieve a measure of personal "liberation" by rejecting the sex-role definitions of the contemporary "monogamous" family, and about the relevance such rejection can have to the furthering of revolutionary aims and consciousness. There has also been considerable argument about the basis for women's inferior position, ranging from the extreme psychobiological view that it results from an innate masculine drive for domination and can be changed only through a single-minded "battle of the sexes," to the extreme economic determinist—and generally masculine— view that since all basic changes ultimately depend on the revolutionary restructuring of society, it is both illusory and diversionary to focus on ameliorating the special problems of women.

While there is still a great deal of abstract argument about the correct position on women's liberation, there is also a growing recognition that it is fruitless to debate the extent to which various parts of the women's movement can or cannot be linked with revolutionary goals, and there is a growing commitment to developing concrete tactics of program and organization around situations where women are in motion on basic issues. It might seem that Engels' discussion of family arrangements that have long ceased to exist in their pristine forms is somewhat esoteric and of little relevance today. However, it is crucial to the organization of women for their liberation to understand that it is the monogamous family as an economic unit, at the heart of class society, that is basic to their subjugation. Such understanding makes clear that child-bearing itself is not responsible for the low status of women, as has been the contention of some radical women's groups. And more important, it indicates the way in which working-class women, not only in their obviously basic fight on the job but also in their seemingly more conservative battles for their families around schools, housing and welfare, are actually posing a more basic challenge than that of the radicals. By demanding that society assume responsibility for their children, they are attacking the nature of the family as an economic unit, the basis of their own oppression and a central buttress of class exploitation. Therefore, while some of the activities of middle-class radical women's groups can be linked with the struggles of working-class women, such as the fight for free legalized abortion, others are so psychologically oriented as to be confusing and diversionary.

The self-declared women's movement in this country has historically been middle class and largely oriented toward a fight for the same options as middle-class men within the system, while the struggles of working-class women have not been conceived as fights for women's liberation as such. This has been true since the close of the Civil War, when the women's movement that had been closely concerned with the fight against slavery and for the rights of women factory workers broke away on its "feminist" course. Today there is more widespread awareness that all oppressive relations are interconnected and embedded in our system as a whole, and that only united effort can effect fundamental change. However, there has been little clear and consistent effort made to achieve such unity. For example, the committees formed by professional women to fight job discrimination are generally prepared to admit forthrightly that their battle is ultimately inseparable from that of working-class and especially Black working-class women, but they have done virtually nothing to find ways of linking the two. And it is commonplace to point out that, despite basic differences between the oppression of women and the oppression of Blacks, there are marked parallels of both an economic and a social-psychological nature—not to mention the fact that half of Black people are women. But again, there has been no solid commitment to building organizational ties between the two movements around specific issues. The theoretical differentiation between the symptoms and the causes of women's oppression can help clarify the issues around which united organization must be built, and can help remove the blocks hampering the enormous potential a women's movement could have for unifying sections of the middle and working classes and bridging some of the disastrous gap between white workers and Black, Puerto Rican, and Mexican American workers. However, in this effort it is important to be wary of a certain suspect quality of many white middle-class women (akin to that of their male counterparts) to be attracted and exhilarated by the assertiveness of the struggle for Black liberation, and to neglect their responsibility to find ways of also building an alliance with white working-class women and men.

Theoretical understanding is sorely needed to help combat the difficulties that will continue to beset the women's movement. Male supremacy, the enormous difficulty men have in facing up to their pathetic feelings of superiority and display of petty power over women, even when theoretically dedicated to revolutionary change, will continue to feed what is often a narrowly anti-men orientation among "movement women;" and the media will continue to exploit this as a gimmick that serves at the same time to sell cigarettes and shampoo, dissipate energies, and divide women from each other and from what should be allied struggles. As with the black-power movement, the sheer possibility of open confrontation will for some serve the need to express a great pent-up anger, and token victories will temporarily serve to give the illusion of some success. The overwhelming need is to keep this powerful anger from being dissipated—to find ways of building upon it through taking organizationally meaningful steps.

THE EMERGENCE OF THE STATE

MORGAN'S DOCUMENTATION of the transition from kin-organized to politically organized society in ancient Greece and Rome emphasized the growth of private property as such, rather than the development of classes based on differential relations to major means and sources of subsistence. In fact, Morgan virtually ignored the fact that Greece was a slave society. Engels, therefore, added to Morgan's data on the Athenian state "their economic content and cause" (171), especially the division of labor and its implications. Within the "structure of society based on kinship groups," Engels writes, "the productivity of labor increasingly develops, and with it private property and exchange, differences of wealth, the possibility of utilizing the labor power of others, and hence the basis of class antagonisms" (72). The incompatibility of these "new social elements" with "the old social order" brings about a complete upheaval. "The gentile constitution . . . [was] shattered by the division of labor and its result, the cleavage of society into classes. It was replaced by the *state"* (228).

The Iroquois confederacy represents the highest stage of political organization possible under the gentile system, Engels continues. Within the limits imposed upon them by the level of their technology, the Iroquois control their own production. In early Greece advancing technology and the creation of a surplus lead to the division of labor between herdsmen and agriculturalists, and between agriculturalists and craftsmen, which "slowly insinuates itself into ... [the] process of production" (233). Goods are transformed into *commodities* for *exchange*: the producers lose control of their products; the accumulation of individual wealth and the separation of society into privileged and non-privileged classes becomes possible. Slavery, made profitable by improved productive techniques, is first limited to prisoners of war, but is then extended to fellow tribesmen. Private estates are built up through the transmission of property within family lines, rather than within the larger kin group, and the family becomes a power against the gens. The gentile constitution had grown out of a society with no internal contradictions and it depended for its effectiveness on the coercive force of public opinion. However, the new developments produced "a society which by all its economic conditions of life had been forced to split itself into freemen and slaves, into the exploiting rich and the exploited poor; a society which not only could never again reconcile these contradictions, but was compelled always to intensify them" (228). The state was the new institution which, as the instrument of the exploiting class, appeared to stand "above the warring classes, suppressed their open conflict and allowed the class struggle to be fought out at most in the economic field, in so-called legal form" (228).

Typically, Engels' argument was nowhere dealt with directly by the Boasian school of American anthropology. However, a leading member and major antagonist of Morgan's, Robert H. Lowie, wrote *The Origin of the State,* in which he took the position that the state was universal, be it in however a rudimentary a form, due to the fact that "illiterate peoples, too, maintain political order within fixed territorial limits" (1929:2). If the "principle of continuity and psychic unity" is correct, he wrote, then we can "discover the processes that could convert a community of the Andamanese model into the elaborate structure of modern times" (1929:6). To Lowie, the evolution of the state involved a purely quantitative change— the strengthening of the feeling for the home territory. In answer to the question of what caused the territorial tie to be strengthened, he wrote: "though permanent concentration of power in a single person's hands is . . . the simplest way to impose the territorial bond, it is not the only one" (1929:116). As another way, he suggested that the "coercive force" might also be vested in a group. Thus he ended where Engels began, with the problem of how power over the rest of society became centralized in the hands of a few, or, in effect, the question of how the state arose at a particular historical juncture.

Although anthropologists in the United States have seldom criticized Lowie's theory of the state directly, it is no longer of much influence. In keeping with a revived evolutionary perspective, there is widespread recognition among contemporary anthropologists that the state emerged as a qualitatively new institution associated with marked economic inequalities, a well developed division of labor, and sizable urban centers. Furthermore, the use of coercive force to control a territorially based citizenry is generally accepted by anthropologists as a central feature of state organization.[18]

Nonetheless, Engels' work is rarely mentioned in the West in scholarly inquiries into the emergence of the state. This is of course typical of the skittishness with which Marxist theory is treated. However, there is another consideration in this case, for Greece

18. For instance, Krader (1968: viii) writes: "This book, then, has a thesis: there is such a thing as the political state, which is found only in certain societies. It has a role in these societies that is uniform throughout, controlling and directing the life of the people under it by centralized social power in the hands of a few." Fried writes, "the emergent state, then . . . is the organization of the power of the society on a supra-kin basis" (1960: 728), and, elsewhere, that "the power (of an emerging state) itself represents a quantum leap over anything previously wielded" (1967: 231). Bohannan (1963: 274) writes: "The state is a special social group charged with allocating authority to use physical force in order to achieve peace and conformance with law and custom on the one hand, and to maintain territorial and cultural integrity against external threats on the other." Bohannan discusses "stateless" society at length (1963, 1964). "Chiefdoms," transitional to the state, are discussed by Sahlins, 1968.

and Rome are unfortunately too late to be good models for state development when applied too narrowly. *Origin* is a relatively brief and pointed book in which a forceful comparison is presented between the communal relations of primitive society and the exploitative relations that arose within it. It throws into sharp relief the nature of the family as an economic unit and the state as the arm of an exploiting class, both institutions that must be abolished if freer relations among people are to be achieved. Unfortunately, however, when Athenian Greece as described by Engels became the model for the transition from classless to class-based society, the concept of a slaveholding "stage" became rigidified in a form that simply could not be applied to the over 2,000 years of prior history during which state-organized and class-based society had existed. To insist on too literal an interpretation of an Athenian model leads to a hopelessly "Eurocentric" position that elevates Greece and Rome to overly important positions, distorts the ancient civilizations of Asia and Northwest Africa, and virtually ignores the states of West Africa and of Central and South America. (Similarly, the implicit acceptance of a specifically European model of feudalism has confused the interpretation by Western scholars of the Orient.)

It has been puzzling to scholars that Engels made no mention of the "Asian" or "Oriental" mode of production Marx spoke of as characterizing some of these societies, and which he illustrated in *Capital* in terms of village India (1965; 1967). In the ancient Indian communities, lands remain held in common by extended family or village groups, and the major part of production is for direct use. Craftsmen and other specialists residing in the community produce goods and services directly for it, and are in return maintained by it. Goods do not become commodities, except for that surplus portion which is taken by the state in the form of goods in kind (1967:334). Marx wrote:

In the ancient Asiatic and other ancient modes of production, we find that the conversion of products into commodities and therefore the conversion of men into producers of commodities, holds a subordinate place, which, however, increases in importance as the primitive communities approach nearer and nearer to their dissolution. Trading nations, properly so called, exist in the ancient world only in its interstices (1967: 79).

Engels refers to this form of relations in *Anti-Dühring* (1939: 165, 337*ff*), though unfortunately not in *Origin*. He does, however, add to his analysis of Morgan's material on Greece and Rome the case of Germany, where the state "springs directly out of the conquest of large territories which the gentile constitution provides no means of governing." In the German conquest of Rome, "the economic basis of society remains . . . as before . . . [and] the gentile constitution is able to survive for many centuries" (228). However, this is a secondary, not primary mechanism of state formation. By contrast to other "conquest theories" of state origin,[19] Engels emphasized that in its "purest" form the state arises "directly and mainly out of the class oppositions which develop within gentile society itself" (228), and he used the Athenian experience to exemplify the process whereby it did so.

Engels wrote in summary:

The stage of commodity production with which civilization begins is distinguished economically by the introduction of (1) metal money and with it money capital, interest and usury, (2) merchants as the class of intermediaries between the producers, (3) private ownership of land and the mortgage system, (4) slave labor as the dominant form of production (234-35).

Associated also were the male-dominated monogamous family as the economic unit of society, the "establishment of a permanent opposition between town and country as basis of the whole social division of labor," and "the introduction of wills, whereby the owner of property is still able to dispose over it even when he is dead" (235). Further: "The central link in civilized society is the state, which in all typical periods is without exception the state of the ruling class and in all cases continues to be essentially a machine for holding down the oppressed, exploited class" (235).

The fact that in seventh century Athens the associated processes outlined by Engels that had been unfolding for thousands of years came to their full fruition makes it both useful and misleading as a

19. Fried (1967) discusses the ongoing process of warfare as important in state formation, by comparison with "conquests" in a literal sense. Similarly, in a recent paper, Carneiro suggests that the concentration of resources in a limited area leads to "warfare over land, and thus to political integration beyond the village level" (1970: 737).

paradigm for the emergence of the state. While useful as an analysis of the interconnections among economy, society and polity associated with what has been called civilization, the case of Athens is misleading when these processes are seen as unfolding in the same sequences in other cases. This is generally true of secondary developments of class and political organization, such as those set off by European conquest, which collapse certain processes into a very short period, thereby sharpening them at the same time as distorting them relative to primary or autonomous developments.

In the Ionian peninsula, the institutions associated with clan society had already been undermined by precisely the type of "Oriental mode" Marx described, and during the classical period, slave-labor and commodity production grew rapidly to predominance. In fact, it was upon the growth of commodity production that the efflorescence of Athens was based. As a small, seafaring, cosmopolitan, trading nation, Athens was one of those "interstices" where trade was carried on by a merchant class, interested in profit, whereas most trade in the ancient Middle East was carried on by a state apparatus associated with a priesthood or aristocracy, for the purpose of acquiring building materials, luxury articles, and slaves. Various forms of money had long been employed in the ancient world, but coinage became necessary when commodity production and trade reached sufficient proportions to warrant it. Its use became widespread rather late, when Athens borrowed it either from Lydia or another of the contemporaneous, trading city-states.[20]

The pristine developments of the state had taken place in ancient Mesopotamia and Egypt over two millenia earlier, and although there is still disagreement about how important slave-holding was before the first millenium BC in Mesopotamia, there is greater agreement that it was not dominant as a form of labor in Egypt until that time. Nor was it dominant, apparently, in the early Chinese states. In both the medieval states of West Africa and the independently evolved states of the Maya, Aztec, Inca and their

20. Lévy (1964: 16*ff*) points out that close approximations to true coins had been used for a long time previously, but had not become standardized by established practice. For a richly documented, if theoretically somewhat confusing, account of early trade, see Polanyi *et al.*, 1957.

predecessors in the New World, production was still based on the peasant-farmer. The farming population supported often despotic aristocracies through feudal-like arrangements whereby they donated goods and services, but retained their inalienable right to land through their connection with a kin or transitional type of kin-community group.

Slavery existed in all of these societies, for it is of course undeniable that slavery of some sort represented the first form of unfree labor. Prisoners of war in primitive societies were often enslaved, and as outsiders with no kinship status within the society, they were consigned to the most onerous tasks; in some societies, they could be killed in ritual sacrifice. Their condition could be dismal enough from a personal point of view; however, they did not, as yet, constitute a significant factor in production. Engels made the point that slavery could not become economically relevant until labor was sufficiently productive to enable slave-labor to produce enough above and beyond the cost of its own maintenance to release a sizable group for exploitative roles in society. Thus, the descendents of slaves in early societies did not necessarily remain slaves, and in many cases, slaves themselves might be adopted into the group and become loved and respected kinsmen.

Slaves in numbers were first attached to temples or palaces where they were often trained as specialists or craftsmen. Although "unfree," their standard of living was well above that of peasant farmers, and their situation was quite different from that of gang-slaves who worked in the fields or mines, or alongside of the corvée labor donated by free men on public works such as irrigation systems, roads, and monumental structures. Thus the term "slavery" covers different kinds of groupings.[21] In comparing central Mexico and ancient Mesopotamia, Adams writes that in both "corporate kin groups, originally preponderating in the control of land, were gradually supplanted by the growth of private estates in the hands of urban elites." In both "there were various social impediments and conditions of servitude, of which slavery was merely the most extreme, and the role of an inferior and in some respects unfree agricultural class was surely far more important

21. For a fuller discussion of this point, see Finley, 1964.

than the numbers of narrowly defined 'slaves' alone would suggest" (1966: 119, 103-04). However, Adams points out that slaves in Mesopotamia, large numbers of whom were women, were important in the production of wool or thread. He writes:

. . . the sale or exchange of this commodity not only played an important part in the local redistributive economy but presumably also served as the basis for long-distance trade in luxuries and vital raw materials like metal. In a sense then, there was a strategic concentration of slaves in precisely those institutions which characterized Mesopotamian urban society as distinguished from preurban society, so to characterize the institution as insignificant, accordingly would misrepresent its importance as a factor in development (1966: 103).

Slavery grew slowly and unevenly in the history of mankind and its significance did not lie in its literal dominance over "free" labor. Greece and Rome were not typical, and although slavery was the first form in which labor was exploited, primitive communal relations were often transformed into feudal relations without slavery becoming predominant. Engels implies this to be the case in Germany; it seems evident for China and the New World; the French Marxist Maurice Godelier has pointed it out for West African society; and many Soviet scholars seem to be in agreement.[22]

The major question that awaits fuller documentation in the light of these considerations is not simply how important slaves were numerically in any given society or period, but how slavery func-

22. The universality of a Mediterranean type of slaveholding "stage" in the history of human society has occasionally been questioned by Soviet scholars (see Danilova, 1966, and Lentsman, 1966). However, the question has been most sharply and conclusively raised in recent times by the French socialist Godelier and his colleagues, in relation to African society. Godelier argues that the communal ownership of land with a surplus appropriated by a chief or king, as found in Africa, corresponds to Marx's concept in which "exploitation of man by man exists without property in land," thereby accelerating "the process of establishment of a class of exploiters." Godelier and his co-workers see this to be a universal form, for which the term "Asian mode" is too narrow. Godelier poses as "two possible paths of development and decay of the Asian mode of production," the Greco-Roman route "to the slaveholding mode of production based upon private property and commodity production," and "the Chinese route" developing toward "a particular form of feudalism," without passing through a slaveholding stage "characterized by the development of private property without the appearance of commodity production" (1965: 39-40).

tioned in the transformation from communal to class society. Despite the many local variations, and the expansion and decline of individual peoples or specific areas the long-term growth of private property and state organization unfolded in a remarkably similar manner in both the Old and the New World. Wherever there is data on the rise of complex societies, one finds that as increasing productivity made exploitation more profitable, the techniques that maintained communal relations and kept goods equitably distributed were eventually undermined by conflicting tendencies. Everywhere the function of priesthoods and chiefly families to maintain tribal reciprocity and integrity conflicted with the institutionalization of the power implicit in the goods and services they had at their disposal. "Civilization" arose as the reciprocal exchanges of goods and services became transmuted into exploitative consumption by a budding upper class and state apparatus.[23]

Priesthoods were often of great importance in the process of state formation, for it was in their interest to establish their position through the building of temple complexes; warfare was usually important, for it necessitated periodic centralization of controls and materials; and in some areas, the reclamation and maintenance of agricultural lands through the building and servicing of irrigation systems contributed to the usurpation of power by an upper class.[24] The enslavement of war prisoners, the temporary and permanent enslavement of kinsmen for debt or other causes, and the slave-labor used to produce agricultural and luxury goods for consumption by an aristocracy or for other enterprises conducted by the state weakened the status of the peasant farmer and the craftsman. Specialization of labor became more prominent and trade more extensive, although for a long time it was controlled by the state apparatus and not allowed to fall completely into the hands of

23. The works of Childe (1939, 1965) and Adams (1966) on the rise of civilization have already been cited. For extensive documentation of Grecian society in terms of the outline offered by Engels, see the work of the British classicist, Thompson (1949, 1955).

24. Referring to Marx's mentioning of irrigation as influential, Wittfogel (1957) has argued that it was basically the social requirements for building large-scale irrigation networks that led to the origin of the ancient states. Adams (1960: 280*ff*) counters Wittfogel's narrow, technological interpretation.

private merchants who were interested in making their own profit. And finally, the focus of these interlinked developmental processes was inevitably to be found in expanding urban centers.

Awaiting fuller synthesis is a wealth of scattered data on how the transformation of some men into chattels, commodities, undercut the status of free men; on how free tribesmen became converted into an exploited class—converted from free farmers, with inalienable rights to land and obligations to the collective as represented by a priest or chief, into serfs, trapped on the land and indebted to a ruling aristocracy or priesthood;[25] and on how these processes were underpinned by the transmutation of goods into commodities—the loss by people of control over their own production. In an analysis of the Inca state, John Murra discusses the function of cloth as a highly valued commodity in a society without money and with relatively small markets. Supposedly generous "gifts" of cloth were made by the Inca to vanquished peoples from the huge supplies kept in state warehouses, but these were, in effect, "the initial pump-priming step in a dependent relationship, since the 'generosity' of the conqueror obligates one to reciprocate, to deliver on a regular, periodic basis, the results of one's workmanship to the Cuzco warehouses." Thenceforth the peasant owes a steady supply of cloth to the state. Murra writes:

> The state was doubly served: the supply of cloth was insured and the onerous nature of the weaving mitta could be phrased in terms of culturally sanctioned reciprocity. But one can also see in this textile "gift" the issuing of Inca citizenship papers, a coercive and yet symbolic reiteration of the peasant's obligations to the state, of his conquered status (1962: 721-22).

It is doubtless through the analysis of commodity production in its early stages that questions about slavery, the "Oriental" mode and other modes mentioned by Marx can be most fully resolved. Despite Marx's important discussion of commodity production in the first section of *Capital,* there has been little follow-through by Marxist scholars on how the acquisition and exchange of a surplus by early states entrapped urban populations as a lower class, while allowing perpetuation of reciprocal relations on a village level—

25. Relevant material is reviewed by Mandel (1968: Chaps. 1-4).

nor of related questions, both empirical and theoretical. When do traders, at first functionaries for the state, perhaps even slaves of a sort, become transformed into or rivaled by independent *merchants?* What is the relation between state trade and direct exchange of goods in the market place, old and widespread in much of the world? When does the latter become converted to a significant extent into exchange in the profit-making sense?

The use of the Athenian city-state as a model obscures how slowly state trade of a surplus acquired through tribute, compulsory dues, and sheer loot gave way to a city-based merchant class that was interested in production for the purpose of profit-making.[26] The early trading ports, where merchants held sway, seldom achieved ascendency in the ancient world. Their rise in Greece, though prophetic, was temporary, and their battle for autonomy forms an important component in the history of medieval Europe.[27]

The rise of full commodity production to dominance essentially lies in the history of urbanization and the rise of the contradiction between urban and rural life. It was in the urban centers that commodity production first transformed relations within the group from direct, personal, and basically cooperative to impersonal and highly competitive, ruled by "mysterious forces" that eluded understanding and control. The full victory of commodity production conducted for profit awaited the development of northwest Europe. A backward area for almost five millenia, here the combination of harbors and waterways, and relatively available coal and iron deposits awaited the historical events that enabled a newly victorious urban merchant class that was expanding northward to realize all the explosive potential of industrial capitalism. Then came the worldwide metamorphosis of human relations into com-

26. See the work of Polanyi and his colleagues (1957) cited above. The book suffers from a confusion between *marketplaces* and *the market* in the profit-making sense, as well as from a meticulous avoidance of anything sounding like a serious discussion of commodity production or classes. However, there are good chapters, such as that on Mexican trade by Chapman and that by Neale documenting the Indian village economy to which Marx had referred. A chapter by Pearson arguing the meaninglessness of a surplus in production is rebutted by Mandel (1962: 68*fn)* and by Harris (1959).

27. On the rise of towns to ascendancy in medieval Europe, see Rörig, 1967.

modity relations, relations among things to be used; a metamorphosis that spread its effects into the remotest hinterlands, with its incredible potential for both enormous creation and for insane—perhaps ultimate—destruction: the heritage of the 20th century.

PROBLEMS OF THEORY AND METHOD

SIXTH CENTURY Greece, aboriginal Australia, pre-Columbian America—such subjects seem remote. However, the theoretical questions posed by studying the transition to class society are crucial to humanity's future. What are the implications of the fact that women's special oppression is ultimately based on the family as an economic unit? What does it mean to eliminate commodity production and the estrangement of interpersonal relations that follow from it at an advanced technological level where elaborate systems of production and exchange are necessary? Is it possible to erase the contradiction between city and country without transforming the world into one vast suburb? What are the steps by which the state can be eliminated?

In his brief discussion of social laws in *Origin,* Engels makes the point that unless they are "laboriously investigated and established," the world seems governed by chance, by "alien, at first often unrecognized powers," and "society is regulated, not by a jointly devised plan, but by blind laws which manifest themselves with elemental violence" (234). However,

. . . chance is only the one pole of a relation whose other pole is named "necessity." In a world of nature where chance also seems to rule, we have long since demonstrated in each separate field the inner necessity and law asserting itself in this chance. But what is true of the natural world is true also of society. The more a social activity, a series of social processes, becomes too powerful for men's conscious control and grows above their heads, and the more it appears a matter of pure chance, then all the more surely within this chance the laws peculiar to it and inherent in it assert themselves as if by natural necessity (233-34).

If humanity is to survive, it will only be through the mastery of social laws, not only by revolutionaries in the capitalist and neo-colonial countries where an economy of waste and destruction now threatens the entire world, but in the socialist countries as well, where any illusion that communism at an advanced level follows smoothly from the initial establishment of socialist power has surely been abandoned.

To reconstruct the social laws, the processes, the mechanisms, whereby class society in all its variations emerged, and the nature of the social forms that preceded it, involves a delicate interweaving of theoretical and empirical considerations. Archaeological and ethnographic data on pre-class societies and on societies where class relations were developing independently of colonial relations established by the powers of Europe and Asia are spotty and ambiguous. Archaeological data on all but the broad outlines of socio-economic organization are generally suggestive, not conclusive, and to find records of a non-literate society means, of course, that it has already come into contact with, and hence been in some way affected by, the relations of commodity production. A basic dilemma, therefore, confronts the attempt to reconstruct the early stages of human history from the evidence at hand. Reconstructing fully communal societies as they functioned before becoming involved in trade and warfare with Europeans or with the state-societies that existed elsewhere in the world necessitates making certain assumptions about the social and political forms that are concomitant with living at simpler technological levels. Yet the reconstructions themselves are needed to demonstrate the correctness of the theoretical assumptions.

Instances where data on pre-class social relations are clear are, therefore, of great importance. Such, for example, is the case of the northeastern Algonkians where unusually detailed records by Jesuit missionaries and others demonstrated the lack of private land-ownership that had been ascribed to them. Where materials are available for ethnohistorical research into a given primitive culture, they reveal fundamental changes of the type that have been taking place independently in various parts of the world or have been developing rapidly during the recent centuries of colonial rule: the breaking down of the corporate kin group into individual families and the individualization of property rights, the downgrading of women's status, the strengthening of rank, and the usurpation of powers by chiefs—in short, the basis for class society. Nonetheless, areas where warfare and trade, often in

slaves as well as goods, have been causing vast upheavals for up
to four and five centuries of European influence and domination are
still commonly treated as if reconstructed 19th century social forms
represent "untouched" institutions.

To add to the resulting theoretical confusion, it is increasingly
common for anthropologists to analyze the forms and processes
of primitive institutions through quantification of what are largely
20th century materials.[28] Furthermore, in the pragmatic atmosphere of United States science, the tendency is to accept quantified
analysis, not as suggesting clues about significant relationships to
be analyzed, but as of itself indicating cause and effect relationships. The fact that quantified comparative analysis separates
traits from their social context is not seen as a serious problem.
The sociologist Talcott Parsons makes this explicit in a statement
of Marx's limitations, a statement worth quoting in full since it
describes so succinctly the limitations of contemporary Western
sociology.

Marx . . . tended to treat the socioeconomic structure of capitalist
enterprise as a single indivisible entity rather than breaking it down
analytically into a set of the distinct variables involved in it. It is this
analytical breakdown which is for present purposes the most distinctive
feature of modern sociological analysis, and which must be done to
take advantage of advances that have taken place. It results both in a
modification of the Marxian view of the system itself and enables the
establishment of relations to other aspects of the total social system,
aspects of which Marx was unaware. This change results in an important modification of Marx's empirical perspective in relation to the
class problem as in other contexts. The primary structural emphasis

28. For a recent review of cross-cultural surveys, see Naroll, 1970. An
early and influential venture in the quantification of ethnographic data was
initiated at Yale University by George Peter Murdock in a project later
known as the Human Relations Area Files. Data on some 250 societies were
coded and punched on IBM cards for the running of cross-tabulations.
Murdock is now continuing his research at the University of Pittsburgh. His
Social Structure (1949) was based on the assumption that correlations among
various social features in a world ethnographic sample would yield valid
generalizations about *primitive* social organization, in spite of the fact that
most of the societies in the sample had been changed by the impact of
conquest and/or colonialization. For a more productive use of statistical
analysis, tied in with a clearer theoretical perspective, see Carneiro's application of scale analysis to the study of evolutionary change (1962, 1968,
1970).

no longer falls on the orientation of capitalistic enterprise to profit and the theory of exploitation but rather the structure of occupational roles within the system of industrial society (1954: 324).

Parson's statement illustrates the type of conclusions that can be reached when social phenomena are naïvely lifted out of context for statistical study. Counting the occurrence of a phenomenon as part of its description and correlating its frequency with that of other phenomena are essential procedures. Problems enter when it is assumed or implied that to codify, quantify, and correlate one aspect of reality with another *ipso facto* reveals causal networks; when, after stating the limitations of statistical analysis for complex social phenomena, the analysis is carried out as if these limitations did not exist. Class status is defined through scaling of occupation and/or income and education, and endlessly correlated with other variables; mental illness is reduced to a scale and measured in different sections of a population; learning ability is tested along some single dimension and individual children are trapped in the confines of some arbitrary number. The net effect—indirectly also the cause—is a mechanical or static view of reality. That which numerically predominates at a given moment, as defined, rated, and counted according to some unstated value scheme of the researcher, is considered "proven" to characterize a situation. Thus measurements *ad infinitum* crowd the social science journals only to obscure rather than reveal, and much less prove, anything fundamental about social process. The upshot is to perpetuate the world of social myth in which we perforce live, to measure it, test it, analyze it, "discover" it—without ever lifting the veil and looking at it!

The contemporary Western social psychological view of experimentation is but an amplification of the same limitations. To put people in a room and manipulate them in various ways will show certain things about behavior, in some cases widely applicable, in most cases probably not, but seldom will it predict how people will act under basically changed circumstances. For this, the laboratory of ongoing history is necessary. The study of voting statistics over the years has indicated with surprising accuracy how people are likely to vote—given the existing framework. However, the question of greater interest, certainly to revolutionaries, remains untouched: what changes are needed in this framework to shift the pattern?

Here there is no substitute for Marx's method of detailed analysis in specific cases, based on a dialectical and materialist theory of relationships that must constantly be tested, elaborated upon, and refined, both through theory and action. Rather than seeking comparabilities in statistical terms among what are all too often superficial features of different situations, *comparabilities must be sought at the level of determinate mechanisms, at the level of processes that are generally hidden from easy view.* Statistical methods can not be allowed to influence theoretical considerations. And hypotheses about social laws or processes are ultimately to be tested in the laboratory of historical experience.

A consideration of the challenge to dialectical materialism put forth in Harris' recent *Rise of Anthropological Theory* (1968) helps clarify the Marxist method of analysis. Harris credits Marx as the pioneer in the "materialist strategy" of research to which he himself subscribes (655, 674), and he writes that, other historians of anthropology notwithstanding, Marx is clearly not irrelevant to anthropology. Instead, Harris points out, it would be closer to the truth to state "that cultural anthropology developed entirely in *reaction* to Marxism" (249, italics his); and he devotes a considerable part of his book to cogent analyses of the "cultural-idealism" or "mentalism" that characterizes the various schools of anthropology. On the other hand, dialectics is, to Harris, "ponderous double-talk" (219), and the Marxist commitment to the inseparability of theory and political action is pernicious to the search for scientific truth (220-22).

However, Harris is guilty of considerable "double-talk" in his efforts to disassociate the concept of social evolution from dialectics. Although he accepts change as "ubiquitous and incessant" (1971: 7), he argues that evolution involves, not "negation" or "contradiction," but "transformation." People may think in terms of dichotomies, and intellectual advances may often follow from "resolving contradictions between the extremes," but history does not proceed in this fashion (71). The description of evolutionary processes as negations of negations "is mere poetic analogy."

If the evolutionary process exemplifies the dialectic of negation, it does so simply by virtue of the absence of workable rules for distinguishing between negative and positive changes. Since evolution means transformation, or difference, it is always possible, in the absence of definite criteria, to declare that each and every evolutionary product is the negation of some earlier condition. . . . What all evolutionary processes have in common is not the "negation" of earlier forms, but *simply their transformation* (68-69, italics added).

Apparently Harris is addressing himself to the casual or conversational usages of the terms contradiction and negation rather than their meaning in the context of how to deal with change as an inherent attribute to all matter. If change is "ubiquitous and incessant," as Harris agrees, then being is becoming as Hegel argued, and reality is not comprised of *things* but of *processes*. Any phenomenon is not, as phrased in classical logic, *either* A *or* not-A; instead, it is *both* A *and* not-A, or in the process of always becoming something else—hence a "unity of opposites," an expression of "struggle," involving "contradiction" or "negation." The use of ordinary terms in a specialized sense is always somewhat awkward, but some such terminology is essential to deal conceptually with the reality of constant change.

Without the concept of contradiction as internal to the processes that we call matter, change is by implication external to any given phenomenon, a result of the interaction between it and other phenomena that are conceived in somewhat static terms. Yet any thoughtful scientist today recognizes that it is not things or states that are interacting, but processes; as the physicist studies the organization of forces in what we call atoms, the chemist the interacting atoms that make up molecules, the biochemist the combinations of these that make up cells, and so on up to the anthropologist who confronts historically evolving societal structures, it is clear that matter, as process, is integrated in a marvelously complex series of successively more inclusive levels. Hence that which can be studied by the scientist as the external "interactions" between two phenomena at one level are in fact internal "contradictions" at the more inclusive level where the two interacting phenomena form a more complex system. This is the understanding of reality that Harris is brushing aside when he decries "Marx's Hegelian infatuation with 'contradictions' " (223).

Harris's disavowal of dialectical concepts leads him to make such statements as that the class struggle, rather than exemplifying contradiction, "is simply an expression of irreconcilable competition between proletarians and bourgeoisie for control of the means of production" (223). Further, where he argues that the advantage of the Marxian model is not that it is dialectical, but that it is "diachronic and evolutionary," he writes:

Any diachronic model is capable of accommodating the fact that strains may accumulate until consistency on the old basis is no longer feasible, and there is a violent collapse in the whole system. But there is another kind of accumulation of dysfunctional strains which defeats the Hegelian dialectic: evolution through the slow accumulation of minor changes wrought by minor adjustments to minor stresses (236).

Two comments must be made. First, it is not just collapse of the old but *replacement* by the new that is essential to the process of evolution that has been called "negation." Second, since Harris agrees that evolution is transformation, there is presumably a point at which the accumulation of minor strains results in transformation or *qualitative change* in accordance with the principles of Marxist-Hegelian dialectic. It is interesting that Harris, in questioning Hegelian dialectics and despite his own materialist convictions, cannot resist a subtle inference of Hegelian idealism: "To the pervasive evolutionism of his times, he added the peculiar notion that entities or events could be comprehended, *or to say the same thing,* exist, only by virtue of their opposite, contradiction or negation" (67, italics added).

Harris's own stategy for analysis calls for the formulation of a materialistic or "etic" data language that will enable a community of scientific observers to treat their material objectively. He characterizes Marxist science as "explicitly bound to a political program," and writes: "If the point is to change the world rather than to interpret it, the Marxist sociologist ought not to hesitate to falsify data in order to make it more useful" (221). However, the Marxist commitment is not to a program as such; instead, the principle underlying the necessary unity of theory and action is that active identification with the presently oppressed but emerging class involves a commitment to the future direction of social change that is basic for full understanding. Some Marxists have indeed crassly distorted and manipulated social data; but, the fact is that such opportunism has not worked in the interest of beneficial change. Furthermore, as the history and sociology of science so amply document, there is no such thing as a community of observers that can avoid acting and reacting in response to their social status as scientists, no matter how detached they may attempt to be.

Harris convincingly, at times brilliantly, illustrates the extent to which idealism in anthropology is bound up with the failure to separate materialistically conceived structures and actions from the subjectively held conceptions of members of the societies being studied. His solution is to make clear a methodological distinction between "emic" and "etic" data (terms recently borrowed from linguistics by social anthropologists). Most ethnographic data are "emic" in that they are organized in terms of informants' views; they deal with distinctions that are "built up out of contrasts and discriminations significant, meaningful, real, accurate, or in some other fashion regarded as appropriate by the actors themselves" (571). For a materialist strategy to be achieved, a new data language must be developed to replace "the predominantly emic corpus of extant ethnography" with etic descriptions (569). Objectively derived, or "etic" data, depend "upon phenomenal distinctions judged appropriate by the community of scientific observers" (575). The emic/etic dichotomy:

rests upon the epistemological significance of describing cultural things through categories and relations which are necessarily isomorphic with those appropriate or meaningful to the actors, as opposed to categories and relations which arise independently in the ethnographer's data language. Thus, actual behavior can be treated in both an emic and etic fashion. An informant's description of what is actually happening . . . need not correspond to what the ethnographer sees or would see in the same situation (580-81).

Harris' concern is to differentiate emic from etic data in order to focus sharply on the material "etic" conditions that determine people's actions (and at times he departs from his own stricture that the emic/etic dichotomy is purely epistemological and applies the term etic to the material conditions of society (1971: 503). As his recent textbook exemplifies, he is deeply committed to exploding myths about the backward or irrational behavior of peasants in the emerging nations or the poor in our own society that buttress neocolonialism and racist institutions. In an earlier work, he demolished the assumption that Indian peasants irrationally and needlessly go undernourished while protecting the sacred cows that uselessly wander the countryside (1965). He pointed out that in addition to milk the cows produce bullocks that are necessary for ploughing; that their dung is essential for cooking fuel and for manure; that their hides are a prime source of leather; that they are free to wander, the better to forage; and that when they die there are plenty of people with no caste to lose by eating them another nice example of Harris' work is his critique of assumptions that culturally patterned attitudinal differences between the early Anglo-Saxon and Latin settlers in the New World were responsible for the differing relations among the races to be found in North and Latin America (1964). Harris documents the fact that differing race relations are instead based on historically developed differences in patterns for the exploitation of labor.

An enormous amount of such reinterpretation needs doing in anthropology, as Harris makes clear. However, his anti-dialectical —and idealist—placement of the observer outside the framework of goals and meanings and extreme separation of the material and ideological dimensions of society leave such reinterpretations incomplete. Harris' own views of the motive forces behind human history stress technological innovation in interaction with environmental influence. He is interested in the "precise demarcation of the sectors of sociocultural systems" and critical of concepts such as "mode of production" which leave so hazy, to him, "the boundary between economics and technology" (233). He quotes Marx's well-known premise from the Preface to the *Critique of Political Economy* that men's "social existence determines their consciousness" (229), and proceeds as if there were no further interaction between ideology and socio-economic structure, or for the role of consciousness in historical process. Instead he speaks of "emic ethnography" and "etic ethnography" as separate enterprises; indeed, a major point is "to insist upon the separateness of emic and etic phenomena and research strategies." He writes: "An etic approach, by definition, avoids the premises of the emic approach. From an etic point of view, the universe of meaning, purposes, goals, motivations, etc., is thus unapproachable" (579). *Yet until one has directly faced the problem of dealing with man's consciousness in material terms, as analyst as well as actor, one has not dealt with man, his history, his culture, or his science.*

By hindsight, mechanical materialism seems to work. The objective conditions—technological, economic, environmental—that preceded—hence "caused"—later developments can necessarily and inevitably be located. The more remote the period studied, the more the role of internal stresses, alternative choices, and revolutionary versus conservative ideologies that defined precisely how, when, and where major changes were initiated are lost in the ambiguities and spottiness of archaeological and historical data. However, for understanding contemporary history, the nature of tensions internal to systems, and the role of understanding as well as misunderstanding are seen to be crucial.

The existence of human consciousness and purpose introduces a type of complexity into the operations of human society that is not found in the rest of nature. In the past it was common to assume that, although society still eluded our grasp, control of natural processes was a mere matter of time. The awesome feat of landing a man on the moon would seem to verify such an assumption had it not come at a time when we have been forced to recognize that the piecemeal approach to natural processes that has characterized Western science is powerless to stop the "blind laws" of nature from asserting themselves at a more complex level and rendering the earth unfit for human life. The world, like society, is a product of history, of meteorological and geological history. Comfortable regularities (in the time and space limits of our solar system) like the atomic progression of minerals and the law of gravity function within the context of interconnecting and changing relationships of unlimited complexity. Now the fact that man is but an aspect of this complex whole has unavoidably asserted itself. Humanity can not for much longer muddle through the mess it has gotten into. It will take understanding to save us, and at the present stage of history, at least, the kind of understanding called Marxist.

October 1971
Polytechnic Institute of Brooklyn.

ACKNOWLEDGMENTS

I should like to thank my colleagues, Constance Sutton, Robert McC. Adams, and Martin Davis for their helpful criticisms of the draft of this introduction. I am also grateful to Martha Livingstone for her help in preparing the manuscript.—E.B.L.

THE ORIGIN OF THE FAMILY, PRIVATE PROPERTY AND THE STATE

by Frederick Engels

PREFACE TO THE FIRST EDITION

THE FOLLOWING chapters are, in a sense, the execution of a bequest. No less a man than Karl Marx had made it one of his future tasks to present the results of Morgan's researches in the light of the conclusions of his own—within certain limits, I may say our—materialistic examination of history, and thus to make clear their full significance. For Morgan in his own way had discovered afresh in America the materialistic conception of history discovered by Marx forty years ago, and in his comparison of barbarism and civilization it had led him, in the main points, to the same conclusions as Marx. And just as the professional economists in Germany were for years as busy in plagiarizing *Capital* as they were persistent in attempting to kill it by silence, so Morgan's *Ancient Society** received precisely the same treatment from the spokesmen of "prehistoric" science in England. My work can offer only a meagre substitute for what my departed friend no longer had the time to do. But I have the critical notes which he made to his extensive extracts from Morgan,[1] and as far as possible I reproduce them here.

According to the materialistic conception, the determining factor in history is, in the final instance, the production and reproduction of immediate life. This, again, is of a twofold character: on the one side, the production of the means of existence, of food, clothing and shelter and the tools necessary for that production; on the other side, the production of human beings themselves, the propagation of the species. The social organization under which the people of a

---

Ancient Society, or Researches in the Lines of Human Progress from Savagery, through Barbarism to Civilization, by Lewis H. Morgan, London, Macmillan & Co., 1877. The book was printed in America and is peculiarly difficult to obtain in London. The author died some years ago. [For the purposes of this edition, all references to *Ancient Society* are from the World Publishing Company edition, 1963, New York.]

1. Marx's Abstract of *Ancient Society* can be found in *Marx-Engels Archives* (in Russian), Vol. IX, 1941, 1-192. Engels' quotations from Marx in the text, unless otherwise stated, are from the Abstract.

particular historical epoch and a particular country live is determined by both kinds of production: by the stage of development
of labor on the one hand and of the family on the other. The
lower the development of labor and the more limited the amount of
its products, and consequently, the more limited also the wealth of
the society, the more the social order is found to be dominated by
kinship groups. However, within this structure of society based on
kinship groups the productivity of labor increasingly develops, and
with it private property and exchange, differences of wealth, the
possibility of utilizing the labor power of others, and hence the
basis of class antagonisms: new social elements, which in the course
of generations strive to adapt the old social order to the new
conditions, until at last their incompatibility brings about a complete upheaval. In the collision of the newly developed social
classes, the old society founded on kinship groups is broken up.
In its place appears a new society, with its control centered in the
state, the subordinate units of which are no longer kinship associations, but local associations; a society in which the system of the
family is completely dominated by the system of property, and
in which there now freely develop those class antagonisms and class
struggles that have hitherto formed the content of all *written*
history.

It is Morgan's great merit that he has discovered and reconstructed in its main lines this prehistoric basis of our written history,
and that in the kinship groups of the North American Indians he
has found the key to the most important and hitherto insoluble
riddles of earliest Greek, Roman and German history. His book
is not the work of a day. For nearly 40 years he wrestled with his
material until he was completely master of it. But that also makes
his book one of the few epoch-making works of our time.

In the following presentation, the reader will in general easily
distinguish what comes from Morgan and what I have added. In the
historical sections on Greece and Rome I have not confined myself
to Morgan's evidence, but have added what was available to me.
The sections on the Celts and the Germans are in the main my
work; Morgan had to rely here almost entirely on secondary
sources, and for German conditions—apart from Tacitus—on the
worthless and liberalistic falsifications of Mr. Freeman. The treat-

ment of the economic aspects, which in Morgan's book was sufficient for his purpose but quite inadequate for mine, has been done afresh by myself. And, finally, I am, of course, responsible for all the conclusions drawn, in so far as Morgan is not expressly cited.

1884. FREDERICK ENGELS

PREFACE TO THE FOURTH EDITION

THE EARLIER large editions of this work have been out of print now for almost half a year, and for some time the publisher has been asking me to prepare a new edition. Until now, more urgent work kept me from doing so. Since the appearance of the first edition seven years have elapsed, during which our knowledge of the primitive forms of the family has made important advances. There was, therefore, plenty to do in the way of improvements and additions; all the more so as the proposed stereotyping of the present text will make any further alterations impossible for some time.

I have accordingly submitted the whole text to a careful revision and made a number of additions which, I hope, take due account of the present state of knowledge. I also give in the course of this preface a short review of the development of the history of the family from Bachofen to Morgan; I do so chiefly because the chauvinistically inclined English anthropologists are still striving their utmost to kill by silence the revolution which Morgan's discoveries have effected in our conception of primitive society, while they appropriate his results without the slightest compunction. Elsewhere also the example of England is in some cases followed only too often.

My work has been translated into a number of other languages: first, Italian—*L'origine della famiglia, della proprietà privata e dello stato, versione riveduta dall'autore, di Pasquale Martignetti,* Benevento, 1885; then, Rumanian—*Origina familiei, proprietatei private si a statului, traducere de Joan Nadejde,* in the Jassy periodical *Contemporanul,* September 1885 to May 1886; further, Danish — *Familjens, Privatejendommens og Statens Oprindelse Dansk, af Forfattern gennemgaaet Udgave, besørgen af Gerson Trier, Köbenhavn,* 1888. A French translation by Henri Ravé, based on the present German edition, is on the press.

Before the beginning of the sixties, one cannot speak of a history of the family. In this field, the science of history was still completely under the influence of the Five Books of Moses. The patriarchal form of the family, which was there described in greater detail than anywhere else, was not only assumed without question to be the oldest form, but it was also identified—minus its polygamy—with the bourgeois family of today, as if the family had really experienced no historical development at all. At most it was admitted that in primitive times there might have been a period of sexual promiscuity. It is true that in addition to the monogamous form of the family, two other forms were known to exist—polygamy in the Orient and polyandry in India and Tibet; but these three forms could not be arranged in any historical order and merely appeared side by side without any connection. That among some peoples of ancient times, as well as among some savages still alive today, descent was reckoned not from the father but from the mother, and that the female line was therefore regarded as alone valid; that among many peoples of the present day in every continent marriage is forbidden within certain large groups which at that time had not been closely studied—these facts were indeed known and fresh instances of them were continually being collected. But nobody knew what to do with them, and even as late as E. B. Tylor's *Researches into the Early History of Mankind, etc.* (1865) they are listed as mere "curious customs," side by side with the prohibition among some savages against touching burning wood with an iron tool and similar religious mumbo jumbo.

The study of the history of the family dates from 1861, from the publication of Bachofen's *Mutterrecht.* [Mother Right]. In this work the author advances the following propositions: (1) That originally man lived in a state of sexual promiscuity, to describe which Bachofen uses the mistaken term "hetaerism"; (2) that such promiscuity excludes any certainty of paternity, that descent could therefore be reckoned only in the female line, according to mother right, and that this was originally the case amongst all the peoples of antiquity; (3) that since women, as mothers, were the only parents of the younger generation that were known with certainty, they held a position of such high respect and honor that it became the foundation, in Bachofen's conception, of a regular rule of women (gyneocracy); (4) that the transition to monogamy, where the women belonged to one man exclusively, involved a violation of a primitive religious law (that is, actually a violation of the traditional right of the other men to this woman), and that in order to expiate this violation or to purchase indulgence for it the woman had to be surrendered for a limited period.

Bachofen finds the proofs of these assertions in innumerable passages of ancient classical literature, which he collected with immense industry. According to him, the development from "hetaerism" to monogamy and from mother right to father right is accomplished, particularly among the Greeks, as the consequence of an advance in religious conceptions, introducing into the old hierarchy of the gods, representative of the old outlook, new divinities, representative of the new outlook, who push the former more and more into the background. Thus, according to Bachofen, it is not the development of men's actual conditions of life, but the religious reflection of these conditions inside their heads, which has brought about the historical changes in the social position of the sexes in relation to each other. In accordance with this view, Bachofen interprets the *Oresteia* of Aeschylus as the dramatic representation of the conflict between declining mother right and the new father right that arose and triumphed in the heroic age. For the sake of her paramour, Aegisthus, Clytemnestra slays her husband, Agamemnon, on his return from the Trojan War; but Orestes, her son by Agamemnon avenges his father's murder by slaying his mother. For this act he is pursued by the Erinyes [Furies], the demonic guardians of mother right, according to which matricide is the gravest and most inexpiable crime. But Apollo, who by the voice of his oracle had summoned Orestes to this deed, and Athena, who is called upon to give judgment—the two deities who here represent the new patriarchal order—take Orestes under their protection; Athena hears both sides. The whole matter of the dispute is briefly summed up in the debate which now takes place between Orestes and the Erinyes. Orestes contends that Clytemnestra has committed a double crime; she has slain *her* husband and thus she has also slain *his* father. Why should the Erinyes pursue him and not her, seeing that she is by far the more guilty? The answer is striking: *"Unrelated by blood* was she to the man she slew."

The murder of a man not related by blood, even if he be the

husband of the murderess, is expiable and does not concern the Erinyes. Their office is solely to punish murder between blood relations, and of such murders the most grave and the most inexpiable, according to mother right, is matricide. Apollo now comes forward in Orestes' defense. Athena calls upon the Areopagites—the Athenian jurors—to vote. The votes for Orestes' condemnation and for his acquittal are equal. Then Athena, as President of the Court, gives her vote for Orestes and acquits him. Father right has triumphed over mother right. The "gods of young descent," as the Erinyes themselves call them, have triumphed over the Erinyes, and the latter then finally allow themselves to be persuaded to take up a new office in the service of the new order.

This new but undoubtedly correct interpretation of the *Oresteia* is one of the best and finest passages in the whole book, but it proves at the same time that Bachofen believes at least as much as Aeschylus did in the Erinyes, Apollo and Athena; for, at bottom, he believes that the overthrow of mother right by father right was a miracle wrought during the Greek heroic age by these divinities. That such a conception, which makes religion the lever of world history, must finally end in pure mysticism, is clear. It is therefore a tough and by no means always a grateful task to plow through Bachofen's solid tome. But all that does not lessen his importance as a pioneer. He was the first to replace the vague phrases about some unknown primitive state of sexual promiscuity by proofs of the following facts: that abundant traces survive in ancient classical literature of a state prior to monogamy among the Greeks and Asiatics when not only did a man have sexual intercourse with several women, but a woman with several men, without offending against morality; that this custom did not disappear without leaving its traces in the limited surrender which was the price women had to pay for the right to monogamy; that therefore descent could originally be reckoned only in the female line, from mother to mother; that far into the period of monogamy, with its certain or at least acknowledged paternity, the female line was still alone recognized; and that the original position of the mothers, as the only certain parents of their children, secured for them, and thus for their whole sex, a higher social status than women have ever enjoyed since. Bachofen did not put these statements as clearly as this, for he was hindered by his mysticism. But he proved them; and in 1861 that was a real revolution.

Bachofen's massive volume was written in German, the language of the nation which at that time interested itself less than any other in the prehistory of the modern family. Consequently, he remained unknown. His first successor in the same field appeared in 1865, without ever having heard of Bachofen.

This successor was J. F. McLennan, the exact opposite of his predecessor. Instead of a mystic of genius, we have the dry-as-dust jurist; instead of the exuberant imagination of a poet, the plausible arguments of a barrister defending his brief. McLennan finds among many savage, barbarian, and even civilized peoples of ancient and modern times a form of marriage in which the bridegroom, alone or with his friends, must carry off the bride from her relations by a show of force. This custom must be the survival of an earlier custom when the men of one tribe did in fact carry off their wives by force from other tribes. What was the origin of this "marriage by capture"? So long as men could find enough women in their own tribe, there was no reason whatever for it. We find, however, no less frequently that among undeveloped peoples there are certain groups (which in 1865 were still often identified with the tribes themselves) within which marriage is forbidden, so that the men are obliged to take their wives, and women their husbands, from outside the group; whereas among other peoples the custom is that the men of one group must take their wives only from within their own group. McLennan calls the first peoples "exogamous" and the second "endogamous"; he then promptly proceeds to construct a rigid opposition between exogamous and endogamous "tribes." And although his own investigations into exogamy force the fact under his nose that in many, if not most or even in all, cases, this opposition exists only in his own imagination, he nevertheless makes it the basis of his whole theory. According to this theory, exogamous tribes can only obtain their wives from other tribes; and since in savagery there is a permanent state of war between tribe and tribe, these wives could only be obtained by capture.

McLennan then goes on to ask: whence this custom of exogamy? The conception of consanguinity and incest could not have anything to do with it, for these things only came much later. But there was another common custom among savages—the custom of killing female children immediately after birth. This would cause a surplus of men in each individual tribe, of which the inevitable and immediate consequence would be that several men possessed a wife in common (polyandry). And this would have the further consequence that it would be known who was the mother of a child, but not who its father was: hence relationship only in the female line, with exclusion of the male line—mother right. And a second consequence of the scarcity of women within a tribe—a scarcity which polyandry mitigated, but did not remove—was precisely this systematic, forcible abduction of women from other tribes.

As exogamy and polyandry are referable to one and the same cause— a want of balance between the sexes—we are forced to regard *all the exogamous races as having originally been polyandrous.* . . . Therefore we must hold it to be beyond dispute that among exogamous races the first system of kinship was that which recognized blood-ties through mothers only (McLennan, *Studies in Ancient History,* 1886. *Primitive Marriage,* 124).[2]

It is McLennan's merit to have directed attention to the general occurrence and great importance of what he calls exogamy. He did not by any means *discover* the existence of exogamous groups; still less did he understand them. Besides the early, scattered notes of many observers (these were McLennan's sources), Latham (*Descriptive Ethnology,* 1859) had given a detailed and accurate description of this institution among the Magars in India, and had said that it was very widespread and occurred in all parts of the world—a passage which McLennan himself cites. Morgan, in 1847, in his letters on the Iroquois (*American Review*) and in 1851 in *The League of the Iroquois,* had already demonstrated the existence of exogamous groups among this tribe and had given an accurate account of them; whereas McLennan, as we shall see, wrought greater confusion here with his legalistic mind than Bachofen wrought in the field of mother right with his mystical

2. John Ferguson McLennan, *Studies in Ancient History, Comprising a Reprint of "Primitive Marriage. An Inquiry into the Origin of the Form of Capture in Marriage Ceremonies,"* London and New York, 1886, 124-25. His book *Primitive Marriage* was first published in Edinburgh in 1865. The first edition of *Studies in Ancient Society* appeared in London in 1876. Later, Engels cites this edition.

fancies. It is also a merit of McLennan that he recognized matrilineal descent as the earlier system, though he was here anticipated by Bachofen, as he later acknowledged. But McLennan is not clear on this either; he always speaks of "kinship through females only," and this term, which is correct for an earlier stage, he continually applies to later stages of development when descent and inheritance were indeed still traced exclusively through the female line, but when kinship on the male side was also recognized and expressed. There you have the pedantic mind of the jurist, who fixes on a rigid legal term and goes on applying it unchanged when changed conditions have made it applicable no longer.

Apparently McLennan's theory, plausible though it was, did not seem any too well established even to its author. At any rate, he himself is struck by the fact that "it is observable that the form of capture is now most distinctly marked and impressive just among those races which have *male* kinship" (should be "descent in the male line") (*ibid.*, 140). And again: "It is a curious fact that nowhere now, that we are aware of, is infanticide *a system* where exogamy and the earliest form of kinship coexist" (*ibid.*, p. 146). Both these facts flatly contradict his method of explanation, and he can only meet them with new and still more complicated hypotheses.

Nevertheless, his theory found great applause and support in England. McLennan was here generally regarded as the founder of the history of the family and the leading authority on the subject. However many exceptions and variations might be found in individual cases, his opposition of exogamous and endogamous tribes continued to stand as the recognized foundation of the accepted view, and to act as blinkers, obstructing any free survey of the field under investigation and so making any decisive advance impossible. Against McLennan's exaggerated reputation in England—and the English fashion is copied elsewhere—it becomes a duty to set down the fact that he has done more harm with his completely mistaken antithesis between exogamous and endogamous "tribes" than he has done good by his research.

Facts were now already coming to light in increasing number which did not fit into his neat framework. McLennan knew only three forms of marriage: polygyny, polyandry and monogamy. But once attention had been directed to the question, more and more proofs were found that there existed among undeveloped peoples forms of marriage in which a number of men possessed a number of women in common, and Lubbock (*The Origin of Civilization,* 1870) recognized this group marriage ("communal marriage") as a historical fact.

Immediately afterwards, in 1871, Morgan came forward with new and, in many ways, decisive evidence. He had convinced himself that the peculiar system of consanguinity in force among the Iroquois was common to all the aboriginal inhabitants of the United States and therefore extended over a whole continent although it directly contradicted the degrees of relationship arising out of the system of marriage as actually practiced by these peoples. He then induced the Federal government to collect information about the systems of consanguinity among the other peoples of the world and to send out for this purpose tables and lists of questions prepared by himself. He discovered from the replies: (1) that the system of consanguinity of the American Indians was also in force among numerous peoples in Asia and, in a somewhat modified form, in Africa and Australia; (2) that its complete explanation was to be found in a form of group marriage which was just dying out in Hawaii and other Australasian islands; and (3) that side by side with this form of marriage a system of consanguinity was in force in the same islands which could only be explained through a still more primitive, now extinct, form of group marriage. He published the collected evidence, together with the conclusions he drew from it, in his *Systems of Consanguinity and Affinity,* 1871, and thus carried the debate on to an infinitely wider field. By starting from the systems of consanguinity and reconstructing from them the corresponding forms of family, he opened a new line of research and extended our range of vision into the prehistory of mankind. If this method proved to be sound, McLennan's pretty theories would be completely demolished.

McLennan defended his theory in a new edition of *Primitive Marriage (Studies in Ancient History,* 1876). Whilst he himself constructs a highly artificial history of the family out of pure hypotheses, he demands from Lubbock and Morgan not merely proofs for every one of their statements, but proofs as indisputably valid as if they were to be submitted in evidence in a Scottish court of law. And this is the man who, from Tacitus' report on the close relationship between maternal uncle and sister's son among the Germans (*Germania*, Chap. 20), from Caesar's report that the Britons in groups of ten or twelve possessed their wives in common, and from all the other reports of classical authors on community of wives among barbarians, calmly draws the conclusion that all these peoples lived in a state of polyandry! One might be listening to a prosecuting counsel who can allow himself every liberty in arguing his own case, but demands from defending counsel the most formal, legally valid proof for his every word.

He maintains that group marriage is pure imagination, and by so doing falls far behind Bachofen. He declares that Morgan's systems of consanguinity are mere codes of conventional politeness, the proof being that the Indians also address a stranger or a white man as "brother" or "father." One might as well say that the terms "father," "mother," "brother," and "sister" are mere meaningless forms of address because Catholic priests and abbesses are addressed as "father" and "mother," and because monks and nuns, and even freemasons and members of English trade unions and associations at their full sessions, are addressed as "brother" and "sister." In a word, McLennan's defense was miserably feeble.

But on one point he had still not been assailed. The opposition of exogamous and endogamous "tribes" on which his whole system rested not only remained unshaken, but was even universally acknowledged as the keystone of the whole history of the family. McLennan's attempt to explain this opposition might be inadequate and in contradiction with his own facts. But the antithesis itself, the existence of two mutually exclusive types of self-sufficient and independent tribes, of which the one type took their wives from within the tribe, while the other type absolutely forbade it—that was sacred gospel. Compare, for example, Giraud-Teulon's *Origines de la famille* (1874) and even Lubbock's *Origin of Civilization* (fourth edition, 1882).

Here Morgan takes the field with his main work, *Ancient Society* (1877), the work that underlies the present study. What Morgan had only dimly guessed in 1871 is now developed in full consciousness. There is no antithesis between endogamy and exogamy; up to the present, the existence of exogamous "tribes" has not been demonstrated anywhere. But at the time when group marriage still prevailed—and in all probability it prevailed everywhere at some time—the tribe was subdivided into a number of groups related by blood on the mother's side, gentes, within which it was strictly forbidden to marry, so that the men of a gens, though they could take their wives from within the tribe and generally did so, were compelled to take them from outside their gens. Thus while each gens was strictly exogamous, the tribe embracing all the gentes was no less endogamous—which finally disposed of the last remains of McLennan's artificial constructions.

But Morgan did not rest here. Through the gens of the American Indians, he was enabled to make his second great advance in his field of research. In this gens, organized according to mother right, he discovered the primitive form out of which had developed the later gens organized according to father right, the gens as we find it among the ancient civilized peoples. The Greek and Roman gens, the old riddle of all historians, now found its explanation in the Indian gens, and a new foundation was thus laid for the whole of primitive history.

This rediscovery of the primitive matriarchal gens as the earlier stage of the patriarchal gens of civilized peoples has the same importance for anthropology as Darwin's theory of evolution has for biology and Marx's theory of surplus value for political economy. It enabled Morgan to outline for the first time a history of the family in which for the present, so far as the material now available permits, at least the classic stages of development in their main outlines are now determined. That this opens a new epoch in the treatment of primitive history must be clear to everyone. The matriarchal gens has become the pivot on which the whole science turns; since its discovery we know where to look and what to look for in our research, and how to arrange the results. And, consequently, since Morgan's book, progress in this field has been made at a far more rapid speed.

Anthropologists, even in England, now generally appreciate, or rather appropriate, Morgan's discoveries. But hardly one of them has the honesty to admit that it is to Morgan that we owe this revolution in our ideas. In England they try to kill his book by silence, and dispose of its author with condescending praise for his *earlier* achievements; they niggle endlessly over details and remain obstinately silent about his really great discoveries. The original edition of *Ancient Society* is out of print; in America there is no sale for such things; in England, it seems, the book was systematically suppressed, and the only edition of this epoch-making work still circulating in the book trade is—the German translation.

Why this reserve? It is difficult not to see in it a conspiracy of silence; for politeness' sake, our recognized anthropologists generally pack their writings with quotations and other tokens of camaraderie. Is it, perhaps, because Morgan is an American, and for the English anthropologists it goes sorely against the grain that, despite their highly creditable industry in collecting material, they should be dependent for their general points of view in the arrangement and grouping of this material, for their ideas in fact, on two foreigners of genius, Bachofen and Morgan? They might put up with the German—but the American? Every Englishman turns patriotic when he comes up against an American, and of this I saw highly entertaining instances in the United States. Moreover, McLennan was, so to speak, the officially appointed founder and leader of the English school of anthropology. It was almost a principle of anthropological etiquette to speak of his artificially constructed historical series—child murder, polygyny, marriage by capture, matriarchal family—in tones only of profoundest respect. The slightest doubt in the existence of exogamous and endogamous "tribes" of absolute mutual exclusiveness was considered rank heresy. Morgan had committed a kind of sacrilege in dissolving all these hallowed dogmas into thin air. Into the bargain, he had done it in such a way that it only needed saying to carry immediate conviction; so that the McLennanites, who had hitherto been helplessly reeling to and fro between exogamy and endogamy, could only beat their brows and exclaim: "How could we be such fools as not to think of that for ourselves long ago?"

As if these crimes had not already left the official school with the option only of coldly ignoring him, Morgan filled the measure to overflowing by not merely criticizing civilization, the society of commodity production, the basic form of present-day society, in a manner reminiscent of Fourier, but also by speaking of a future transformation of this society in words which Karl Marx might have used. He had therefore amply merited McLennan's indignant reproach that "the historical method is antipathetical to Mr. Morgan's mind," and its echo as late as 1884 from Professor Giraud-Teulon of Geneva. In (1874) *Origines de la famille* this same gentleman was still groping helplessly in the maze of the McLennanite exogamy, from which Morgan had to come and rescue him!

Of the other advances which primitive anthropology owes to Morgan, I do not need to speak here; they are sufficiently discussed in the course of this study. The 14 years which have elapsed since the publication of his chief work have greatly enriched the material available for the study of the history of primitive human societies. The anthropologists, travelers and primitive historians by profession have now been joined by the comparative jurists, who have contributed either new material or new points of view. As a result, some of Morgan's minor hypotheses have been shaken or even disproved. But not one of the great leading ideas of his work has been ousted by this new material. The order which he introduced into primitive history still holds in its main lines today. It is, in fact, winning recognition to the same degree in which Morgan's responsibility for the great advance is carefully concealed.*[3]

FREDERICK ENGELS

London, June 16, 1891

* On the voyage back from New York in September 1888, I met a former member of Congress for the district of Rochester, who had known Lewis Morgan. Unfortunately, he could not tell me very much about him. He said that Morgan had lived in Rochester as a private individual, occupied only with his studies. His brother was a colonel, and had held a post in the War Department in Washington; it was through him that Morgan had managed to interest the government in his researches and to get several of his works published at public expense. While he was a member of Congress, my informant had also on more than one occasion used his influence on Morgan's behalf.

3. An excellent biography of Morgan has been written recently by Carl Resek: *Lewis Henry Morgan: American Scholar,* Chicago, University of Chicago Press, 1960. See also Leslie White's introduction to Lewis H. Morgan's *Ancient Society,* Cambridge, Belknap Press of Harvard University Press, 1964.

CHAPTER I

STAGES OF PREHISTORIC CULTURE

MORGAN WAS the first person with expert knowledge to attempt to introduce a definite order into the history of primitive man; so long as no important additional material makes changes necessary, his classification will undoubtedly remain in force.

Of the three main epochs—savagery, barbarism, and civilization —he is concerned, of course, only with the first two and the transition to the third. He divides both savagery and barbarism into lower, middle, and upper stages according to the progress made in the production of food; for, he says:

> Upon their skill in this direction, the whole question of human supremacy on the earth depended. Mankind are the only beings who may be said to have gained an absolute control [Engels inserts "almost"] over the production of food. . . . It is accordingly probable that the great epochs of human progress have been identified, more or less directly, with the enlargement of the sources of subsistence [1963: 19].

The development of the family takes a parallel course, but here the periods have not such striking marks of differentiation.

1. SAVAGERY

(a) *Lower stage.* Childhood of the human race. Man still lived in his original habitat, in tropical or subtropical forests, and was partially at least a tree-dweller, for otherwise his survival among huge beasts of prey cannot be explained. Fruit, nuts and roots served him for food. The development of articulate speech is the main result of this period. Of all the peoples known to history none was still at this primitive level. Though this period may have lasted thousands of years[4] we have no direct evidence to prove its exist-

4. The period of transition from early hominids, as represented by Austra-lopithecus of Africa, to Homo sapiens is now estimated at 2,000,000 years or more. The evidence suggests that Australopithecus evolved in savannah country and relied on group cooperation and intelligence for survival. *See* 247.

ence; but once the evolution of man from the animal kingdom is admitted, such a transitional stage must necessarily be assumed.

(b) *Middle stage.* Begins with the utilization of fish for food (including crabs, mussels, and other aquatic animals) and with the use of fire. The two are complementary, since fish becomes fully available only by the use of fire. With this new source of nourishment, men now became independent of climate and locality; even as savages, they could, by following the rivers and coasts, spread over most of the earth. Proof of these migrations is the distribution over every continent of the crudely worked, unpolished flint tools of the earlier Stone Age, known as "paleoliths," all or most of which date from this period. New environments, ceaseless exercise of his inventive faculty, and the ability to produce fire by friction led man to discover new kinds of food: farinaceous roots and tubers, for instance, were baked in hot ashes or in ground ovens. With the invention of the first weapons, club and spear, game could sometimes be added to the fare. But the tribes which figure in books as living entirely, that is, exclusively, by hunting never existed in reality; the yield of the hunt was far too precarious. At this stage, owing to the continual uncertainty of food supplies, cannibalism seems to have arisen and was practiced from now onwards for a long time. The Australian aborigines and many of the Polynesians are still in this middle stage of savagery today.[5]

(c) *Upper stage.* Begins with the invention of the bow and arrow, whereby game became a regular source of food, and hunting a normal form of work. Bow, string, and arrow already constitute a very complex instrument, whose invention implies long, ac-

---

5. The totally erroneous allocation of the Polynesians to such a stage of technological development was commonly cited in my student days as evidence of the uselessness of Morgan's entire formulation. To go further, not only would the complex horticultural societies of Polynesia not fit "middle savagery", but neither would the Australians or any other living hunter-gatherers. With the appearance of Homo sapiens some 40,000 years ago, a technological level equivalent to Morgan's formulation of the "upper stage of savagery" was achieved. The *regular* use of human meat as a source of food has been documented for no known group, although ritual eating both of dead relatives and enemies is very widespread and sometimes leads to individual cannibalistic acts. A few archaeological sites are suggestive of cannibalism although the evidence is far from clear; that human groups ever depended to any extent on human meat remains doubtful.

cumulated experience and sharpened intelligence and therefore knowledge of many other inventions as well. We find, in fact, that the peoples acquainted with the bow and arrow but not yet with pottery (from which Morgan dates the transition to barbarism) are already making some beginnings towards settlement in villages and have gained some control over the production of means of subsistence; we find wooden vessels and utensils; finger-weaving (without looms) with filaments of bark; plaited baskets of bast or osier; sharpened (neolithic) stone tools. With the discovery of fire and the stone ax, dugout canoes now become common; beams and planks are also sometimes used for building houses. We find all these advances, for instance, among the Indians of northwest America, who are acquainted with the bow and arrow but not with pottery.[6] The bow and arrow was for savagery what the iron sword was for barbarism and firearms for civilization—the decisive weapon.

2. BARBARISM

(a) *Lower stage.* Dates from the introduction of pottery.[7] In many cases it has been proved, and in all it is probable, that the first pots originated from the habit of covering baskets or wooden vessels with clay to make them fireproof; in this way it was soon discovered that the clay mold answered the purpose without any inner vessel.

Thus far we have been able to follow a general line of development applicable to all peoples at a given period without distinction of place. With the beginning of barbarism, however, we have reached a stage when the difference in the natural endowments of the two hemispheres of the earth comes into play. The characteristic feature of the period of barbarism is the domestication and breeding of animals and the cultivation of plants. Now, the Eastern

6. To this stage would belong most hunter-gatherers, but not the Northwest Coast Indians. Their regular and seasonal supply of salmon, which they smoke-dried and stored, afforded them an economy equivalent to that of horticulturalists. For further discussion of these stages, *see* Leacock's introduction to Morgan's *Ancient Society,* I, xi-xv.

7. In most cases pottery is associated with the cultivation of plants, but not always. In Polynesia wooden bowls and coconut shells were used instead.

Hemisphere, the so-called Old World, possessed nearly all the animals adaptable to domestication, and all the varieties of cultivable cereals except one; the Western Hemisphere, America, had no mammals that could be domesticated except the llama, which, moreover, was only found in one part of South America, and of all the cultivable cereals only one, though that was the best, namely, maize. Owing to these differences in natural conditions, the population of each hemisphere now goes on its own way, and different landmarks divide the particular stages in each of the two cases.

(b) *Middle stage.* Begins in the Eastern Hemisphere with domestication of animals; in the Western, with the cultivation, by means of irrigation, of plants for food, and with the use of adobe (sun-dried) bricks and stone for building.

We will begin with the Western Hemisphere, as here this stage was never superseded before the European conquest.

At the time when they were discovered, the Indians at the lower stage of barbarism (comprising all the tribes living east of the Mississippi) were already practicing some horticulture of maize and possibly also of pumpkins, melons, and other garden plants, from which they obtained a very considerable part of their food. They lived in wooden houses in villages protected by stockades. The tribes in the northwest, particularly those in the region of the Columbia River, were still at the upper stage of savagery and acquainted neither with pottery nor with any form of horticulture. The so-called Pueblo Indians of New Mexico, however, and the Mexicans, Central Americans, and Peruvians at the time of the Conquest were at the middle stage of barbarism. They lived in houses like fortresses, made of adobe brick or of stone, and cultivated maize and other plants, varying according to locality and climate, in artificially irrigated plots of ground, which supplied their main source of food; some animals even had also been domesticated—the turkey and other birds by the Mexicans, the llama by the Peruvians. They could also work metals, but not iron; hence they were still unable to dispense with stone weapons and tools. The Spanish Conquest then cut short any further independent development.

In the Eastern Hemisphere the middle stage of barbarism began with the domestication of animals providing milk and meat, but horticulture seems to have remained unknown far into this period.[8] It was, apparently, the domestication and breeding of animals and the formation of herds of considerable size that led to the differentiation of the Aryans and Semites from the mass of barbarians. The European and Asiatic Aryans still have the same names for cattle, but those for most of the cultivated plants are already different.

In suitable localities, the keeping of herds led to a pastoral life; the Semites lived upon the grassy plains of the Euphrates and Tigris, and the Aryans upon those of India, of the Oxus and Jaxartes,[9] and of the Don and the Dnieper. It must have been on the borders of such pasture lands that animals were first domesticated. To later generations, consequently, the pastoral tribes appear to have come from regions which, so far from being the cradle of mankind, were almost uninhabitable for their savage ancestors and even for man at the lower stages of barbarism. But having once accustomed themselves to pastoral life in the grassy plains of the rivers, these barbarians of the middle period would never have dreamed of returning willingly to the native forests of their ancestors. Even when they were forced further to the north and west, the Semites and Aryans could not move into the forest regions of western Asia and of Europe until by cultivation of grain they had made it possible to pasture and especially to winter their herds on this less favorable land. It is more than probable that among these tribes the cultivation of grain originated from the need for cattle fodder and only later became important as a human food supply.

The plentiful supply of milk and meat and especially the beneficial effect of these foods on the growth of the children account perhaps for the superior development of the Aryan and Semitic races. It is a fact that the Pueblo Indians of New Mexico, who are reduced to an almost entirely vegetarian diet, have a smaller brain than the Indians at the lower stage of barbarism, who eat more meat and fish.[10] In any case, cannibalism now gradually dies out, sur-

8. The priority of animal domestication over horticulture in the Old World is doubtful. Present evidence suggests the close association of both developments.

9. Ancient names of the Central Asian rivers: the Amu Darya and Syr Darya.

10. Gross brain size, once within the range of the human species, has, of course, no relation to ability. Brain size correlates with body size; larger people are not more intelligent than smaller people.

viving only as a religious act or as a means of working magic, which is here almost the same thing.

(c) *Upper stage.* Begins with the smelting of iron ore and passes into civilization with the invention of alphabetic writing and its use for literary records. This stage (as we have seen, only the Eastern Hemisphere passed through it independently) is richer in advances in production than all the preceding stages together. To it belong the Greeks of the heroic age, the tribes of Italy shortly before the foundation of Rome, the Germans of Tacitus and the Norsemen of the Viking age.

Above all, we now first meet the iron plowshare drawn by cattle, which made large-scale agriculture, the cultivation of fields, possible and thus created a practically unrestricted food supply in comparison with previous conditions. This led to the clearance of forest land for tillage and pasture, which in turn was impossible on a large scale without the iron ax and the iron spade. Population rapidly increased in number, and in small areas became dense. Prior to field agriculture, conditions must have been very exceptional if they allowed half a million people to be united under a central organization; probably such a thing never occurred.[11]

We find the upper stage of barbarism at its highest in the Homeric poems, particularly in the *Iliad*. Fully developed iron tools, the bellows, the hand mill, the potter's wheel, the making of oil and wine, metal work developing almost into a fine art, the wagon and the war chariot, shipbuilding with beams and planks, the beginnings of architecture as art, walled cities with towers and battlements, the Homeric epic and a complete mythology—these are the chief legacy brought by the Greeks from barbarism into civilization. When we compare the descriptions which Caesar and even Tacitus give of the Germans, who stood at the beginning of the cultural stage from which the Homeric Greeks were just preparing to make the next advance, we realize how rich was the development of production within the uppe · stage of barbarism.

---

11. Here again, although in many cases a specific technological innovation will signal a major advance in productivity, the same advance may be made in other ways. For example, the Andean Indians lacked iron or cattle but nonetheless built a productive enough agriculture, using fertilization, terracing and irrigation, to support a large empire. The Inca empire comprised some six million subjects.

The sketch which I have given here, following Morgan, of the development of mankind through savagery and barbarism to the beginnings of civilization, is already rich enough in new features; what is more, they cannot be disputed since they are drawn directly from the process of production. Yet my sketch will seem flat and feeble compared with the picture to be unrolled at the end of our travels; only then will the transition from barbarism to civilization stand out in full light and in all its striking contrasts. For the time being, Morgan's division may be summarized thus: Savagery—the period in which man's appropriation of products in their natural state predominates; the products of human art are chiefly instruments which assist this appropriation. Barbarism— the period during which man learns to breed domestic animals and to practice agriculture, and acquires methods of increasing the supply of natural products by human activity. Civilization—the period in which man learns a more advanced application of work to the products of nature, the period of industry proper and of art.

CHAPTER II

THE FAMILY

MORGAN, WHO spent a great part of his life among the Iroquois Indians—settled to this day in New York State—and was adopted into one of their tribes (the Senecas), found in use among them a system of consanguinity which was in contradiction to their actual family relationships. There prevailed among them a form of monogamy easily terminable on both sides, which Morgan calls the "pairing family." The issue of the married pair was therefore known and recognized by everybody: there could be no doubt about whom to call father, mother, son, daughter, brother, sister. But these names were actually used quite differently. The Iroquois calls not only his own children his sons and daughters, but also the children of his brothers; and they call him father. The children of his sisters, however, he calls his nephews and nieces, and they call him their uncle. The Iroquois woman, on the other hand, calls her sisters' children, as well as her own, her sons and daughters, and they call her mother. But her brothers' children she calls her nephews and nieces, and she is known as their aunt. Similarly, the children of brothers call one another brother and sister, and so do the children of sisters. A woman's own children and the children of her brother, on the other hand, call one another cousins. And these are not mere empty names, but expressions of actual conceptions of nearness and remoteness, of equality and difference in the degrees of consanguinity: these conceptions serve as the foundation of a fully elaborated system of consanguinity through which several hundred different relationships of one individual can be expressed. What is more, this system is not only in full force among all American Indians (no exception has been found up to the present), but also retains its validity almost unchanged among the aborigines of India, the Dravidian tribes in the Deccan and the Gaura tribes in Hindustan. To this day the Tamils of southern India and the

Iroquois Seneca Indians in New York State still express more than two hundred degrees of consanguinity in the same manner. And among these tribes of India, as among all the American Indians, the actual relationships arising out of the existing form of the family contradict the system of consanguinity.

How is this to be explained? In view of the decisive part played by consanguinity in the social structure of all savage and barbarian peoples, the importance of a system so widespread cannot be dismissed with phrases. When a system is general throughout America and also exists in Asia among peoples of a quite different race, when numerous instances of it are found with greater or less variation in every part of Africa and Australia, then that system has to be historically explained, not talked out of existence, as McLennan, for example, tried to do. The names of father, child, brother and sister are no mere complimentary forms of address; they involve quite definite and very serious mutual obligations which together make up an essential part of the social constitution of the peoples in question.

The explanation was found. In the Sandwich Islands (Hawaii) there still existed in the first half of the 19th century a form of family in which the fathers and mothers, brothers and sisters, sons and daughters, uncles and aunts, nephews and nieces were exactly what is required by the American and ancient Indian system of consanguinity. But now comes a strange thing. Once again, the system of consanguinity in force in Hawaii did not correspond to the actual form of the Hawaiian family. For according to the Hawaiian system of consanguinity all children of brothers and sisters are without exception brothers and sisters of one another and are considered to be the common children not only of their mother and her sisters or of their father and his brothers, but of all the brothers and sisters of both their parents without distinction. While, therefore, the American system of consanguinity presupposes a more primitive form of the family which has disappeared in America, but still actually exists in Hawaii, the Hawaiian system of consanguinity, on the other hand, points to a still earlier form of the family which, though we can nowhere prove it to be still in existence, nevertheless *must* have existed; for otherwise the corresponding system of consanguinity could never have arisen.

The family [says Morgan] represents an active principle. It is never stationary, but advances from a lower to a higher form as society advances from a lower to a higher condition. . . . Systems of consanguinity, on the contrary, are passive; recording the progress made by the family at long intervals apart, and only changing radically when the family has radically changed [1963: 444].

"And," adds Marx, "the same is true of the political, juridical, religious, and philosophical systems in general." While the family undergoes living changes, the system of consanguinity ossifies; while the system survives by force of custom, the family outgrows it. But just as Cuvier could deduce from the marsupial bone of an animal skeleton found near Paris that it belonged to a marsupial animal and that extinct marsupial animals once lived there, so with the same certainty we can deduce from the historical survival of a system of consanguinity that an extinct form of family once existed which corresponded to it.

The systems of consanguinity and the forms of the family we have just mentioned differ from those of today in the fact that every child has more than one father and mother. In the American system of consanguinity, to which the Hawaiian family corresponds, brother and sister cannot be the father and mother of the same child; but the Hawaiian system of consanguinity, on the contrary, presupposes a family in which this was the rule. Here we find ourselves among forms of family which directly contradict those hitherto generally assumed to be alone valid. The traditional view recognizes only monogamy, with, in addition, polygamy on the part of individual men, and at the very most polyandry on the part of individual women; being the view of moralizing philistines, it conceals the fact that in practice these barriers raised by official society are quietly and calmly ignored. The study of primitive history, however, reveals conditions where the men live in polygamy and their wives in polyandry at the same time, and their common children are therefore considered common to them all—and these conditions in their turn undergo a long series of changes before they finally end in monogamy. The trend of these changes is to narrow more and more the circle of people comprised within the common bond of marriage, which was originally very wide, until at last it includes only the single pair, the dominant form of marriage today.

Reconstructing thus the past history of the family, Morgan, in agreement with most of his colleagues, arrives at a primitive stage when unrestricted sexual freedom prevailed within the tribe, every woman belonging equally to every man and every man to every woman. Since the 18th century there had been talk of such a primitive state, but only in general phrases. Bachofen—and this is one of his great merits—was the first to take the existence of such a state seriously and to search for its traces in historical and religious survivals. Today we know that the traces he found do not lead back to a social stage of promiscuous sexual intercourse, but to a much later form—namely, group marriage. The primitive social stage of promiscuity, if it ever existed, belongs to such a remote epoch that we can hardy expect to prove its existence *directly* by discovering its social fossils among backward savages. Bachofen's merit consists in having brought this question to the forefront for examination.*

Lately it has become fashionable to deny the existence of this initial stage in human sexual life. Humanity must be spared this "shame." It is pointed out that all direct proof of such a stage is lacking, and particular appeal is made to the evidence from the rest of the animal world; for, even among animals, according to the numerous facts collected by Letourneau (*Evolution du mariage et de la famille,* 1888), complete promiscuity in sexual intercourse marks a low stage of development. But the only conclusion I can draw from all these facts, so far as man and his primitive conditions of life are concerned, is that they prove nothing whatever. That vertebrates mate together for a considerable period is sufficiently explained by physiological causes—in the case of birds, for example, by the female's need for help during the brooding period;

---

* Bachofen proves how little he understood his own discovery, or rather his guess, by using the term "hetaerism" to describe this primitive state. For the Greeks, when they introduced the word, hetaerism meant intercourse of men, unmarried or living in monogamy, with unmarried women; it always presupposes a definite form of marriage outside which this intercourse takes place and includes at least the possibility of prostitution. The word was never used in any other sense, and it is in this sense that I use it with Morgan. Bachofen everywhere introduces into his extremely important discoveries the most incredible mystifications through his notion that in their historical development the relations between men and women had their origin in men's contemporary religious conceptions, not in their actual conditions of life.

examples of faithful monogamy among birds prove nothing about man for the simple reason that men are not descended from birds. And if strict monogamy is the height of all virtue, then the palm must go to the tapeworm, which has a complete set of male and female sexual organs in each of its 50 to 200 proglottides or sections, and spends its whole life copulating in all its sections with itself. Confining ourselves to mammals, however, we find all forms of sexual life—promiscuity, indications of group marriage, polygyny, monogamy. Polyandry alone is lacking—it took human beings to achieve that. Even our nearest relations, the quadrumana, exhibit every possible variation in the grouping of males and females; and if we narrow it down still more and consider only the four anthropoid apes, all that Letourneau has to say about them is that they are sometimes monogamous, sometimes polygamous, while Saussure, quoted by Giraud-Teulon, maintains that they are monogamous. The more recent assertions of the monogamous habits of the anthropoid apes which are cited by Westermarck (*The History of Human Marriage,* London, 1891) are also very far from proving anything. In short, our evidence is such that honest Letourneau admits: "Among mammals there is no strict relation between the degree of intellectual development and the form of sexual life." And Espinas (*Des sociétés animales,* 1877) says in so many words:

The herd is the highest social group which we can observe among animals. It is composed, *so it appears,* of families, but from the start *the family and the herd are in conflict with one another* and develop in inverse proportion.

As the above shows, we know practically nothing definite about the family and other social groupings of the anthropoid apes; the evidence is flatly contradictory, which is not to be wondered at. The evidence with regard to savage human tribes is contradictory enough, requiring very critical examination and sifting, and ape societies are far more difficult to observe than human. For the present, therefore, we must reject any conclusion drawn from such completely unreliable reports.

The sentence quoted from Espinas, however, provides a better starting point. Among the higher animals the herd and the family are not complementary to one another, but antagonistic. Espinas shows very well how the jealousy of the males during the mating season loosens the ties of every social herd or temporarily breaks it up.

When the family bond is close and exclusive, herds form only in exceptional cases. When on the other hand free sexual intercourse or polygamy prevails, the herd comes into being almost spontaneously. . . . Before a herd can be formed, family ties must be loosened and the individual must have become free again. This is the reason why organized flocks are so rarely found among birds. . . . We find more or less organized societies among mammals, however, precisely because here the individual is not merged in the family. . . . In its first growth, therefore, the common feeling of the herd has no greater enemy than the common feeling of the family. We state it without hesitation: only by absorbing families which had undergone a radical change could a social form higher than the family have developed; at the same time, these families were thereby enabled later to constitute themselves afresh under infinitely more favorable circumstances [Espinas, *op. cit.*, quoted by Giraud-Teulon, *Origines du mariage et de la famille*, 1884, 518-20].

Here we see that animal societies are, after all, of some value for drawing conclusions about human societies; but the value is only negative. So far as our evidence goes, the higher vertebrates know only two forms of family—polygyny or separate couples; each form allows only *one* adult male, only one husband. The jealousy of the male, which both consolidates and isolates the family, sets the animal family in opposition to the herd. The jealousy of the males prevents the herd, the higher social form, from coming into existence, or weakens its cohesion, or breaks it up during the mating period; at best, it attests to its development. This alone is sufficient proof that animal families and primitive human society are incompatible, and that when primitive men were working their way up from the animal creation, they either had no family at all or a form that does not occur among animals. In small numbers, an animal so defenseless as evolving man might struggle along even in conditions of isolation, with no higher social grouping than the single male and female pair, such as Westermarck, following the reports of hunters, attributes to the gorillas and the chimpanzees. For man's development beyond the level of the animals, for the achievement of the greatest advance nature can show, something more was needed: the power of defense lacking to the individual had to be made good by the united strength and cooperation of the herd. To explain the transition to humanity from conditions such as those in which the anthropoid apes live today would be quite impossible; it looks much more as if these apes had strayed off the line of evolution and were gradually dying out or at least degenerating. That alone is sufficient ground for rejecting all attempts based on parallels drawn between their forms of family and those of primitive man. Mutual toleration among the adult males, freedom from jealousy, was the first condition for the formation of those larger, permanent groups in which alone animals could become men. And what, in fact, do we find to be the oldest and most primitive form of family whose historical existence we can indisputably prove and which in one or two parts of the world we can still study today?—group marriage, the form of family in which whole groups of men and whole groups of women mutually possess one another, and which leaves little room for jealousy. And at a later stage of development we find the exceptional form of polyandry, which positively revolts every jealous instinct and is therefore unknown among animals. But, as all known forms of group marriage are accompanied by such peculiarly complicated regulations that they necessarily point to earlier and simpler forms of sexual relations, and therefore in the last resort to a period of promiscuous intercourse corresponding to the transition from the animal to the human, the references to animal marriages only bring us back to the very point from which we were to be led away for good and all.

What, then, does promiscuous sexual intercourse really mean? It means the absence of prohibitions and restrictions which are or have been in force. We have already seen the barrier of jealousy go down. If there is one thing certain, it is that the feeling of jealousy develops relatively late. The same is true of the conception of incest. Not only were brother and sister originally man and wife, sexual intercourse between parents and children is still permitted among many peoples today. Bancroft (*The Native Races of the Pacific States of North America,* 1875, Vol. I), testifies to it among the Kaviats on the Bering Straits, the Kadiaks near Alaska, and the Tinneh in the interior of British North America. Letourneau compiled reports of it among the Chippewa Indians, the Cucus in Chile, the Caribs, the Karens in Burma—to say nothing of the stories told by the old Greeks and Romans about the Parthians, Persians, Scythians, Huns, and so on.[12] Before incest was invented—for incest *is* an invention, and a very valuable one, too—sexual intercourse between parents and children did not arouse any more repulsion than sexual intercourse between other persons of different generations, and that occurs today even in the most philistine countries without exciting any great horror; even "old maids" of over 60, if they are rich enough, sometimes marry young men in their 30's. But if we consider the most primitive known forms of family apart from their conceptions of incest—conceptions which are totally different from ours and frequently in direct contradiction to them—then the form of sexual intercourse can only be described as promiscuous—promiscuous in so far as the restrictions later established by custom did not yet exist. But in everyday practice that by no means necessarily implies general mixed mating. Temporary pairings of one man with one woman were not in any way excluded, just as in the cases of group marriages today the majority of relationships are of this character. And when Westermarck, the latest writer to deny the existence of such a primitive state, applies the term "marriage" to every relationship in which the two sexes remain mated until the birth of the offspring, we must point out that this kind of marriage can very well occur under the conditions of promiscuous intercourse without contradicting the principle of promiscuity—the absence of any restriction imposed by custom on sexual intercourse. Westermarck, however, takes the standpoint that promiscuity "involves a suppression of individual inclinations," and that therefore "the most genuine form of it is prostitution." In my opinion, any understanding of primitive society is impossible to people who only see it as a brothel. We will return to this point when discussing group marriage.

According to Morgan, from this primitive state of promiscuous intercourse there developed, probably very early:

12. Parent-child marriage has not been firmly documented for any culture. Cases where it has been reported often turn out to be marriage with *categorical* parents according to kinship terminologies, not with biological parents. In pastoral nomadic cultures such as those cited, a man of rank may inherit his father's wives, but does not have intercourse with his own mother.

1. THE CONSANGUINE FAMILY, THE FIRST STAGE OF THE FAMILY

Here the marriage groups are separated according to generations: all the grandfathers and grandmothers within the limits of the family are all husbands and wives of one another; so are also their children, the fathers and mothers; the latter's children will form a third circle of common husbands and wives; and their children, the great-grandchildren of the first group, will form a fourth. In this form of marriage, therefore, only ancestors and progeny, and parents and children, are excluded from the rights and duties (as we should say) of marriage with one another. Brothers and sisters, male and female cousins of the first, second, and more remote degrees, are all brothers and sisters of one another, and *precisely for that reason* they are all husbands and wives of one another. At this stage the relationship of brother and sister also includes as a matter of course the practice of sexual intercourse with one another.* In its typical form, such a family would consist of the descendants of a single pair, the descendants of these

---

* In a letter written in the spring of 1882, Marx expresses himself in the strongest terms about the complete misrepresentation of primitive times in Wagner's text to the *Nibelungen:* "Have such things been heard, that brother embraced sister as a bride?" To Wagner and his "lecherous gods" who, quite in the modern manner, spice their love affairs with a little incest, Marx replies: "In primitive times the sister *was* the wife, *and that was moral."*

[*To the Fourth edition.*] A French friend of mine [Bonnier] who is an admirer of Wagner is not in agreement with this note. He observes that already in the Elder Edda, on which Wagner based his story, in the *Oegisdrecka,* Loki makes the reproach to Freya: "In the sight of the gods thou didst embrace thine own brother." Marriage between brother and sister, he argues, was therefore forbidden already at that time. The *Oegisdrecka* is the expression of a time when belief in the old myths had completely broken down; it is purely a satire on the gods, in the style of Lucian. If Loki as Mephistopheles makes such a reproach to Freya, it tells rather against Wagner. Loki also says some lines later to Njord: "With thy sister didst thou breed such a son" *(vidh systur thinni gaztu slikan mög).* Njord is not, indeed, an Asa, but a Vana, and says in the Ynglinga saga that marriages between brothers and sisters are usual in Vanaland, which was not the case among the Asas. This would seem to show that the Vanas were more ancient gods than the Asas. At any rate, Njord lives among the Asas as one of themselves, and therefore the *Oegisdrecka* is rather a proof that at the time when the Norse sagas of the gods arose, marriages between brothers and sisters, at any rate among the gods, did not yet excite any horror. If one wants to find excuses for Wagner, it would perhaps be better to cite Goethe instead of the Edda, for in his ballad of the God and the Bayadere Goethe commits a similar mistake in regard to the religious surrender of women, which he makes far too similar to modern prostitution.

descendants in each generation being again brothers and sisters, and therefore husbands and wives, of one another.

The consanguine family is extinct. Even the most primitive peoples known to history provide no demonstrable instance of it. But that it *must* have existed, we are compelled to admit; for the Hawaiian system of consanguinity still prevalent today throughout the whole of Polynesia expresses degrees of consanguinity which could only arise in this form of family; and the whole subsequent development of the family presupposes the existence of the consanguine family as a necessary preparatory stage.

2. THE PUNALUAN FAMILY

If the first advance in organization consisted in the exclusion of parents and children from sexual intercourse with one another, the second was the exclusion of sister and brother. On account of the greater nearness in age, this second advance was infinitely more important, but also more difficult, than the first. It was effected gradually, beginning probably with the exclusion from sexual intercourse of one's own brothers and sisters (children of the same mother) first in isolated cases and then by degrees as a general rule (even in this century exceptions were found in Hawaii), and ending with the prohibition of marriage even between collateral brothers and sisters, or, as we should say, between first, second, and third cousins. It affords, says Morgan, "a good illustration of the operation of the principle of natural selection." There can be no question that the tribes among whom inbreeding was restricted by this advance were bound to develop more quickly and more fully than those among whom marriage between brothers and sisters remained the rule and the law. How powerfully the influence of this advance made itself felt is seen in the institution which arose directly out of it and went far beyond it—the gens, which forms the basis of the social order of most, if not all, barbarian peoples of the earth and from which in Greece and Rome we step directly into civilization.

After a few generations at most, every original family was bound to split up. The practice of living together in a primitive communistic household which prevailed without exception till late in the middle stage of barbarism set a limit, varying with the conditions but fairly definite in each locality, to the maximum size of the family community. As soon as the conception arose that sexual intercourse between children of the same mother was wrong, it was bound to exert its influence when the old households split up and new ones were founded (though these did not necessarily coincide with the family group). One or more lines of sisters would form the nucleus of the one household and their own brothers the nucleus of the other. It must have been in some such manner as this that the form which Morgan calls the punaluan family originated out of the consanguine family. According to the Hawaiian custom, a number of sisters, natural or collateral (first, second or more remote cousins) were the common wives of their common husbands, from among whom, however, their own brothers were excluded. These husbands now no longer called themselves brothers, for they were no longer necessarily brothers, but *punalua*— that is, intimate companion, or partner. Similarly, a line of natural or collateral brothers had a number of women, *not* their sisters, as common wives, and these wives called one another *punalua*. This was the classic form of family structure [*Familienformation*], in which later a number of variations was possible, but whose essential feature was the mutually common possession of husbands and wives within a definite family circle, from which, however, the brothers of the wives—first one's own and later also collateral— and conversely also the sisters of the husbands, were excluded.

This form of the family provides with the most complete exactness the degrees of consanguinity expressed in the American system. The children of my mother's sisters are still her children, just as the children of my father's brothers are also his children; and they are all my brothers and sisters. But the children of my mother's brothers are now her nephews and nieces, the children of my father's sisters are his nephews and nieces, and they are all my cousins. For while the husbands of my mother's sisters are still her husbands, and the wives of my father's brothers are still his wives (in right, if not always in fact), the social ban on sexual intercourse between brothers and sisters has now divided the children of brothers and sisters, who had hitherto been treated as one's own brothers and sisters, into two classes. Those in the one class remain brothers and sisters as before (collateral, according to our system). Those in the other class, the children of my mother's brother in the one case and of my father's sister in the other, *cannot* be brothers and sisters any longer; they can no longer have common parents, neither father nor mother nor both, and therefore now for the first time the class of nephews and nieces, male and female cousins, becomes necessary, which in the earlier composition of the family would have been senseless. The American system of consanguinity, which appears purely nonsensical in any form of family based on any variety of monogamy, finds, down to the smallest details, its rational explanation and its natural foundation in the punaluan family. The punaluan family or a form similar to it must have been at the very least as widespread as this system of consanguinity.

Evidence of this form of family, whose existence has actually been proved in Hawaii, would probably have been received from all over Polynesia if the pious missionaries, like the Spanish monks of former days in America, had been able to see in such unchristian conditions anything more than a sheer "abomination."* Caesar's report of the Britons, who were at that time in the middle stage of barbarism, "every ten or twelve have wives in common, especially brothers with brothers and parents with children," is best explained as group marriage. Barbarian mothers do not have ten or twelve sons of their own old enough to keep wives in common, but the American system of consanguinity, which corresponds to the punaluan family, provides numerous brothers, because all a man's cousins, near and distant, are his brothers. Caesar's mention of "parents with children" may be due to misunderstanding on his part; it is not, however, absolutely impossible under this system that father and son or mother and daughter should be included in the same marriage group, though not father and daughter or mother and son. This or a similar form of group marriage also provides the simplest explanation of the accounts in Herodotus and other ancient

---

* There can no longer be any doubt that the traces which Bachofen thought he had found of unrestricted sexual intercourse, or what he calls "spontaneous generation in the slime," [*Sumpfzeugung*], go back to group marriage. "If Bachofen considers these punaluan marriages 'lawless,' a man of that period would consider most of the present-day marriages between near and remote cousins on the father's or mother's side to be incestuous, as being marriages between blood brothers and sisters" (Marx).

writers about community of wives among savages and barbarian peoples. The same applies also to the reports of Watson and Kaye in their book, *The People of India,* about the Tikurs in Oudh (north of the Ganges): "Both sexes have but a nominal tie on each other, and they change connection without compunction; living together, almost indiscriminately, in many large families."

In the very great majority of cases the institution of the gens seems to have originated directly out of the punaluan family. It is true that the Australian classificatory system also provides an origin for it: the Australians have gentes, but not yet the punaluan family; instead, they have a cruder form of group marriage.

In all forms of group family, it is uncertain who is the father of a child; but it is certain who its mother is. Though she calls *all* the children of the whole family her children and has a mother's duties toward them, she nevertheless knows her own children from the others. It is therefore clear that in so far as group marriage prevails, descent can only be proved on the *mother's* side and that therefore only the *female* line is recognized. And this is in fact the case among all peoples in the period of savagery or in the lower stage of barbarism. It is the second great merit of Bachofen that he was the first to make this discovery. To denote this exclusive recognition of descent through the mother and the relations of inheritance which in time resulted from it, he uses the term "mother right," which for the sake of brevity I retain. The term is, however, ill-chosen, since at this stage of society there cannot yet be any talk of "right" in the legal sense.

If we now take one of the two standard groups of the punaluan family, namely a line of natural and collateral sisters (that is, one's own sisters' children in the first, second or more remote degree), together with their children and their own collateral brothers on the mother's side (who, according to our assumption, are *not* their husbands), we have the exact circle of persons whom we later find as members of a gens, in the original form of that institution. They all have a common ancestral mother, by virtue of their descent from whom the female offspring in each generation are sisters. The husbands of these sisters, however, can no longer be their brothers and therefore cannot be descended from the same ancestral mother; consequently, they do not belong to the same consanguine group, the later gens. The children of these sisters, however, do belong to this group, because descent on the mother's side alone counts, since it alone is certain. As soon as the ban had been established on sexual intercourse between all brothers and sisters, including the most remote collateral relatives on the mother's side, this group transformed itself into a gens—that is, it constituted itself as a firm circle of blood relations in the female line between whom marriage was prohibited; and henceforward by other common institutions of a social and religious character, it increasingly consolidated and differentiated itself from the other gentes of the same tribe (more of this later). When we see, then, that the development of the gens follows, not only necessarily, but also perfectly naturally from the punaluan family, we may reasonably infer that at one time this form of family almost certainly existed among all peoples among whom the presence of gentile institutions can be proved—that is, practically all barbarians and civilized peoples.

At the time Morgan wrote his book, our knowledge of group marriage was still very limited. A little information was available about the group marriages of the Australians, who were organized in classes, and Morgan had already in 1871 published the reports he had received concerning the punaluan family in Hawaii. The punaluan family provided, on the one hand, the complete explanation of the system of consanguinity in force among the American Indians, which had been the starting point of all Morgan's researches; on the other hand, the origin of the matriarchal gens could be derived directly from the punaluan family; further, the punaluan family represented a much higher stage of development than the Australian classificatory system. It is therefore comprehensible that Morgan should have regarded it as the necessary stage of development before pairing marriage and should believe it to have been general in earlier times. Since then we have become acquainted with a number of other forms of group marriage, and we now know that Morgan here went too far. However, in his punaluan family he had had the good fortune to strike the highest, the classic form of group marriage, from which the transition to a higher stage can be explained most simply.

For the most important additions to our knowledge of group marriage, we are indebted to the English missionary, Lorimer Fison, who for years studied this form of the family in its classic home, Australia. He found the lowest stage of development among the Australian aborigines of Mount Gambier in South Australia. Here the whole tribe is divided into two great exogamous classes or moieties, Kroki and Kumite. Sexual intercourse within each of these moieties is strictly forbidden; on the other hand, every man in the one moiety is the husband by birth of every woman in the other moiety and she is by birth his wife. Not the individuals, but the entire groups are married, moiety with moiety. And observe that there is no exclusion on the ground of difference in age or particular degrees of affinity, except such as is entailed by the division of the tribe into two exogamous classes. A Kroki has every Kumite woman lawfully to wife; but, as his own daughter according to mother right is also a Kumite, being the daughter of a Kumite woman, she is by birth the wife of every Kroki, including, therefore, her father. At any rate, there is no bar against this in the organization into moieties as we know it. Hence, either this organization arose at a time when, in spite of the obscure impulse toward the restriction of inbreeding, sexual intercourse between parents and children was still not felt to be particularly horrible—in which case the moiety system must have originated directly out of a state of sexual promiscurity—or else intercourse between parents and children was *already* forbidden by custom when the moieties arose—and in that case the present conditions point back to the consanguine family and are the first step beyond it. The latter is more probable. There are not, to my knowledge, any instances from Australia of sexual cohabitation between parents and children, and as a rule the later form of exogamy, the matriarchal gens, also tacitly presupposes the prohibition of this relationship as already in force when the gens came into being.

The system of *two* moieties is found, not only at Mount Gambier in South Australia, but also on the Darling River further to the east and in Queensland in the northeast; it is therefore widely distributed. It excludes marriages only between brothers and sisters, between the children of brothers and between the children of sisters on the mother's side, because these belong to the same moiety; the children of sisters and brothers, however, may marry. A further step toward the prevention of inbreeding was taken by the Kamilaroi on the Darling River in New South Wales; the two original moieties are split up into four, and again each of these four sections is married *en bloc* to another. The first two sections are husbands and wives of one another by birth; according to whether the mother belonged to the first or second section, the children go into the third or fourth; the children of these last two sections, which are also married to one another, come again into the first and second sections. Thus one generation always belongs to the first and second sections, the next to the third and fourth, and the generation after that to the first and second again. Under this system, first cousins (on the mother's side) cannot be man and wife, but second cousins can. This peculiarly complicated arrangement is made still more intricate by having matriarchal gentes grafted onto it (at any rate later), but we cannot go into the details of this now. What is significant is how the urge toward the prevention of inbreeding asserts itself again and again, feeling its way, however, quite instinctively, without clear consciousness of its aim.

Group marriage which in these instances from Australia is still marriage of sections, mass marriage of an entire section of men often scattered over the whole continent with an equally widely distributed section of women—this group marriage, seen close at hand, does not look quite so terrible as the philistines, whose minds cannot get beyond brothels, imagine it to be. On the contrary, for years its existence was not even suspected and has now quite recently been questioned again. All that the superficial observer sees in group marriage is a loose form of monogamous marriage, here and there polygyny, and occasional infidelities. It takes years, as it took Fison and Howitt, to discover beneath these marriage customs, which in their actual practice should seem almost familiar to the average European, their controlling law: the law by which the Australian aborigine, wandering hundreds of miles from his home among people whose language he does not understand, nevertheless often finds in every camp and every tribe women who give themselves to him without resistance and without resentment—the law by which the man with several wives gives one up for the night to his guest. Where the European sees immorality and lawlessness, strict law rules in reality. The women belong to the marriage group of the stranger, and therefore they are his wives by birth;

that same law of custom which gives the two to one another forbids under penalty of outlawry all intercourse outside the marriage groups that belong together. Even when wives are captured, as frequently occurs in many places, the law of the exogamous classes is still carefully observed.

Marriage by capture, it may be remarked, already shows signs of the transition to monogamous marriage, at least in the form of pairing marriage. When the young man has captured or abducted a girl with the help of his friends, she is enjoyed by all of them in turn, but afterwards she is regarded as the wife of the young man who instigated her capture. If, on the other hand, the captured woman runs away from her husband and is caught by another man, she becomes his wife and the first husband loses his rights. Thus, while group marriage continues to exist as the general form, side by side with group marriage and within it exclusive relationships begin to form, pairings for a longer or shorter period, also polygyny; thus group marriage is dying out here too, and the only question is which will disappear first under European influence, group marriage or the Australian aborigines who practice it.

Marriage between entire sections, as it prevails in Australia, is in any case a very low and primitive form of group marriage, whereas the punaluan family, so far as we know, represents its highest stage of development. The former appears to be the form corresponding to the social level of vagrant savages, while the latter already presupposes relatively permanent settlements of communistic communities and leads immediately to the successive higher phase of development. But we shall certainly find more than one intermediate stage between these two forms; here lies a newly discovered field of research which is still almost completely unexplored.

3. THE PAIRING FAMILY

A certain amount of pairing, for a longer or shorter period, already occurred in group marriage or even earlier; the man had a chief wife among his many wives (one can hardly yet speak of a favorite wife), and for her he was the most important among her husbands. This fact has contributed considerably to the confusion of the missionaries, who have regarded group marriage sometimes as promiscuous community of wives, sometimes as unbridled adultery. But these customary pairings were bound to grow more stable as the gens developed and the classes of "brothers" and "sisters" between whom marriage was impossible became more numerous. The impulse given by the gens to the prevention of marriage between blood relatives extended still further. Thus among the Iroquois and most of the other Indians at the lower stage of barbarism, we find that marriage is prohibited between *all* relatives enumerated in their system—which includes several hundred degrees of kinship. The increasing complication of these prohibitions made group marriages more and more impossible; they were displaced by the *pairing family.* In this stage, one man lives with one woman, but the relationship is such that polygamy and occasional infidelity remain the right of the men, even though for economic reasons polygamy is rare, while from the woman the strictest fidelity is generally demanded throughout the time she lives with the man and adultery on her part is cruelly punished. The marriage tie can, however, be easily dissolved by either partner; after separation, the children still belong as before to the mother alone.

In this ever extending exclusion of blood relatives from the bond of marriage, natural selection continues its work. In Morgan's words:

> The influence of the new practice, which brought unrelated persons into the marriage relation, tended to create a more vigorous stock physically and mentally. . . . When two advancing tribes, with strong mental and physical characters, are brought together and blended into one people by the accidents of barbarous life, the new skull and brain would widen and lengthen to the sum of the capabilities of both [1963: 468].[13]

Tribes with gentile constitution were thus bound to gain supremacy over more backward tribes, or else to carry them along by their example.

Thus the history of the family in primitive times consists in the

13. A most infelicitous statement, worthy of quotation only as an example of how much we have learned about genetics since Morgan's and Engels' time.

progressive narrowing of the circle, originally embracing the whole tribe, within which the two sexes have a common conjugal relation. The continuous exclusion, first of nearer, then of more and more remote relatives, and at last even of relatives by marriage, ends by making any kind of group marriage practically impossible. Finally, there remains only the single, still loosely linked pair, the molecule with whose dissolution marriage itself ceases. This in itself shows what a small part individual sex love, in the modern sense of the word, played in the rise of monogamy. Yet stronger proof is afforded by the practice of all peoples at this stage of development. Whereas in the earlier forms of the family, men never lacked women but, on the contrary, had too many rather than too few, women had now become scarce and highly sought after. Hence it is with the pairing marriage that there begins the capture and purchase of women—widespread *symptoms,* but no more than symptoms, of the much deeper change that had occurred. These symptoms, mere methods of procuring wives, the pedantic Scot McLennan has transmogrified into special classes of families under the names of "marriage by capture" and "marriage by purchase." In general, whether among the American Indians or other peoples (at the same stage), the conclusion of a marriage is the affair not of the two parties concerned, who are often not consulted at all, but of their mothers. Two persons entirely unknown to each other are often thus affianced; they only learn that the bargain has been struck when the time for marrying approaches. Before the wedding the bridegroom gives presents to the bride's gentile relatives (to those on the mother's side, therefore, not to the father and his relations) which are regarded as gift payments in return for the girl. The marriage is still terminable at the desire of either partner, but among many tribes, the Iroquois for example, public opinion has gradually developed against such separations. When differences arise between husband and wife, the gens relatives of both partners act as mediators, and only if these efforts prove fruitless does a separation take place, the wife then keeping the children and each partner being free to marry again.

The pairing family, itself too weak and unstable to make an independent household necessary or even desirable, in no wise destroys the communistic household inherited from earlier times.

Communistic housekeeping, however, means the supremacy of women in the house; just as the exclusive recognition of the female parent, owing to the impossibility of recognizing the male parent with certainty, means that the women—the mothers—are held in high respect. One of the most absurd notions taken over from 18th century enlightenment is that in the beginning of society woman was the slave of man. Among all savages and all barbarians of the lower and middle stages, and to a certain extent of the upper stage also, the position of women is not only free, but honorable. As to what it still is in the pairing marriage, let us hear the evidence of Ashur Wright, for many years missionary among the Iroquois Senecas:

As to their family system, when occupying the old long houses [communistic households comprising several families], it is probable that some one clan [gens] predominated, the women taking in husbands, however, from the other clans [gentes]. . . . Usually, the female portion ruled the house. . . . The stores were in common; but woe to the luckless husband or lover who was too shiftless to do his share of the providing. No matter how many children, or whatever goods he might have in the house, he might at any time be ordered to pick up his blanket and budge; and after such orders it would not be healthful for him to attempt to disobey. The house would be too hot for him; and . . . he must retreat to his own clan [gens]; or, as was often done, go and start a new matrimonial alliance in some other. The women were the great power among the clans [gentes], as everywhere else. They did not hesitate, when occasion required, "to knock off the horns," as it was technically called, from the head of a chief, and send him back to the ranks of the warriors [Morgan, 1963: 464 *fn*].

The communistic household, in which most or all of the women belong to one and the same gens, while the men come from various gentes, is the material foundation of that supremacy of the women which was general in primitive times, and which it is Bachofen's third great merit to have discovered. The reports of travelers and missionaries, I may add, to the effect that women among savages and barbarians are overburdened with work in no way contradict what has been said. The division of labor between the two sexes is determined by quite other causes than by the position of woman in society. Among peoples where the women have to work far harder than we think suitable, there is often much more real respect for women than among our Europeans. The lady of civilization, surrounded by false homage and estranged from all real work, has an infinitely lower social position than the hard-working woman of barbarism, who was regarded among her people as a real lady (lady, *frowa, Frau*—mistress) and who was also a lady in character.

Whether pairing marriage has completely supplanted group marriage in America today is a question to be decided by closer investigation among the peoples still at the upper stage of savagery in the northwest, and particularly in South America. Among the latter, so many instances of sexual license are related that one can hardly assume the old group marriage to have been completely overcome here. At any rate, all traces of it have not yet disappeared. In at least 40 North American tribes the man who marries an eldest sister has the right to take all her other sisters as his wives as soon as they are old enough—a relic of the time when a whole line of sisters had husbands in common.[14] And Bancroft reports of the Indians of the California peninsula (upper stage of savagery) that they have certain festivals when several "tribes" come together for the purpose of promiscuous sexual intercourse. These "tribes" are clearly gentes, who preserve in these feasts a dim memory of the time when the women of one gens had all the men of the other as their common husbands, and conversely. The same custom still prevails in Australia. We find among some peoples that the older men, the chieftains and the magician-priests, exploit the community of wives and monopolize most of the women for themselves; at certain festivals and great assemblies of the people, however, they have to restore the old community of women and allow their wives to enjoy themselves with the young men. Westermarck (*History of Human Marriage*, 1891, 28, 29) quotes a whole series of instances of such periodic Saturnalian feasts when for a short time the old freedom of sexual intercourse is again restored; examples are given among the Hos, the Santals, the Punjas and Kotars in India, among some African peoples, and so forth. Curiously

14. The sororate, a widespread custom, can just as readily be explained in terms of the ongoing functioning of clan societies, as in terms of a survival. The series of relationships set up by the initial marriage are reinforced by the second. The functional significance of the practice is demonstrated very clearly by a parallel custom, that of the levirate, whereby a widowed woman marries her dead husband's brother, and the disruption of the family is minimized.

enough, Westermarck draws the conclusion that these are survivals not of the group marriage which he totally rejects, but of the mating season which primitive man had in common with the other animals.

Here we come to Bachofen's fourth great discovery—the widespread transitional form between group marriage and pairing. What Bachofen represents as a penance for the transgression of the old divine laws—the penance by which the woman purchases the right of chastity—is in fact only a mystical expression of the penance by which the woman buys herself out of the old community of husbands and acquires the right to give herself to *one* man only. This penance consists in a limited surrender; the Babylonian women had to give themselves once a year in the temple of Mylitta; other peoples of Asia Minor sent their girls for years to the temple of Anaitis, where they had to practice free love with favorites of their own choosing before they were allowed to marry. Similar customs in religious disguise are common to almost all Asiatic peoples between the Mediterranean and the Ganges. The sacrifice of atonement by which the woman purchases her freedom becomes increasingly lighter in course of time, as Bachofen already noted:

> Instead of being repeated annually, the offering is made once only; the hetaerism of the matrons is succeeded by the hetaerism of the maidens; hetaerism during marriage by hetaerism before marriage; surrender to all without choice by surrender to some (*Mutterrecht,* xix).

Among other peoples the religious disguise is absent. In some cases—among the Thracians, Celts, and others, in classical times; many of the original inhabitants of India, and to this day among the Malayan peoples, the South Sea Islanders and many American Indians—the girls enjoy the greatest sexual freedom up to the time of their marriage. This is especially the case almost everywhere in South America as everyone who has gone any distance into the interior can testify. Thus Agassiz (*A Journey in Brazil,* Boston and New York, 1868, 266) tells this story of a rich family of Indian extraction. When he was introduced to the daughter, he asked after her father, presuming him to be her mother's husband, who was fighting as an officer in the war against Paraguay; but the mother answered with a smile: *"Naõ tem pai, é filha da fortuna"* (She has no father, she is a child of chance):

It is the way the Indian or half-breed women here always speak of their illegitimate children . . . without an intonation of sadness or of blame. . . . So far is this from being an unusual case, that . . . the opposite seems the exception. Children are frequently quite ignorant of their parentage. They know about their mother, for all the care and responsibility falls upon her, but they have no knowledge of their father; nor does it seem to occur to the woman that she or her children have any claim upon him.

What seems strange here to civilized people is simply the rule according to mother right and group marriage.

Among other peoples, again, the friends and relatives of the bridegroom or the wedding guests claim their traditional right to the bride at the wedding itself, and the bridegroom's turn only comes last; this was the custom in the Balearic Islands and among the Augilers of Africa in ancient times; it is still observed among the Bareas of Abyssinia. In other cases, an official personage, the head of the tribe or the gens, *cacique,* shaman, priest, prince or whatever he may be called, represents the community and exercises the right of the first night with the bride. Despite all neo-romantic whitewashing, this *jus primae noctis* (right of first night) still persists today as a relic of group marriage among most of the natives of the Alaska region (Bancroft, *Native Races,* I, 81), the Tahus of North Mexico (*ibid.,* 584) and other peoples; and at any rate in the countries originally Celtic, where it was handed down directly from group marriage, it existed throughout the whole of the middle ages, for example in Aragon. While in Castile the peasants were never serfs, in Aragon there was serfdom of the most shameful kind right up till the decree of Ferdinand the Catholic in 1486. This document states:

We judge and declare that the aforementioned lords (señors, barons) . . . when the peasant takes himself a wife, shall neither sleep with her on the first night; nor shall they during the wedding night, when the wife has laid herself in her bed, step over it and the aforementioned wife as a sign of lordship; nor shall the aforementioned lords use the daughter or the son of the peasant, with payment or without payment, against their will (quoted in the original Catalan by Sugenheim, *Serfdom,* Petersburg, 1861, 35).

Bachofen is also prefectly right when he consistently maintains that the transition from what he calls "hetaerism" or *"Sumpfzeu-*

gung" to monogamy was brought about primarily through the women. The more the traditional sexual relations lost the naive primitive character of forest life, owing to the development of economic conditions with consequent undermining of the old communism and growing density of population, the more oppressive and humiliating must the women have felt them to be, and the greater their longing for the right of chastity, of temporary or permanent marriage with one man only, as a way of release. This advance could not in any case have originated with the men if only because it has never occurred to them, even to this day, to renounce the pleasures of actual group marriage. Only when the women had brought about the transition to pairing marriage were the men able to introduce strict monogamy—though indeed only for women.

The first beginnings of the pairing family appear on the dividing line between savagery and barbarism; they are generally to be found already at the upper stage of savagery, but occasionally not until the lower stage of barbarism. The pairing family is the form characteristic of barbarism, as group marriage is characteristic of savagery and monogamy of civilization. To develop it further, to strict monogamy, other causes were required than those we have found active hitherto. In the single pair the group was already reduced to its final unit, its two-atom molecule: one man and one woman. Natural selection, with its progressive exclusions from the marriage community, had accomplished its task; there was nothing more for it to do in this direction. Unless new, *social* forces came into play, there was no reason why a new form of family should arise from the single pair. But these new forces did come into play.

We now leave America, the classic soil of the pairing family. No sign allows us to conclude that a higher form of family developed here or that there was ever permanent monogamy anywhere in America prior to its discovery and conquest. But not so in the Old World.

Here the domestication of animals and the breeding of herds had developed a hitherto unsuspected source of wealth and created entirely new social relations. Up to the lower stage of barbarism, permanent wealth had consisted almost solely of house, clothing, crude ornaments and the tools for obtaining and preparing food—boat, weapons, and domestic utensils of the simplest kind. Food had to be won afresh day by day. Now, with their herds of horses, camels, asses, cattle, sheep, goats, and pigs, the advancing pastoral peoples —the Semites on the Euphrates and the Tigris, and the Aryans in the Indian country of the Five Streams (Punjab), in the Ganges region, and in the steppes then much more abundantly watered by the Oxus and the Jaxartes—had acquired property which only needed supervision and the rudest care to reproduce itself in steadily increasing quantities and to supply the most abundant food in the form of milk and meat. All former means of procuring food now receded into the background; hunting, formerly a necessity, now became a luxury.

But to whom did this new wealth belong? Originally to the gens, without a doubt. Private property in herds must have already started at an early period, however. Is it difficult to say whether the author of the so-called first book of Moses regarded the patriarch Abraham as the owner of his herds in his own right as head of a family community or by right of his position as actual hereditary head of a gens. What is certain is that we must not think of him as a property owner in the modern sense of the word. And it is also certain that at the threshold of authentic history we already find the herds everywhere separately owned by heads of families, as are the artistic products of barbarism (metal implements, luxury articles and, finally, the human cattle—the slaves).

For now slavery had also been invented. To the barbarian of the lower stage, a slave was valueless. Hence the treatment of defeated enemies by the American Indians was quite different from that at a higher stage. The men were killed or adopted as brothers into the tribe of the victors; the women were taken as wives or otherwise adopted with their surviving children. At this stage human labor power still does not produce any considerable surplus over and above its maintenance costs. That was no longer the case after the introduction of cattle breeding, metalworking, weaving and, lastly, agriculture. Just as the wives whom it had formerly been so easy to obtain had now acquired an exchange value and were bought, so also with labor power, particularly since the herds had definitely become family possessions. The family did not multiply so rapidly as the cattle. More people were needed to look after them; for this purpose use could be made of the enemies captured in war, who could also be bred just as easily as the cattle themselves.

Once it had passed into the private possession of families and there rapidly begun to augment, this wealth dealt a severe blow to the society founded on pairing marriage and the matriarchal gens. Pairing marriage had brought a new element into the family. By the side of the natural mother of the child it placed its natural and attested father with a better warrant of paternity, probably, than that of many a "father" today. According to the division of labor within the family at that time, it was the man's part to obtain food and the instruments of labor necessary for the purpose. He therefore also owned the instruments of labor, and in the event of husband and wife separating, he took them with him, just as she retained her household goods. Therefore, according to the social custom of the time, the man was also the owner of the new source of subsistence, the cattle, and later of the new instruments of labor, the slaves. But according to the custom of the same society, his children could not inherit from him. For as regards inheritance, the position was as follows:

At first, according to mother right—so long, therefore, as descent was reckoned only in the female line—and according to the original custom of inheritance within the gens, the gentile relatives inherited from a deceased fellow member of their gens. His property had to remain within the gens. His effects being insignificant, they probably always passed in practice to his nearest gentile relations—that is, to his blood relations on the mother's side. The children of the dead man, however, did not belong to his gens, but to that of their mother; it was from her that they inherited, at first conjointly with her other blood-relations, later perhaps with rights of priority; they could not inherit from their father because they did not belong to his gens within which his property had to remain. When the owner of the herds died, therefore, his herds would go first to his brothers and sisters and to his sister's children, or to the issue of his mother's sisters. But his own children were disinherited.

Thus on the one hand, in proportion as wealth increased it made the man's position in the family more important than the woman's, and on the other hand created an impulse to exploit this strengthened position in order to overthrow, in favor of his children, the traditional order of inheritance. This, however, was impossible so long as descent was reckoned according to mother right. Mother right, therefore, had to be overthrown, and overthrown it was. This was by no means so difficult as it looks to us today. For this revolution—one of the most decisive ever experienced by humanity—could take place without disturbing a single one of the living members of a gens. All could remain as they were. A simple decree sufficed that in the future the offspring of the male members should remain within the gens, but that of the female should be excluded by being transferred to the gens of their father. The reckoning of descent in the female line and the matriarchal law of inheritance were thereby overthrown, and the male line of descent and the paternal law of inheritance were substituted for them. As to how and when this revolution took place among civilized peoples, we have no knowledge. It falls entirely within prehistoric times. But that it *did* take place is more than sufficiently proved by the abundant traces of mother right which have been collected, particularly by Bachofen. How easily it is accomplished can be seen in a whole series of American Indian tribes where it has only recently taken place and is still taking place under the influence, partly of increasing wealth and a changed mode of life (transference from forest to prairie), and partly of the moral pressure of civilization and missionaries. Of eight Missouri tribes, six observe the male line of descent and inheritance; two still observe the female. Among the Shawnees, Miamis and Delawares the custom has grown up of giving the children a gentile name of their father's gens in order to transfer them into it, thus enabling them to inherit from him.

Man's innate casuistry! To change things by changing their names! And to find loopholes for violating tradition while maintaining tradition, when direct interest supplied sufficient impulse (Marx).

The result was hopeless confusion, which could only be remedied and to a certain extent was remedied by the transition to father right. "In general, this seems to be the most natural transition" (Marx). For the theories proffered by comparative jurisprudence regarding the manner in which this change was effected among the civilized peoples of the Old World—though they are almost pure hypothesis—see M. Kovalevsky, (*Tableau des origines et de l'évolution de la famille et de la propriété*, Stockholm, 1890).

The overthrow of mother right was the *world historical defeat of the female sex*. The man took command in the home also; the woman was degraded and reduced to servitude; she became the slave of his lust and a mere instrument for the production of children. This degraded position of the woman, especially conspicuous among the Greeks of the heroic and still more of the classical age, has gradually been palliated and glossed over, and sometimes clothed in a milder form; in no sense has it been abolished.

The establishment of the exclusive supremacy of the man shows its effects first in the patriarchal family, which now emerges as an intermediate form. Its essential characteristic is not polygyny, of which more later, but "the organization of a number of persons, bond and free, into a family under paternal power for the purpose of holding lands and for the care of flocks and herds. . . . (In the Semitic form) the chiefs, at least, lived in polygamy. . . . Those held to servitude and those employed as servants lived in the marriage relation" [Morgan, 1963: 474].

Its essential features are the incorporation of unfree persons and paternal power; hence the perfect type of this form of family is the Roman. The original meaning of the word "family" (*familia*) is not that compound of sentimentality and domestic strife which forms the ideal of the present-day philistine; among the Romans it did not at first even refer to the married pair and their children but only to the slaves. *Famulus* means domestic slave, and *familia* is the total number of slaves belonging to one man. As late as the time of Gaius, the *familia, id est patrimonium* (family, that is, the patrimony, the inheritance) was bequeathed by will. The term was invented by the Romans to denote a new social organism whose head ruled over wife and children and a number of slaves, and was invested under Roman paternal power with rights of life and death over them all.

This term, therefore, is no older than the ironclad family system of the Latin tribes, which came in after field agriculture and after legalized servitude, as well as after the separation of the Greeks and Latins [Morgan, 1963: 478].

Marx adds:

The modern family contains in germ not only slavery (*servitus*) but also serfdom, since from the beginning it is related to agricultural services. It contains *in miniature* all the contradictions which later extend throughout society and its state.

Such a form of family shows the transition of the pairing family to monogamy. In order to make certain of the wife's fidelity and therefore of the paternity of the children, she is delivered over unconditionally into the power of the husband; if he kills her, he is only exercising his rights.

With the patriarchal family, we enter the field of written history, a field where comparative jurisprudence can give valuable help. And it has in fact brought an important advance in our knowledge. We owe to Maxim Kovalevsky (*Tableau, etc.,* 60-100) the proof that the patriarchal household community, as we still find it today among the Serbs and the Bulgars under the name of *zádruga* (which may be roughly translated "bond of friendship") or *bratstvo* (brotherhood), and in a modified form among the Oriental peoples, formed the transitional stage between the matriarchal family deriving from group marriage and the single family of the modern world. For the civilized peoples of the Old World, for the Aryans and Semites at any rate, this seems to be established.

The Southern Slav *zádruga* provides the best instance of such a family community still in actual existence. It comprises several generations of the descendants of one father, together with their wives, who all live together in one homestead, cultivate their fields in common, feed and clothe themselves from a common stock, and possess in common the surplus from their labor. The community is under the supreme direction of the head of the house (*domácin*), who acts as its representative outside, has the right to sell minor objects, and controls the funds, for which, as for the regular organization of business, he is responsible. He is elected, and it is not at all necessary that he should be the oldest in the community. The women and their work are under the control of the mistress of the house (*domácica*), who is generally the wife of the *domácin*. She also has an important and often a decisive voice in the choice of husbands for the girls. Supreme power rests, however, with the family council, the assembly of all the adult members of the household, women as well as men. To this assembly the master of the house renders account; it takes all important decisions, exercises jurisdiction over the members, decides on sales and purchases of any importance, especially of land and so on.

It is only within the last ten years or so that such great family communities have been proved[15] to be still in existence in Russia; it is now generally recognized that they are as firmly rooted in the customs of the Russian people as the *obshchina* or village community. They appear in the oldest Russian code of laws, the *Pravda* of Yaroslav, under the same name as in the Dalmatian laws (*vervj*), and references to them can also be traced in Polish and Czech historical sources.

Among the Germans also, according to Heusler (*Institutionen des deutschen Rechts*), the economic unit was originally not the single family in the modern sense but the "house community," which consisted of several generations or several single families, and often enough included unfree persons as well. The Roman family is now also considered to have originated from this type, and consequently the absolute power of the father of the house and the complete absence of rights among the other members of the family in relation to him have recently been strongly questioned. It is supposed that similar family communities also existed among the Celts in Ireland; in France, under the name of *parçonneries,* they survived in Nivernais until the French Revolution, and in the Franche Comté they have not completely died out even today [1891]. In the district of Louhans (Saône et Loire), large peasant houses can be seen in which live several generations of the same family; the house has a lofty common hall reaching to the roof, and surrounding it the sleeping rooms to which stairs of six or eight steps give access.

In India the household community with common cultivation of the land is already mentioned by Nearchus in the time of Alexander the Great, and it still exists today in the same region, in the Punjab and the whole of northwest India. Kovalevsky was himself able to prove its existence in the Caucasus. In Algeria it survives among the Kabyles. It is supposed to have occurred even in America, and the *calpullis* which Zurita describes in old Mexico have been identified with it; on the other hand, Cunow has proved fairly clearly (in the journal *Ausland,* 1890, Nos. 42-44) that in Peru at the time of the conquest there was a form of constitution based on

15. M. M. Kovalesky, *Primitive Law, Book I, Gens,* Moscow, 1886, cites data on the family community in Russia collected by Orshansky in 1875 and Yefimenko in 1878.

marks (called, curiously enough, *marca*) with periodical allotment of arable land and consequently with individual tillage.[16]

In any case, the patriarchal household community with common ownership and common cultivation of the land now assumes an entirely different significance than hitherto. We can no longer doubt the important part it played as a transitional form between the matriarchal family and the single family among civilized and other peoples of the Old World. Later we will return to the further conclusion drawn by Kovalevsky that it was also the transitional form out of which developed the village or mark community with individual tillage and the allotment, first periodical and then permanent, of arable and pasture land.

With regard to the family life within these communities, it must be observed that at any rate in Russia the master of the house has a reputation for violently abusing his position toward the younger women of the community, especially his daughters-in-law, whom he often converts into his harem; the Russian folk songs have more than a little to say about this.

Before we go on to monogamy, which developed rapidly with the overthrow of mother right, a few words about polygyny and polyandry. Both forms can only be exceptions, historical luxury products as it were, unless they occur side by side in the same country, which is of course not the case. As the men excluded from polygyny cannot console themselves with the women left over from polyandry, and as hitherto, regardless of social institutions, the number of men and women has been fairly equal, it is obviously impossible for either of these forms of marriage to be elevated to the general form. Polygyny on the part of one individual man was, in fact, obviously a product of slavery and confined to a few people in exceptional positions. In the Semitic patriarchal family it was only the patriarch himself, and a few of his sons at most, who lived in polygyny; the rest had to content themselves with one wife. This still holds throughout the whole of the Orient; polygyny is the privilege of the wealthy and of the nobility, the women being recruited chiefly through purchase as slaves; the mass of the people live in monogamy.

16. Day-to-day work was individual, but the common practice here and generally among such peoples was for the heavy labor of planting and harvesting to be done by cooperative work groups.

A similar exception is the polyandry of India and Tibet, the origin of which in group marriage requires closer examination and would certainly prove interesting. It seems to be much more easy-going in practice than the jealous harems of the Mohammedans. At any rate, among the Nayar in India, where three or four men have a wife in common, each of them can have a second wife in common with another three or more men, and similarly a third and a fourth and so on.[17] It is a wonder that McLennan did not discover in these marriage clubs, to several of which one could belong and which he himself describes, a new class of *club marriage!* This marriage-club system, however, is not real polyandry at all; on the contrary, as Giraud-Teulon has already pointed out, it is a specialized form of group marriage; the men live in polygyny, the women in polyandry.

4. THE MONOGAMOUS FAMILY

It develops out of the pairing family, as previously shown, in the transitional period between the upper and middle stages of barbarism; its decisive victory is one of the signs that civilization is beginning. It is based on the supremacy of the man, the express purpose being to produce children of undisputed paternity; such paternity is demanded because these children are later to come into their father's property as his natural heirs. It is distinguished from pairing marriage by the much greater strength of the marriage tie, which can no longer be dissolved at either partner's wish. As a rule, it is now only the man who can dissolve it and put away his wife. The right of conjugal infidelity also remains secured to him, at any rate by custom (the *Code Napoléon* explicitly accords it to the husband as long as he does not bring his concubine into the house), and as social life develops he exercises his right more and more; should the wife recall the old form of sexual life and attempt to revive it, she is punished more severely than ever.

We meet this new form of the family in all its severity among the Greeks. While the position of the goddesses in their mythology, as Marx points out, refers to an earlier period when the position of

17. For a discussion of Nayar marriage and its theoretical implications, see E. K. Gough, "The Nayars and the Definition of Marriage," *Journal of the Royal Anthropological Institute,* 1959, pp. 23-34.

women was freer and more respected, in the heroic age we find the
woman already being humiliated by the domination of the man
and by competition from girl slaves. Note how Telemachus in the
Odyssey silences his mother.[18] In Homer young women are booty
and are handed over to the pleasure of the conquerors, the hand-
somest being picked by the commanders in order of rank; the entire
Iliad, it will be remembered, turns on the quarrel of Achilles and
Agamemnon over one of these slaves. If a hero is of any importance, Homer also mentions the captive girl with whom he shares his
tent and his bed. These girls were also taken back to Greece and
brought under the same roof as the wife, as Cassandra was brought
by Agamemnon in Aeschylus; the sons begotten of them received a
small share of the paternal inheritance and had the full status of
freemen. Teucer, for instance, is a natural son of Telamon by one
of these slaves and has the right to use his father's name. The
legitimate wife was expected to put up with all this, but herself to
remain strictly chaste and faithful. In the heroic age a Greek
woman is, indeed, more respected than in the period of civilization,
but to her husband she is after all nothing but the mother of his
legitimate children and heirs, his chief housekeeper and the super-
visor of his female slaves, whom he can and does take as concubines
if he so fancies. It is the existence of slavery side by side with
monogamy, the presence of young, beautiful slaves belonging un-
reservedly to the *man,* that stamps monogamy from the very beginning with its specific character of monogamy *for the woman only,*
but not for the man. And that is the character it still has today.

Coming to the later Greeks, we must distinguish between Dorians
and Ionians. Among the former—Sparta is the classic example—
marriage relations are in some ways still more archaic than even in
Homer. The recognized form of marriage in Sparta was a pairing
marriage, modified according to the Spartan conceptions of the
state, in which there still survived vestiges of group marriage.
Childless marriages were dissolved; King Anaxandridas (about
650 B.C.), whose first wife was childless, took a second and kept
two households; about the same time, King Ariston, who had two

18. The reference is to a passage where Telemachus, son of Odysseus and
Penelope, tells his mother to get on with her weaving and leave the men to
mind their own business (*Odyssey,* Bk. 21, 11, 350ff.).

unfruitful wives, took a third but dismissed one of the other two. On the other hand, several brothers could have a wife in common; a friend who preferred his friend's wife could share her with him; and it was considered quite proper to place one's wife at the disposal of a sturdy "stallion," as Bismarck would say, even if he was not a citizen. A passage in Plutarch where a Spartan woman refers an importunate wooer to her husband seems to indicate, according to Schömann, even greater freedom. Real adultery, secret infidelity by the woman without the husband's knowledge, was therefore unheard of. On the other hand, domestic slavery was unknown in Sparta, at least during its best period; the unfree helots were segregated on the estates and the Spartans were therefore less tempted to take the helots' wives. Inevitably in these conditions women held a much more honored position in Sparta than anywhere else in Greece. The Spartan women and the élite of the Athenian *hetaerae* are the only Greek women of whom the ancients speak with respect and whose words they thought it worth while to record.

The position is quite different among the Ionians; here Athens is typical. Girls only learned spinning, weaving, and sewing, and at most a little reading and writing. They lived more or less behind locked doors and had no company except other women. The women's apartments formed a separate part of the house on the upper floor or at the back where men, especially strangers, could not easily enter and to which the women retired when men visited the house. They never went out without being accompanied by a female slave; indoors they were kept under regular guard. Aristophanes speaks of Molossian dogs kept to frighten away adulterers, and, at any rate in the Asiatic towns, eunuchs were employed to keep watch over the women—making and exporting eunuchs was an industry in Chios as early as Herodotus' time, and, according to Wachsmuth, it was not only the barbarians who bought the supply. In Euripides [*Orestes*] a woman is called an *oikurema,* a thing (the word is neuter) for looking after the house, and, apart from her business of bearing children, that was all she was for the Athenian—his chief female domestic servant. The man had his athletics and his public business from which women were barred; in addition, he often had female slaves at his disposal and during the most flourishing days of Athens an extensive system of prostitution which the state at least favored. It was precisely through this system of prostitution that the only Greek women of personality were able to develop, and to acquire that intellectual and artistic culture by which they stand out as high above the general level of classic womanhood as the Spartan women by their qualities of character. But that a woman had to be a *hetaera* before she could be a woman is the worst condemnation of the Athenian family.

This Athenian family became in time the accepted model for domestic relations not only among the Ionians but to an increasing extent among all the Greeks of the mainland and colonies also. But, in spite of locks and guards, Greek women found plenty of opportunity for deceiving their husbands. The men, who would have been ashamed to show any love for their wives, amused themselves by all sorts of love affairs with *hetaerae;* but this degradation of the women was avenged on the men and degraded them also till they fell into the abominable practice of sodomy and degraded alike their gods and themselves with the myth of Ganymede.

This is the origin of monogamy as far as we can trace it back among the most civilized and highly developed people of antiquity. It was not in any way the fruit of individual sex love, with which it had nothing whatever to do; marriages remained as before marriages of convenience. It was the first form of the family to be based not on natural but on economic conditions—on the victory of private property over primitive, natural communal property. The Greeks themselves put the matter quite frankly: the sole exclusive aims of monogamous marriage were to make the man supreme in the family and to propagate, as the future heirs to his wealth, children indisputably his own. Otherwise, marriage was a burden, a duty which had to be performed whether one liked it or not to gods, state, and one's ancestors. In Athens the law exacted from the man not only marriage but also the performance of a minimum of so-called conjugal duties.

Thus when monogamous marriage first makes its appearance in history, it is not as the reconciliation of man and woman, still less as the highest form of such a reconciliation. Quite the contrary monogamous marriage comes on the scene as the subjugation of the one sex by the other; it announces a struggle between the sexes unknown throughout the whole previous prehistoric period. In an old unpublished manuscript written by Marx and myself in 1846,[19] I find the words: "The first division of labor is that between man and woman for the propagation of children." And today I can add: The first class opposition that appears in history coincides with the development of the antagonism between man and woman in monogamous marriage, and the first class oppression coincides with that of the female sex by the male. Monogamous marriage was a great historical step forward; nevertheless, together with slavery and private wealth, it opens the period that has lasted until today in which every step forward is also relatively a step backward, in which prosperity and development for some is won through the misery and frustration of others. It is the cellular form of civilized society in which the nature of the oppositions and contradictions fully active in that society can be already studied.

The old comparative freedom of sexual intercourse by no means disappeared with the victory of pairing marriage or even of monogamous marriage:

> The old conjugal system, now reduced to narrower limits by the gradual disappearance of the punaluan groups, still environed the advancing family, which it was to follow to the verge of civilization. . . . It finally disappeared in the new form of hetaerism, which still follows mankind in civilization as a dark shadow upon the family [Morgan, 1963: 511].

By "hetaerism" Morgan understands the practice, *coexistent with monogamous marriage,* of sexual intercourse between men and unmarried women outside marriage, which, as we know, flourishes in the most varied forms throughout the whole period of civilization and develops more and more into open prostitution. This hetaerism derives quite directly from group marriage, from the ceremonial surrender by which women purchased the right of chastity. Surrender for money was at first a religious act; it took place in the temple of the goddess of love, and the money originally went into the temple treasury. The hierodules [temple slaves] of Anaitis in Armenia and of Aphrodite in Corinth, like the sacred dancing girls

19. The reference here is to the *Deutsche Ideologie (German Ideology),* written by Marx and Engels in Brussels in 1845-46 and first published in 1932 by the Marx-Engels-Lenin Institute in Moscow. *See* Marx-Engels, 1970:51.

attached to the temples of India, the so-called bayaderes (the word is a corruption of the Portuguese word *bailadeira* meaning female dancer), were the first prostitutes. Originally the duty of every woman, this surrender was later performed by these priestesses alone as representatives of all other women.[20] Among other peoples, hetaerism derives from the sexual freedom allowed girls before marriage—again, therefore, a relic of group marriage, but handed down in a different way. With the rise of the inequality of property —already at the upper stage of barbarism, therefore—wage labor appears sporadically side by side with slave labor, and at the same time, as its necessary correlate, the professional prostitution of free women side by side with the forced surrender of the slave. Thus the heritage which group marriage has bequeatherd to civilization is double-edged, just as everything civilization brings forth is double-edged, double-tongued, divided against itself, contradictory: here monogamy, there hetaerism with its most extreme form, prostitution. For hetaerism is as much a social institution as any other; it continues the old sexual freedom—to the advantage of the men. Actually, not merely tolerated but gaily practiced by the ruling classes particularly, it is condemned in words. But in reality this condemnation never falls on the men concerned, but only on the women; they are despised and outcast in order that the unconditional supremacy of men over the female sex may be once more proclaimed as a fundamental law of society.

But a second contradiction thus develops within monogamous marriage itself. At the side of the husband who embellishes his existence with hetaerism stands the neglected wife. And one cannot have one side of this contradiction without the other, any more than a man has a whole apple in his hand after eating half. But that seems to have been the husbands' notion, until their wives

20. That the institution of professional prostitution survived as a "vestige" of group marriage, through the intermediate step of "ceremonial surrender" for the "right of chastity," seems rather forced as a line of analysis. The desire for sexual diversity hardly needs such a cumbersome explanation. That it was allowed for men at the expense of women is sufficiently explained by Engel's discussion of monogamous marriage and its origin. Despite his generally empathetic and sensitive handling of women's status, Engels' phrasings frequently reflect a Victorian bias—women should by nature value chastity.

taught them better. With monogamous marriage, two constant social types, unknown hitherto, make their appearance on the scene—the wife's attendant lover and the cuckold husband. The husbands had won the victory over the wives, but the vanquished magnanimously provided the crown. Together with monogamous marriage and hetaerism, adultery became an unavoidable social institution—denounced, severely penalized, but impossible to suppress. At best, the certain paternity of the children rested on moral conviction as before, and to solve the insoluble contradiction the *Code Napoléon,* Article 312, decreed: *"L'enfant conçu pendant le mariage a pour père le mari,"* the father of a child conceived during marriage is—the husband. Such is the final result of three thousand years of monogamous marriage.

Thus, wherever the monogamous family remains true to its historical origin and clearly reveals the antagonism between the man and the woman expressed in the man's exclusive supremacy, it exhibits in miniature the same oppositions and contradictions as those in which society has been moving, without power to resolve or overcome them, ever since it split into classes at the beginning of civilization. I am speaking here, of course, only of those cases of monogamous marriage where matrimonial life actually proceeds according to the original character of the whole institution but where the wife rebels against the husband's supremacy. Not all marriages turn out thus, as nobody knows better than the German philistine who can no more assert his rule in the home than he can in the state and whose wife, with every right, wears the trousers he is unworthy of. But, to make up for it, he considers himself far above his French companion in misfortune to whom, oftener than to him, something much worse happens.

However, monogamous marriage did not by any means appear always and everywhere in the classically harsh form it took among the Greeks. Among the Romans, who as future world-conquerors had a larger, if a less fine, vision than the Greeks, women were freer and more respected. A Roman considered that his power of life and death over his wife sufficiently guaranteed her conjugal fidelity. Here, moreover, the wife equally with the husband could dissolve the marriage at will. But the greatest progress in the development of individual marriage certainly came with the entry of the Germans into history, and for the reason that the Germans—on account of their poverty, very probably—were still at a stage where monogamy seems not yet to have become perfectly distinct from pairing marriage. We infer this from three facts mentioned by Tacitus. First, though marriage was held in great reverence—"they content themselves with one wife, the women live hedged round with chastity"—polygamy was the rule for the distinguished members and the leaders of the tribe, a condition of things similar to that among the Americans, where pairing marriage was the rule. Secondly, the transition from mother right to father right could only have been made a short time previously, for the brother on the mother's side—the nearest gentile male relation according to mother right—was still considered almost closer of kin than the father, corresponding again to the standpoint of the American Indians among whom Marx, as he often said, found the key to the understanding of our own primitive past. And thirdly, women were greatly respected among the Germans and also influential in public affairs, which is in direct contradiction to the supremacy of men in monogamy. In almost all these points the Germans agree with the Spartans, among whom also, as we saw, pairing marriage had not yet been completely overcome. Thus, here again an entirely new influence came to power in the world with the Germans. The new monogamy, which now developed from the mingling of peoples amid the ruins of the Roman world, clothed the supremacy of the men in milder forms and gave women a position which, outwardly at any rate, was much more free and respected than it had ever been in classical antiquity. Only now were the conditions realized in which through monogamy—within it, parallel to it, or in opposition to it, as the case might be—the greatest moral advance we owe to it could be achieved: modern individual sex love, which had hitherto been unknown to the entire world.[21]

21. This hypothesis about the historical development of individual sex love is one that merits further research. While it is true that the notion of basing marriage on "love" is not general in primitive society, yet romantic love and courtship are by no means unknown. And the mature love of married couples may be deep and profound. There is of course great individual variation here in all societies, but Engels' further point—that "individual sex love" can characteristically be expressed more fully outside marriage than within it in our society—suggests that marital relationships may well have been more fulfilling than ours, not less, in primitive societies.

This advance, however, undoubtedly sprang from the fact that the Germans still lived in pairing families and grafted the corresponding position of women onto the monogamous system so far as that was possible. It most decidedly did not spring from the legendary virtue and wonderful moral purity of the German character, which was nothing more than the freedom of the pairing family from the crying moral contradictions of monogamy. On the contrary, in the course of their migrations the Germans had morally much deteriorated, particularly during their southeasterly wanderings among the nomads of the Black Sea steppes from whom they acquired not only equestrian skill but also gross, unnatural vices, as Ammianus expressly states of the Taifali and Procopius of the Heruli.

But if monogamy was the only one of all the known forms of the family through which modern sex love could develop, that does not mean that within monogamy modern sexual love developed exclusively or even chiefly as the love of husband and wife for each other. That was precluded by the very nature of strictly monogamous marriage under the rule of the man. Among all historically active classes—that is, among all ruling classes—matrimony remained what it had been since the pairing marriage, a matter of convenience which was arranged by the parents. The first historical form of sexual love as passion, a passion recognized as natural to all human beings (at least if they belonged to the ruling classes), and as the highest form of the sexual impulse—and that is what constitutes its specific character—this first form of individual sexual love, the chivalrous love of the middle ages, was by no means conjugal. Quite the contrary, in its classic form among the Provençals, it heads straight for adultery, and the poets of love celebrated adultery. The flower of Provençal love poetry are the Albas [songs of dawn], in German, *Tagelieder*. They describe in glowing colors how the knight lies in bed beside his love—the wife of another— while outside stands the watchman who calls to him as soon as the first gray of dawn (*alba*) appears so that he can get away unobserved; the parting scene then forms the climax of the poem. The northern French and also the worthy Germans adopted this kind of poetry together with the corresponding fashion of chivalrous love; old Wolfram of Eschenbach has left us three wonderfully beautiful songs of dawn on this same improper subject which I like better than his three long heroic poems.

Nowadays there are two ways of concluding a bourgeois marriage. In Catholic countries the parents, as before, procure a suitable wife for their young bourgeois son, and the consequence is, of course, the fullest development of the contradiction inherent in monogamy: the husband abandons himself to hetaerism and the wife to adultery. Probably the only reason why the Catholic Church abolished divorce was because it had convinced itself that there is no more a cure for adultery than there is for death. In Protestant countries, on the other hand, the rule is that the son of a bourgeois family is allowed to choose a wife from his own class with more or less freedom; hence there may be a certain element of love in the marriage as, indeed, in accordance with Protestant hypocrisy is always assumed for decency's sake. Here the husband's hetaerism is a more sleepy kind of business, and adultery by the wife is less the rule. But since in every kind of marriage people remain what they were before and since the bourgeois of Protestant countries are mostly philistines, all that this Protestant monogamy achieves, taking the average of the best cases, is a conjugal partnership of leaden boredom, known as "domestic bliss." The best mirror of these two methods of marrying is the novel—the French novel for the Catholic manner, the German for the Protestant. In both, the hero "gets it": in the German, the young man gets the girl; in the French, the husband gets the horns. Which of them is worse off is sometimes questionable. This is why the French bourgeois is as much horrified by the dullness of the German novel as the German philistine is by the "immorality" of the French. However, now that "Berlin is a world capital," the German novel is beginning with a little less timidity to use as part of its regular stock-in-trade the hetaerism and adultery long familiar to that town.

In both cases, however, the marriage is conditioned by the class position of the parties and is to that extent always a marriage of convenience. In both cases this marriage of convenience turns often enough into the crassest prostitution—sometimes of both partners, but far more commonly of the woman, who only differs from the ordinary courtesan in that she does not let out her body on piecework as a wage worker, but sells it once and for all into slavery.

And of all marriages of convenience Fourier's words hold true: "As in grammar two negatives make an affirmative, so in matrimonial morality two prostitutions pass for a virtue."[22] Sex love in the relationship with a woman becomes and can only become the real rule among the oppressed classes, which means today among the proletariat—whether this relation is officially sanctioned or not. But here all the foundations of typical monogamy are cleared away. Here there is no property, for the preservation and inheritance of which monogamy and male supremacy were established; hence there is no incentive to make this male supremacy effective. What is more, there are no means of making it so. Bourgeois law, which protects this supremacy, exists only for the possessing class and their dealings with the proletarians. The law costs money and, on account of the worker's poverty, it has no validity for his relation to his wife. Here quite other personal and social conditions decide. And now that large-scale industry has taken the wife out of the home onto the labor market and into the factory, and made her often the breadwinner of the family, no basis for any kind of male supremacy is left in the proletarian household, except, perhaps, for something of the brutality toward women that has spread since the introduction of monogamy. The proletarian family is therefore no longer monogamous in the strict sense, even where there is passionate love and firmest loyalty on both sides and maybe all the blessings of religious and civil authority. Here, therefore, the eternal attendants of monogamy, hetaerism and adultery, play only an almost vanishing part.[23] The wife has in fact regained the right to dissolve the marriage, and if two people cannot get on with one another, they prefer to separate. In short, proletarian marriage is monogamous in the etymological sense of the word, but not at all in its historical sense.

Our jurists, of course, find that progress in legislation is leaving women with no further ground of complaint. Modern civilized systems of law increasingly acknowledge first, that for a marriage to be legal it must be a contract freely entered into by both partners

22. Charles Fourier, *Théorie de l'Unité Universelle,* Paris, 1841-45, III, 120.
23. A trend that has certainly reversed itself, possibly as the result of a shorter working day!

and secondly, that also in the married state both partners must stand on a common footing of equal rights and duties. If both these demands are consistently carried out, say the jurists, women have all they can ask.

This typically legalist method of argument is exactly the same as that which the radical republican bourgeois uses to put the proletarian in his place. The labor contract is to be freely entered into by both partners. But it is considered to have been freely entered into as soon as the law makes both parties equal on *paper*. The power conferred on the one party by the difference of class position, the pressure thereby brought to bear on the other party—the real economic position of both—that is not the law's business. Again, for the duration of the labor contract, both parties are to have equal rights in so far as one or the other does not expressly surrender them. That economic relations compel the worker to surrender even the last semblance of equal rights—here again, that is no concern of the law.

In regard to marriage, the law, even the most advanced, is fully satisfied as soon as the partners have formally recorded that they are entering into the marriage of their own free consent. What goes on in real life behind the juridical scenes, how this free consent comes about—that is not the business of the law and the jurist. And yet the most elementary comparative jurisprudence should show the jurist what this free consent really amounts to. In the countries where an obligatory share of the paternal inheritance is secured to the children by law and they cannot therefore be disinherited—in Germany, in the countries with French law and elsewhere—the children are obliged to obtain their parents' consent to their marriage. In the countries with English law, where parental consent to a marriage is not legally required, the parents on their side have full freedom in the testamentary disposal of their property and can disinherit their children at their pleasure. It is obvious that in spite and precisely because of this fact freedom of marriage among the classes with something to inherit is in reality not a whit greater in England and America than it is in France and Germany.

As regards the legal equality of husband and wife in marriage, the position is no better. The legal inequality of the two partners bequeathed to us from earlier social conditions is not the cause but the effect of the economic oppression of the woman. In the old communistic household, which comprised many couples and their children, the task entrusted to the women of managing the household was as much a public, a socially necessary industry as the procuring of food by the men. With the patriarchal family and still more with the single monogamous family, a change came. Household management lost its public character. It no longer concerned society. It became a *private service;* the wife became the head servant, excluded from all participation in social production. Not until the coming of modern large-scale industry was the road to social production opened to her again—and then only to the proletarian wife. But it was opened in such a manner that, if she carries out her duties in the private service of her family, she remains excluded from public production and unable to earn; and if she wants to take part in public production and earn independently, she cannot carry out family duties. And the wife's position in the factory is the position of women in all branches of business, right up to medicine and the law. The modern individual family is founded on the open or concealed domestic slavery of the wife, and modern society is a mass composed of these individual families as its molecules.

In the great majority of cases today, at least in the possessing classes, the husband is obliged to earn a living and support his family, and that in itself gives him a position of supremacy without any need for special legal titles and privileges. Within the family he is the bourgeois, and the wife represents the proletariat. In the industrial world, the specific character of the economic oppression burdening the proletariat is visible in all its sharpness only when all special legal privileges of the capitalist class have been abolished and complete legal equality of both classes established. The democratic republic does not do away with the opposition of the two classes; on the contrary, it provides the clear field on which the fight can be fought out. And in the same way, the peculiar character of the supremacy of the husband over the wife in the modern family, the necessity of creating real social equality between them and the way to do it, will only be seen in the clear light of day when both possess legally complete equality of rights. Then it will be plain that the first condition for the liberation of the wife is to bring the whole female sex back into public industry, and that this in turn demands that the characteristic of the monogamous family as the economic unit of society be abolished.

We thus have three principal forms of marriage which correspond broadly to the three principal stages of human development: for the period of savagery, group marriage; for barbarism, pairing marriage; for civilization, monogamy supplemented by adultery and prostitution. Between pairing marriage and monogamy intervenes a period in the upper stage of barbarism when men have female slaves at their command and polygamy is practiced.

As our whole presentation has shown, the progress which manifests itself in these successive forms is connected with the peculiarity that women, but not men, are increasingly deprived of the sexual freedom of group marriage. In fact, for men group marriage actually still exists even to this day. What for the woman is a crime entailing grave legal and social consequences is considered honorable in a man or, at the worst, a slight moral blemish which he cheerfully bears. But the more the hetaerism of the past is changed in our time by capitalist commodity production and brought into conformity with it, the more, that is to say, it is transformed into undisguised prostitution, the more demoralizing are its effects. And it demoralizes men far more than women. Among women, prostitution degrades only the unfortunate ones who become its victims, and even these by no means to the extent commonly believed. But it degrades the character of the whole male world. A long engagement particularly is in nine cases out of ten a regular preparatory school for conjugal infidelity.

We are now approaching a social revolution in which the economic foundations of monogamy as they have existed hitherto will disappear just as surely as those of its complement—prostitution. Monogamy arose from the concentration of considerable wealth in the hands of a single individual—a man—and from the need to bequeath this wealth to the children of that man and of no other. For this purpose, the monogamy of the woman was required, not that of the man, so this monogamy of the woman did not in any way interfere with open or concealed polygamy on the part of the man. But by transforming by far the greater portion, at any rate, of permanent, heritable wealth—the means of production—into social property, the coming social revolution will reduce to a minimum all this anxiety about bequeathing and inheriting. Having arisen from economic causes, will monogamy then disappear when these causes disappear?

One might answer, not without reason: far from disappearing, it will on the contrary begin to be realized completely. For with the transformation of the means of production into social property there will disappear also wage labor, the proletariat, and therefore the necessity for a certain—statistically calculable—number of women to surrender themselves for money. Prostitution disappears; monogamy, instead of collapsing, at last becomes a reality—also for men.

In any case, therefore, the position of men will be very much altered. But the position of women, of *all* women, also undergoes significant change. With the transfer of the means of production into common ownership, the single family ceases to be the economic unit of society. Private housekeeping is transformed into a social industry. The care and education of the children becomes a public affair; society looks after all children alike, whether they are legitimate or not. This removes all the anxiety about the "consequences," which today is the most essential social—moral as well as economic —factor that prevents a girl from giving herself completely to the man she loves. Will not that suffice to bring about the gradual growth of unconstrained sexual intercourse and with it a more tolerant public opinion in regard to a maiden's honor and a woman's shame? And finally, have we not seen that in the modern world monogamy and prostitution are indeed contradictions, but inseparable contradictions, poles of the same state of society? Can prostitution disappear without dragging monogamy with it into the abyss?

Here a new element comes into play, an element which at the time when monogamy was developing existed at most in embryo— individual sex love.

Before the Middle Ages we cannot speak of individual sex love. That personal beauty, close intimacy, similarity of tastes and so forth awakened in people of opposite sex the desire for sexual intercourse, that men and women were not totally indifferent regarding the partner with whom they entered into this most intimate relationship—that goes without saying. But it is still a very long way to our sexual love. Throughout the whole of antiquity, marriages were arranged by the parents, and the partners calmly accepted their choice. What little love there was between husband and wife in antiquity is not so much subjective inclination as objective duty, not the cause of the marriage but its corollary. Love relationships in the modern sense only occur in antiquity outside official society. The shepherds of whose joys and sorrows in love Theocritus and Moschus sing, the Daphnis and Chloe of Longus, are all slaves who have no part in the state, the free citizen's sphere of life. Except among slaves, we find love affairs only as products of the disintegration of the old world and carried on with women who also stand outside official society, with *hetaerae*—that is, with foreigners or freed slaves: in Athens from the eve of its decline, in Rome under the Caesars. If there were any real love affairs between free men and free women, these occurred only in the course of adultery. And to the classical love poet of antiquity, old Anacreon, sexual love in our sense mattered so little that it did not even matter to him which sex his beloved was.

Our sex love differs essentially from the simple sexual desire, the Eros, of the ancients. In the first place, it assumes that the person loved returns the love; to this extent the woman is on an equal footing with the man, whereas in the Eros of antiquity she was often not even asked. Secondly, our sex love has a degree of intensity and duration which makes both lovers feel that non-possession and separation are a great, if not the greatest, calamity; to possess one another, they risk high stakes, even life itself. In the ancient world this happened only, if at all, in adultery. And finally, there arises a new moral standard in the judgment of a sexual relationship. We do not only ask, was it within or outside marriage, but also, did it spring from love and reciprocated love or not? Of course, this new standard has fared no better in feudal or bourgeois practice than all the other standards of morality—it is ignored. But neither does it fare any worse. It is recognized, like all the rest, in theory, on paper. And for the present more than this cannot be expected.

At the point where antiquity broke off its advance to sexual love, the Middle Ages took it up again—in adultery. We have already described the knightly love which gave rise to the songs of dawn. From the love which strives to break up marriage to the love which is to be its foundation there is still a long road, which chivalry never fully traversed. Even when we pass from the frivolous Latins to the virtuous Germans we find in the *Nibelungenlied* that although in her heart Kriemhild is as much in love with Siegfried as he is with her, yet when Gunther announces that he has promised her to a knight he does not name, she simply replies: "You have no need to ask me; as you bid me, so will I ever be; whom you, lord, give me as husband, him will I gladly take in troth." It never enters her head that her love can be even considered. Gunther asks for Brünhild in marriage and Etzel for Kriemhild, though they have never seen them. Similarly, in *Gutrun,* Sigebant of Ireland asks for the Norwegian Ute, whom he has never seen, Hetel of Hegelingen for Hilde of Ireland, and finally Siegfried of Morland, Hartmut of Ormany and Herwig of Seeland for Gutrun—and here Gutrun's acceptance of Herwig is for the first time voluntary. As a rule, the young prince's bride is selected by his parents if they are still living or, if not, by the prince himself with the advice of the great feudal lords, who have a weighty word to say in all these cases. Nor can it be otherwise. For the knight or baron, as for the prince of the land himself, marriage is a political act, an opportunity to increase power by new alliances; the interest of the *house* must be decisive, not the wishes of an individual. What chance then is there for love to have the final word in the making of a marriage?

The same thing holds for the guild member in the medieval towns. The very privileges protecting him, the guild charters with all their clauses and rubrics, the intricate distinctions legally separating him from other guilds, from the members of his own guild or from his journeymen and apprentices, already made the circle narrow enough within which he could look for a suitable wife. And who in the circle was the most suitable was decided under this complicated system most certainly not by his individual preference but by the family interests.

In the vast majority of cases, therefore, marriage remained up to the close of the middle ages what it had been from the start—a matter which was not decided by the partners. In the beginning, people were already born married—married to an entire group of the opposite sex. In the later forms of group marriage similar relations probably existed, but with the group continually contracting. In the pairing marriage it was customary for the mothers to settle the marriages of their children; here, too, the decisive considerations are the new ties of kinship which are to give the young pair a stronger position in the gens and tribe. And when, with the preponderance of private over communal property and the interest in its bequeathal father right and monogamy gained supremacy, the dependence of marriages on economic considerations became complete. The *form* of marriage by purchase disappears; the actual practice is steadily extended until not only the woman but also the man acquires a price—not according to his personal qualities but according to his property. That the mutual affection of the people concerned should be the one paramount reason for marriage, outweighing everything else, was and always had been absolutely unheard of in the practice of the ruling classes; that sort of thing only happened in romance—or among the oppressed classes, who did not count.

Such was the state of things encountered by capitalist production when it began to prepare itself, after the epoch of geographical discoveries, to win world power by world trade and manufacture. One would suppose that this manner of marriage exactly suited it, and so it did. And yet—there are no limits to the irony of history—capitalist production itself was to make the decisive breach in it. By changing all things into commodities, it dissolved all inherited and traditional relationships, and in place of time-honored custom and historic right, it set up purchase and sale, "free" contract. And the English jurist H. S. Maine thought he had made a tremendous discovery when he said that our whole progress in comparison with former epochs consisted in the fact that we had passed "from status to contract," from inherited to freely contracted conditions—which, in so far as it is correct was already in *The Communist Manifesto* [Chapter II].

But a contract requires people who can dispose freely of their persons, actions, and possessions and meet each other on the footing of equal rights. To create these "free" and "equal" people was one of the main tasks of capitalist production. Even though at the start it was carried out only half-consciously, and under a religious disguise at that, from the time of the Lutheran and Calvinist Reformation the principle was established that man is only fully responsible for his actions when he acts with complete freedom of will, and that it is a moral duty to resist all coercion to an immoral act. But how did this fit in with the hitherto existing practice in the arrangement of marriages? Marriage according to the bourgeois conception was a contract, a legal transaction, and the most important one of all because it disposed of two human beings, body and mind, for life. Formally, it is true, the contract at that time was entered into voluntarily; without the assent of the persons concerned, nothing could be done. But everyone knew only too well how this assent was obtained and who were the real contracting parties in the marriage. But if real freedom of decision was required for all other contracts, then why not for this? Had not the two young people to be coupled also the right to dispose freely of themselves, of their bodies and organs? Had not chivalry brought sex love into fashion, and was not its proper bourgeois form, in contrast to chivalry's adulterous love, the love of husband and wife? And if it was the duty of married people to love each other, was it not equally the duty of lovers to marry each other and nobody else? Did not this right of the lovers stand higher than the right of parents, relations, and other traditional marriage brokers and matchmakers? If the right of free, personal discrimination broke boldly into the Church and religion, how should it halt before the intolerable claim of the older generation to dispose of the body, soul, property, happiness, and unhappiness of the younger generation?

These questions inevitably arose at a time which was loosening all the old ties of society and undermining all traditional conceptions. The world had suddenly grown almost ten times bigger; instead of one quadrant of a hemisphere, the whole globe lay before the gaze of the West Europeans who hastened to take the other seven quadrants into their possession. And with the old narrow barriers of their homeland fell also the thousand-year-old barriers of the prescribed medieval way of thought. To the outward and the inward eye of man opened an infinitely wider horizon. What did a young man care about the approval of respectability or honorable guild privileges handed down for generations when the wealth of India beckoned to him, the gold and the silver mines of Mexico and Potosi? For the bourgeoisie it was the time of knight-errantry; they, too, had their romance and their raptures of love, but on a bourgeois footing and, in the last analysis, with bourgeois aims.

So it came about that the rising bourgeoisie, especially in Protestant countries where existing conditions had been most severely shaken, increasingly recognized freedom of contract also in marriage, and carried it into effect in the manner described. Marriage remained class marriage, but within the class the partners were conceded a certain degree of freedom of choice. And on paper, in ethical theory and in poetic description, nothing was more immutably established than that every marriage is immoral which does not rest on mutual sexual love and really free agreement of husband and wife. In short, the love marriage was proclaimed as a human right, and indeed not only as a *droit de l'homme*, one of the rights of man, but also, for once in a way, as *droit de la femme*, one of the rights of woman.

This human right, however, differed in one respect from all other so-called human rights. While the latter in practice remain restricted to the ruling class (the bourgeoisie) and are directly or indirectly curtailed for the oppressed class (the proletariat), in the case of the former the irony of history plays another of its tricks. The ruling class remains dominated by the familar economic influences and therefore only in exceptional cases does it provide instances of really freely contracted marriages, while among the oppressed class, as we have seen, these marriages are the rule.

Full freedom of marriage can therefore only be generally established when the abolition of capitalist production and of the property relations created by it has removed all the accompanying economic considerations which still exert such a powerful influence on the choice of a marriage partner. For then there is no other motive left except mutual inclination.

And as sexual love is by its nature exclusive—although at present this exclusiveness is fully realized only in the woman—the marriage based on sexual love is by its nature individual marriage. We have seen how right Bachofen was in regarding the advance from group marriage to individual marriage as primarily due to the women. Only the step from pairing marriage to monogamy can be put down to the credit of the men, and historically the essence of this was to make the position of the women worse and the infidelities of the men easier. If now the economic considerations also disappear which made women put up with the habitual infidelity of their husbands—concern for their own means of existence and still more for their children's future—then, according to all previous experience, the equality of woman thereby achieved will tend infinitely more to make men really monogamous than to make women polyandrous.

But what will quite certainly disappear from monogamy are all the features stamped upon it through its origin in property relations; these are, in the first place, supremacy of the man and secondly, the indissolubility of marriage. The supremacy of the man in marriage is the simple consequence of his economic supremacy, and with the abolition of the latter will disappear of itself. The indissolubility of marriage is partly a consequence of the economic situation in which monogamy arose, partly tradition from the period when the connection between this economic situation and monogamy was not yet fully understood and was carried to extremes under a religious form. Today it is already broken through at a thousand points. If only the marriage based on love is moral, then also only the marriage is moral in which love continues. But the intense emotion of individual sex love varies very much in duration from one individual to another, especially among men, and if affection definitely comes to an end or is supplanted by a new passionate love, separation is a benefit for both partners as well as for society—only people will then be spared having to wade through the useless mire of a divorce case.

What we can now conjecture about the way in which sexual relations will be ordered after the impending overthrow of capitalist production is mainly of a negative character, limited for the most part to what will disappear. But what will there be new? That will be answered when a new generation has grown up: a generation of men who never in their lives have known what it is to buy a woman's surrender with money or any other social instrument of power; a generation of women who have never known what it is to give themselves to a man from any other considerations than real love or to refuse to give themselves to their lover from fear of the economic consequences. When these people are in the world, they will care precious little what anybody today thinks they ought to do; they will make their own practice and their corresponding public opinion about the practice of each individual—and that will be the end of it.

Let us, however, return to Morgan, from whom we have moved a considerable distance. The historical investigation of the social institutions developed during the period of civilization goes beyond the limits of his book. How monogamy fares during this epoch, therefore, only occupies him very briefly. He, too, sees in the further development of the monogamous family a step forward, an approach to complete equality of the sexes, though he does not regard this goal as attained. But, he says:

When the fact is accepted that the family has passed through four successive forms and is now in a fifth, the question at once arises whether this form can be permanent in the future. The only answer that can be given is that it must advance as society advances, and change as society changes, even as it has done in the past. It is the creature of the social system, and will reflect its culture. As the mono-gamian family has improved greatly since the commencement of civilization, and very sensibly in modern times, it is at least supposable that it is capable of still further improvement until the equality of the sexes is attained. Should the monogamian family in the distant future fail to answer the requirements of society . . . it is impossible to predict the nature of its successor [1963: 499].

CHAPTER III

THE IROQUOIS GENS

WE NOW come to another discovery made by Morgan, which is at least as important as the reconstruction of the family in its primitive form from the systems of consanguinity. The proof that the kinship organizations designated by animal names in a tribe of American Indians are essentially identical with the *genea* of the Greeks and the *gentes* of the Romans; that the American is the original form and the Greek and Roman forms are later and derivative; that the whole social organization of the primitive Greeks and Romans into gens, phratry, and tribe finds its faithful parallel in that of the American Indians; that the gens is an institution common to all barbarians until their entry into civilization and even afterward (so far as our sources go up to the present)—this proof has cleared up at one stroke the most difficult questions in the most ancient periods of Greek and Roman history, providing us at the same time with an unsuspected wealth of information about the fundamental features of social constitution in primitive times, before the introduction of the *state*. Simple as the matter seems once it is understood, Morgan only made his discovery quite recently. In his previous work, published in 1871,[24] he had not yet penetrated this secret, at whose subsequent revelation the English anthropologists, usually so self-confident, became for a time as quiet as mice.

The Latin word *gens,* which Morgan uses as a general term for such kinship organizations, comes, like its Greek equivalent, *genos,* from the common Aryan root *gan* (in German, where following the law[25] Aryan *g* is regularly replaced by *k, kan*), which means to beget. *Gens, Genos,* Sanscrit *jánas,* Gothic *kuni* (following the same law as above), Old Norse and Anglo-Saxon *kyn,* English *kin,* Middle High German *künne,* all signify lineage, descent. *Gens* in

---

24. *Systems of Consanguinity and Affinity of the Human Family,* Smithsonian Publications, 1871.
25. Engels refers here to Grimm's law of the shifting of consonants in the Indo-European languages.

Latin and *genos* in Greek are, however, used specifically to denote the form of kinship organization which prides itself on its common descent (in this case from a common ancestral father) and is bound together by social and religious institutions into a distinct community, though to all our historians its origin and character have hitherto remained obscure.

We have already seen in connection with the punaluan family what is the composition of a gens in its original form. It consists of all the persons who in punaluan marriage, according to the conceptions necessarily prevailing under it, form the recognized descendants of one particular ancestral mother, the founder of the gens. In this form of family, as paternity is uncertain, only the female line counts. Since brothers may not marry their sisters but only women of different descent, the children begotten by them with these alien women cannot according to mother right belong to the father's gens. Therefore only the offspring of the *daughters* in each generation remain within the kinship organization; the offspring of the sons go into the gentes of their mothers. What becomes of this consanguine group when it has constituted itself a separate group distinct from similar groups within the tribe?

As the classic form of this original gens, Morgan takes the gens among the Iroquois and especially in the Seneca tribe. In this tribe there are eight gentes, named after animals: (1) Wolf, (2) Bear, (3) Turtle, (4) Beaver, (5) Deer, (6) Snipe, (7) Heron, (8) Hawk. In every gens the following customs are observed:

1. The gens elects its sachem (head of the gens in peace) and its chief (leader in war). The sachem had to be chosen from among the members of the gens, and his office was hereditary within the gens in the sense that it had to be filled immediately as often as a vacancy occurred. The military leader could be chosen from outside the gens, and for a time the office might even be vacant. A son was never chosen to succeed his father as sachem since mother right prevailed among the Iroquois, and the son consequently belonged to a different gens; but the office might and often did pass to a brother of the previous sachem or to his sister's son. All voted in the elections, both men and women. The election, however, still required the confirmation of the seven remaining gentes, and only then was the new sachem ceremonially invested with his office by

the common council of the whole Iroquois confederacy. The significance of this will appear later. The authority of the sachem within the gens was paternal and purely moral in character; he had no means of coercion. By virtue of his office he was also a member of the tribal council of the Senecas and also of the federal council of all the Iroquois. The war chief could only give orders on military expeditions.

2. The gens deposes the sachem and war chief at will. This also is done by men and women jointly. After a sachem or chief had been deposed, they became simple braves, private persons, like the other members. The tribal council also had the power to depose sachems, even against the will of the gens.

3. No member is permitted to marry within the gens. This is the fundamental law of the gens, the bond which holds it together. It is the negative expression of the very positive blood relationship by virtue of which the individuals it comprises become a gens. By his discovery of this simple fact Morgan has revealed for the first time the nature of the gens. How little the gens was understood before is obvious from the earlier reports about savages and barbarians in which the various bodies out of which the gentile organization is composed are ignorantly and indiscriminately referred to as tribe, clan, *thum,* and so forth, and then sometimes designated as bodies within which marriage is prohibited. Thus was created the hopeless confusion which gave Mr. McLennan his chance to appear as Napoleon, establishing order by his decree: All tribes are divided into those within which marriage is prohibited (exogamous) and those within which it is permitted (endogamous). Having now made the muddle complete, he could give himself up to the profoundest inquiries as to which of his two absurd classes was the older—exogamy or endogamy. All this nonsense promptly stopped of itself with the discovery of the gens and of its basis in consanguinity, involving the exclusion of its members from intermarriage with one another. Obviously, at the stage at which we find the Iroquois the prohibition of marriage within the gens was stringently observed.

4. The property of deceased persons passed to the other members of the gens; it had to remain in the gens. As an Iroquois had only things of little value to leave, the inheritance was shared by

his nearest gentile relations; in the case of a man, by his own brothers and sisters and maternal uncle; in the case of a woman, by her children and own sisters, but not by her brothers. For this reason man and wife could not inherit from one another, nor children from their father.

5. The members of the gens owed each other help, protection, and especially assistance in avenging injury by strangers. The individual looked for his security to the protection of the gens and could rely upon receiving it; to wrong him was to wrong his whole gens. From the bonds of blood uniting the gens sprang the obligation of blood revenge, which the Iroquois unconditionally recognized. If any person from outside the gens killed a gentile member, the obligation of blood revenge rested on the entire gens of the slain man. First, mediation was tried; the gens of the slayer sat in council and made proposals of settlement to the council of the gens of the slain, usually offering expressions of regret and presents of considerable value. If these were accepted, the matter was disposed of. In the contrary case, the wronged gens appointed one or more avengers whose duty it was to pursue and kill the slayer. If this was accomplished, the gens of the slayer had no ground of complaint; accounts were even and closed.

6. The gens has special names or classes of names which may not be used by any other gens in the whole tribe, so that the name of the individual indicates the gens to which he belongs. A gentile name confers of itself gentile rights.

7. The gens can adopt strangers and thereby admit them into the whole tribe. Thus among the Senecas the prisoners of war who were not killed became through adoption into a gens members of the tribe, receiving full gentile and tribal rights. The adoption took place on the proposal of individual members of the gens; if a man adopted, he accepted the stranger as brother or sister; if a woman, as son or daughter. The adoption had to be confirmed by ceremonial acceptance into the tribe. Frequently, a gens which was exceptionally reduced in numbers was replenished by mass adoption from another gens, with its consent. Among the Iroquois the ceremony of adoption into the gens was performed at a public council of the tribe and therefore was actually a religious rite.

8. Special religious ceremonies can hardly be found among the

Indian gentes; the religious rites of the Indians are, however, more or less connected with the gens. At the six yearly religious festivals of the Iroquois, the sachems and war chiefs of the different gentes were included *ex officio* among the "Keepers of the Faith" and had priestly functions.

9. The gens has a common burial place. Among the Iroquois of New York State, who are hedged in on all sides by white people, this has disappeared, but it existed formerly. It exists still among other Indians—for example, among the Tuscaroras, who are closely related to the Iroquois; although they are Christians, each gens has a separate row in the cemetery; the mother is therefore buried in the same row as her children, but not the father. And among the Iroquois also the whole gens of the deceased attends the burial, prepares the grave, delivers funeral addresses, and so forth.

10. The gens has a council, the democratic assembly of all male and female adult gentiles, all with equal votes. This council elected sachems, war chiefs and also the other "Keepers of the Faith" and deposed them. It took decisions regarding blood revenge or payment of atonement for murdered gentiles; it adopted strangers into the gens. In short, it was the sovereign power in the gens.

Such were the rights and privileges of a typical Indian gens.

All the members of an Iroquois gens were personally free, and they were bound to defend each other's freedom; they were equal in privileges and in personal rights, the sachem and chiefs claiming no superiority; and they were a brotherhood bound together by the ties of kin. Liberty, equality, and fraternity, though never formulated, were cardinal principles of the gens. These facts are material, because the gens was the unit of a social and governmental system, the foundation upon which Indian society was organized. . . . It serves to explain that sense of independence and personal dignity universally an attribute of Indian character [1963: 85-86].

The Indians of the whole of North America at the time of its discovery were organized in gentes under mother right. The gentes had disappeared only in some tribes, as among the Dakotas; in others, as among the Ojibwas and the Omahas, they were organized according to father right.

Among very many Indian tribes with more than five or six gentes, we find every three, four, or more gentes united in a special group which Morgan, rendering the Indian name faithfully by its Greek equivalent, calls a "phratry" (brotherhood). Thus the Senecas have two phratries: the first comprises gentes (1) to (4), the second gentes (5) to (8). Closer investigation shows that these phratries generally represent the original gentes into which the tribe first split up; for since marriage was prohibited within the gens, there had to be at least two gentes in any tribe to enable it to exist independently. In the measure in which the tribe increased, each gens divided again into two or more gentes, each of which now appears as a separate gens, while the original gens, which includes all the daughter gentes, continues as the phratry.

Among the Senecas and most other Indians, the gentes within one phratry are brother gentes to one another while those in the other phratry are their cousin gentes—terms which in the American system of consanguinity have, as we have seen, a very real and expressive meaning. Originally no Seneca was allowed to marry within his phratry, but this restriction has long since become obsolete and is now confined to the gens. According to Senecan tradition, the Bear and the Deer were the two original gentes from which the others branched off. After this new institution had once taken firm root, it was modified as required; if the gentes in one phratry died out, entire gentes were sometimes transferred into it from other phratries to make the numbers even. Hence we find gentes of the same name grouped in different phratries in different tribes.

Among the Iroquois the functions of the phratry are partly social, partly religious. (1) In the ball game one phratry plays against an other. Each phratry puts forward its best players, while the other members, grouped according to phratries, look on and bet against one another on the victory of their players. (2) In the tribal council the sachems and the war chiefs of each phratry sit together, the two groups facing one another; each speaker addresses the representatives of each phratry as a separate body. (3) If a murder had been committed in the tribe and the slayer and the slain belonged to different phratries, the injured gens often appealed to its brother gentes; these held a council of the phratry and appealed in a body to the other phratry that it also should assemble its council to effect a settlement. Here the phratry reappears as the original gens and with greater prospect of success than the weaker single gens, its offspring. (4) At the death of prominent persons the opposite phratry saw to the interment and the burial ceremonies, while the phratry of the dead person attended as mourners. If a sachem died, the opposite phratry reported to the federal council of the Iroquois that the office was vacant. (5) The council of the phratry also played a part in the election of a sachem. That the election would be confirmed by the brother gentes was more or less taken for granted, but the gentes of the opposite phratry might raise an objection. In this case the council of the opposite phratry was assembled; if it maintained the objection, the election was void. (6) The Iroquois formerly had special religious mysteries, called medicine lodges by the white men. Among the Senecas, these mysteries were celebrated by two religious brotherhoods into which new members were admitted by formal initiation; there was one such brotherhood in each of the two phratries. (7) If, as is almost certain, the four lineages occupying the four quarters of Tlascalá at the time of the Conquest [of Mexico] were four phratries, we here have proof that the phratries were also military units, like the phratries among the Greeks and similar kinship organizations among the Germans; these four lineages went into battle as separate groups each with its own uniform and flag and under its own leader.

As several gentes make up a phratry, so in the classic form several phratries make up a tribe; in some cases, when tribes have been much weakened, the intermediate form, the phratry, is absent. What distinguishes an Indian tribe in America?

1. *Its own territory and name.* In addition to its actual place of settlement, every tribe further possessed considerable territory for hunting and fishing. Beyond that lay a broad strip of neutral land reaching to the territory of the neighboring tribe; it was smaller between tribes related in language, larger between tribes not so related. It is the same as the boundary forest of the Germans, the waste made by Caesar's Suevi around their territory, the *îsarnholt* (in Danish, *jarnved, limes Danicus*) between Danes and Germans, the Saxon forest, and the *branibor* (Slav, "protecting wood") between Germans and Slavs, from which Brandenburg takes its name. The territory delimited by these uncertain boundaries was the common land of the tribe, recognized as such by neighboring tribes and

defended by the tribe itself against attacks. In most cases the uncertainty of the boundaries only became a practical disadvantage when there had been a great increase in population. The names of the tribes seem generally to have arisen by chance rather than to have been deliberately chosen; in the course of time it often happened that a tribe was called by another name among the neighboring tribes than that which it used itself, just as the Germans were first called Germans by the Celts.

2. *A distinct dialect, peculiar to this tribe alone.* Tribe and dialect are substantially coextensive; the formation through segmentation of new tribes and dialects was still proceeding in America until quite recently, and most probably has not entirely stopped even today. When two weakened tribes have merged into one, the exceptional case occurs of two closely related dialects being spoken in the same tribe. The average strength of American tribes is under 2,000 members; the Cherokees, however, number about 26,000, the greatest number of Indians in the United States speaking the same dialect.

3. *The right to install into office the sachems and war chiefs elected by the gentes and the right to depose them,* even against the will of their gens. As these sachems and war chiefs are members of the council of the tribe, these rights of the tribe in regard to them explain themselves. Where a confederacy of tribes had been formed with all the tribes represented in a federal council, these rights were transferred to the latter.

4. *The possession of common religious conceptions (mythology) and ceremonies.* "After the fashion of barbarians the American Indians were a religious people" [Morgan; 1963: 117]. Their mythology has not yet been studied at all critically. They already embodied their religious ideas—spirits of every kind—in human form; but the lower stage of barbarism which they had reached still knows no plastic representations, so-called idols. Their religion is a cult of nature and of elemental forces in process of development to polytheism. The various tribes had their regular festivals with definite rites, especially dances and games. Dancing particularly was an essential part of all religious ceremonies; each tribe held its own celebration separately.

5. *A tribal council for the common affairs of the tribe.* It was

composed of all the sachems and war chiefs of the different gentes, who were genuinely representative because they could be deposed at any time. It held its deliberations in public surrounded by the other members of the tribe, who had the right to join freely in the discussion and to make their views heard. The decision rested with the council. As a rule, everyone was given a hearing who asked for it; the women could also have their views expressed by a speaker of their own choice. Among the Iroquois the final decision had to be unanimous, as was also the case in regard to many decisions of the German mark communities. The tribal council was responsible especially for the handling of relations with other tribes; it received and sent embassies, declared war and made peace. If war broke out, it was generally carried on by volunteers. In principle, every tribe was considered to be in a state of war with every other tribe with which it had not expressly concluded a treaty of peace. Military expeditions against such enemies were generally organized by prominent individual warriors; they held a war dance, and whoever joined in the dance announced thereby his participation in the expedition. The column was at once formed and started off. The defense of the tribal territory when attacked was also generally carried out by volunteers. The departure and return of such columns were always an occasion of public festivities. The consent of the tribal council was not required for such expeditions, and was neither asked nor given. They find their exact counterpart in the private war expeditions of the German retinues described by Tacitus, only with the difference that among the Germans the retinues have already acquired a more permanent character forming a firm core already organized in peacetime to which the other volunteers are attached in event of war. These war parties are seldom large; the most important expeditions of the Indians, even to great distances, were undertaken with insignificant forces. If several such parties united for operations on a large scale, each was under the orders only of its own leader. Unity in the plan of campaign was secured well or ill by a council of these leaders. It is the same manner of warfare as we find described by Ammianus Marcellinus among the Alemanni on the Upper Rhine in the fourth century.

6. *Among some tribes we find a head chief whose powers, how-*

ever, are very slight. He is one of the sachems, and in situations demanding swift action he has to take provisional measures until the council can assemble and make a definite decision. His function represents the first feeble attempt at the creation of an official with executive power, though generally nothing more came of it; as we shall see, the executive official developed in most cases, if not in all, out of the chief military commander.

The great majority of the American Indians did not advance to any higher form of association than the tribe. Living in small tribes, separated from one another by wide tracts between their frontiers, weakened by incessant wars, they occupied an immense territory with few people. Here and there alliances between related tribes came into being in the emergency of the moment and broke up when the emergency had passed. But in certain districts tribes which were originally related and had then been dispersed joined together again in permanent federations, thus taking the first step toward the formation of nations. In the United States we find the most developed form of such a federation among the Iroquois. Emigrating from their homes west of the Mississippi where they probably formed a branch of the great Dakota family, they settled after long wanderings in what is now the State of New York. They were divided into five tribes: Senecas, Cayugas, Onondagas, Oneidas and Mohawks. They subsisted on fish, game and the products of a crude horticulture, and lived in villages which were generally protected by a stockade. Never more than 20,000 strong, they had a number of gentes common to all the five tribes, spoke closely related dialects of the same language, and occupied a continuous stretch of territory which was divided up among the five tribes. As they had newly conquered this territory, these tribes were naturally accustomed to stand together against the inhabitants they had driven out. From this developed at the beginning of the fifteenth century at latest a regular "everlasting league," a sworn confederacy, which in the consciousness of its new strength immediately assumed an aggressive character and at the height of its power, about 1675 conquered wide stretches of the surrounding country, either expelling the inhabitants or making them pay tribute. The Iroquois confederacy represents the most advanced social organization achieved by any Indians still at the lower stage of barbarism (excluding, therefore, the Mexicans, New Mexicans and Peruvians).

The main provisions of the confederacy were as follows:

1. Perpetual federation of the five consanguineous tribes on the basis of complete equality and independence in all internal matters of the tribe. This bond of kin represented the real basis of the confederacy. Of the five tribes, three were known as father tribes and were brother tribes to one another; the other two were known as son tribes and were likewise brother tribes to one another. Three gentes, the oldest, still had their living representatives in all five tribes, and another three in three tribes; the members of each of these gentes were all brothers of one another throughout all the five tribes. Their common language, in which there were only variations of dialect, was the expression and the proof of their common descent.

2. The organ of the confederacy was a federal council of fifty sachems, all equal in rank and authority; the decisions of this council were final in all matters relating to the confederacy.

3. The fifty sachems were distributed among the tribes and gentes at the foundation of the confederacy to hold the new offices specially created for federal purposes. They were elected by the respective gentes whenever a vacancy occurred and could be deposed by the gentes at any time; but the right of investing them with their office belonged to the federal council.

4. These federal sachems were also sachems in their respective tribes, and had a seat and a vote in the tribal council.

5. All decisions of the federal council had to be unanimous.

6. Voting was by tribes, so that for a decision to be valid every tribe and all members of the council in every tribe had to signify their agreement.

7. Each of the five tribal councils could convene the federal council, but it could not convene itself.

8. The meetings of the council were held in the presence of the assembled people; every Iroquois could speak; the council alone decided.

9. The confederacy had no official head or chief executive officer.

10. On the other hand, the council had two principal war chiefs, with equal powers and equal authority (the two "kings" of the Spartans, the two consuls in Rome).

That was the whole public constitution under which the Iroquois lived for over 400 years and are still living today. I have described it fully, following Morgan, because here we have the opportunity of studying the organization of society which still has no *state*. The state presupposes a special public power separated from the body of the people, and Maurer, who with a true instinct recognizes that the constitution of the German mark is a purely social institution differing essentially from the state though later providing a great part of its basis, consequently investigates in all his writings the gradual growth of the public power out of and side by side with the primitive constitutions of marks, villages, homesteads, and towns. Among the North American Indians we see how an originally homogeneous tribe gradually spreads over a huge continent; how through division tribes become nations, entire groups of tribes; how the languages change until they not only become unintelligible to other tribes but also lose almost every trace of their original identity; how at the same time within the tribes each gens splits up into several gentes, how the old mother gentes are preserved as phratries, while the names of these oldest gentes nevertheless remain the same in widely distant tribes that have long been separated—the Wolf and the Bear are still gentile names among a majority of all Indian tribes. And the constitution described above applies in the main to them all, except that many of them never advanced as far as the confederacy of related tribes.

But once the gens is given as the social unit we also see how the whole constitution of gentes, phratries, and tribes is almost necessarily bound to develop from this unit, because the development is natural. Gens, phratry, and tribe are all groups of different degrees of consanguinity, each self-contained and ordering its own affairs, but each supplementing the other. And the affairs which fall within their sphere comprise all the public affairs of barbarians of the lower stage. When we find a people with the gens as their social unit, we may therefore also look for an organization of the tribe similar to that here described; and when there are adequate sources as in the case of the Greeks and the Romans, we shall not find it, but we shall also be able to convince ourselves that where the sources fail us comparison with the American social constitution helps us over the most difficult doubts and riddles.

And a wonderful constitution it is, this gentile constitution, in all its childlike simplicity! No soldiers, no gendarmes or police, no nobles, kings, regents, prefects, or judges, no prisons, or lawsuits— and everything takes its orderly course. All quarrels and disputes are settled by the whole of the community affected, by the gens or the tribe, or by the gentes among themselves; only as an extreme and exceptional measure is blood revenge threatened—and our capital punishment is nothing but blood revenge in a civilized form, with all the advantages and drawbacks of civilization. Although there were many more matters to be settled in common than today —the household is maintained by a number of families in common and is communistic; the land belongs to the tribe, only the small gardens are allotted provisionally to the households—yet there is no need for even a trace of our complicated administrative apparatus with all its ramifications. The decisions are taken by those concerned, and in most cases everything has been already settled by the custom of centuries. There cannot be any poor or needy— the communal household and the gens know their responsibilities toward the old, the sick, and those disabled in war. All are equal and free—the women included. There is no place yet for slaves, nor, as a rule, for the subjugation of other tribes. When about the year 1651 the Iroquois had conquered the Eries and the "Neutral Nation," they offered to accept them into the confederacy on equal terms; it was only after the defeated tribes had refused that they were driven from their territory. And what men and women such a society breeds is proved by the admiration inspired in all white people who have come into contact with unspoiled Indians, by the personal dignity, uprightness, strength of character, and courage of these barbarians.

We have seen examples of this courage quite recently in Africa. The Zulus a few years ago and the Nubians a few months ago[26]—

26. The reference is to the war between the British and the Zulus in 1879 and between the British and the Nubians in 1883.

both of them tribes in which gentile institutions have not yet died out—did what no European army can do. Armed only with lances and spears, without firearms, under a hail of bullets from the breech-loaders of the English infantry—acknowledged the best in the world at fighting in close order—they advanced right up to the bayonets and more than once threw the lines into disorder and even broke them, in spite of the enormous inequality of weapons and in spite of the fact that they have no military service and know nothing of drill. Their powers of endurance and performance are shown by the complaint of the English that a Kaffir travels farther and faster in 24 hours than a horse. His smallest muscle stands out hard and firm like whipcord, says an English painter.

That is what men and society were before the division into classes. And when we compare their position with that of the overwhelming majority of civilized men today, an enormous gulf separates the present-day proletarian and small peasant from the free member of the old gentile society.

That is the one side. But we must not forget that this organization was doomed. It did not go beyond the tribe. The confederacy of tribes already marks the beginning of its collapse, as we shall see later, and was already apparent in the attempts at subjugation by the Iroquois. Outside the tribe was outside the law. Wherever there was not an explicit treaty of peace, tribe was at war with tribe, and wars were waged with the cruelty which distinguishes man from other animals and which was only mitigated later by self-interest. The gentile constitution in its best days, as we saw it in America, presupposed an extremely undeveloped state of production and therefore an extremely sparse population over a wide area. Man's attitude to nature was therefore one of almost complete subjection to a strange incomprehensible power, as is reflected in his childish religious conceptions. Man was bounded by his tribe, both in relation to strangers from outside the tribe and to himself; the tribe, the gens, and their institutions were sacred and inviolable, a higher power established by nature to which the individual subjected himself unconditionally in feeling, thought, and action. However impressive the people of this epoch appear to us, they are completely undifferentiated from one another; as Marx says, they are still attached to the navel string of the primitive community.[27] The power of this primitive community had to be broken, and it was broken. But it was broken by influences which from the very start appear as a degradation, a fall from the simple moral greatness of the old gentile society. The lowest interests—base greed, brutal appetites, sordid avarice, selfish robbery of the common wealth—inaugurate the new, civilized, class society. It is by the vilest means —theft, violence, fraud, treason—that the old classless gentile society is undermined and overthrown. And the new society itself during all the 2,500 years of its existence has never been anything else but the development of the small minority at the expense of the great exploited and oppressed majority; today it is so more than ever before.

27. "Those ancient social organisms of production are, as compared with bourgeois society, extremely simple and transparent. But they are founded either on the immature development of man individually, who has not yet severed the umbilical cord that unites him with his fellow men in a primitive tribal community, or upon direct relations of domination and subjection" (Marx, 1967: 79).

CHAPTER IV

THE GREEK GENS

FROM PREHISTORIC times Greeks and Pelasgians alike, and other peoples of kindred stock, had been organized in the same organic series as the Americans: gens, phratry, tribe, confederacy of tribes. The phratry might be absent, as among the Dorians, and the confederacy of tribes was not necessarily fully developed everywhere as yet; but in every case the gens was the unit. At the time of their entry into history, the Greeks are on the threshold of civilization; between them and the American tribes, of whom we spoke above, lie almost two entire great periods of development by which the Greeks of the heroic age are ahead of the Iroquois. The gens of the Greeks is therefore no longer the archaic gens of the Iroquois; the impress of group marriage is beginning to be a good deal blurred. Mother right has given way to father right; increasing private wealth has thus made its first breach in the gentile constitution. A second breach followed naturally from the first. After the introduction of father right, the property of a rich heiress would have passed to her husband and thus into another gens on her marriage, but the foundation of all gentile law was now violated and in such a case the girl was not only permitted but *ordered* to marry within the gens, in order that her property should be retained for the gens.

According to Grote's *A History of Greece* [III, 54-55], the Athenian gens in particular was held together by the following institutions and customs:

1. Common religious rites and the exclusive privilege of priesthood in honor of a particular god, the supposed ancestral father of the gens, who in this attribute was designated by a special surname.

2. A common burial place (*see* Demosthenes' *Eubulides*).

3. Mutual right of inheritance.

4. Mutual obligations of help, protection, and assistance in case of violence.

5. Mutual right and obligation to marry within the gens in certain cases, especially for orphan girls and heiresses.

6. Possession, at least in some cases, of common property with a special archon (chief magistrate) and treasurer.

Next, several gentes were united in the phratry, but less closely; though here also we find mutual rights and obligations of a similar kind, particularly the common celebration of certain religious ceremonies and the right to avenge the death of a phrator. Similarly, all the phratries of a tribe held regularly recurring religious festivals in common at which a leader of the tribe (*phylobasileus*), elected from the nobility (eupatrida), officiated.

Thus Grote, and Marx adds: "In the Greek gens, the savage (for example, Iroquois) shows through unmistakably." He becomes still more unmistakable when we investigate further.

For the Greek gens has also the following characteristics:

7. Descent in the male line.

8. Prohibition of marriage within the gens except in the case of heiresses. This exception and its formulation as an ordinance prove the old rule to be valid. This is further substantiated by the universally accepted principle that at her marriage the woman renounced the religious rites of her gens and went over to those of her husband, being also inscribed in his phratry. This custom and a famous passage in Dicaearchus both show that marriage outside the gens was the rule, and Becker in *Charicles* directly assumes that nobody might marry within his own gens.

9. The right of adoption into the gens. This was exercised through adoption into the family but required public formalities and was exceptional.

10. The right to elect chieftains and to depose them. We know that every gens had its archon; but it is nowhere stated that the office was hereditary in certain families. Until the end of barbarism the probability is always against strict heredity, which is quite incompatible with conditions in which rich and poor had completely equal rights within the gens.

Not only Grote but also Niebuhr, Mommsen and all the other historians of classical antiquity have come to grief over the gens. Though they correctly noted many of its characteristics, they always took it to be a *group of families,* thus making it impossible for themselves to understand the nature and origin of the gens. Under the gentile constitution, the family was never an organizational unit and could not be so, for man and wife necessarily belonged to two different gentes. The whole gens was incorporated within the phratry and the whole phratry within the tribe; but the family belonged half to the gens of the man and half to the gens of the woman. In public law the state also does not recognize the family; up to this day, the family only exists for private law. And yet all our histories have hitherto started from the absurd assumption, which since the 18th century in particular has become inviolable, that the monogamous single family, which is hardly older than civilization, is the core around which society and state have gradually crystallized.

Mr. Grote will also please note [Marx throws in] that though the Greeks derive their gentes from mythology, the gentes are older than the mythology which *they themselves* created with all its gods and demigods.

Morgan prefers to quote Grote because he is not only an impressive but also a trustworthy witness. Grote goes on to say that every Athenian gens had a name derived from its supposed ancestor; that it was the general custom before Solon, and even after Solon, in the absence of a will for the property of a deceased person to pass to the members of his gens (*gennêtes*); and that in the case of a murder it was the right and the duty, first of the relatives of the murdered man, then of the members of his gens, and lastly of his phratry, to prosecute the criminal before the tribunals: "All that we hear of the most ancient Athenian laws is based upon the gentile and phratric divisions" [Grote, 1869: III, 66].

The descent of the gentes from common ancestors has caused the "pedantic philistines," as Marx calls them, a lot of brain-racking. As they of course declare the common ancestors to be pure myths, they are at an utter loss to explain how the gens originated out of a number of separate and originally quite unrelated families; yet they have to perform this feat in order to explain how the gentes exist at all. So they argue in a whirlpool of words, never getting any further than the statement: the ancestral tree is a fairy tale, but the gens is a reality. And finally Grote declares (interpolations by Marx):

We hear of this genealogy but rarely because it is only brought before the public in certain cases pre-eminent and venerable. But the humbler gentes had their common rites [this is strange, Mr. Grote!], and common superhuman ancestor and genealogy, as well as the more celebrated [this is most strange, Mr. Grote, among *humbler* gentes!]: the scheme and ideal basis [my good sir, not *ideal,* but carnal, *germanic fleishlich!*] was the same in all [Grote, 1869: III, 60].

Marx summarizes Morgan's reply to this as follows:

The system of consanguinity corresponding to the original form of the gens—and the Greeks like other mortals once possessed such a gens—preserved the knowledge of the mutual relations between all the members of the gens. It was of decisive importance for them, and they learned it by practice from childhood upwards. With the monogamous family, this knowledge was forgotten. The gentile name created an ancestral tree, beside which that of the individual family appeared insignificant. It was now the function of this name to preserve the fact of the common descent of those who bore it; but the lineage of the gens went back so far that its members could not prove the actual relationship existing between them, except in a limited number of cases through more recent common ancestors. The name 'itself was proof of common descent and conclusive proof, apart from cases of adoption. Actually to deny, like Grote and Niebuhr, all relationship between the members of the gens, thus changing the gens into a purely fictitious and imaginary creation, is worthy of "ideal," that is, pedantic bookworms. Because the ties of kinship, especially with the rise of monogamy, are pushed back into remote times and the reality of the past appears reflected in mythological phantasies, our good philistines concluded, and conclude, that the imaginary pedigree created the real gentes!

The phratry, as among the Americans, was a mother gens that had split up into several daughter gentes and now united them; often it still traced all the gentes back to its own common ancestral father. According to Grote, "all the contemporary members of the phratry of Hekataeus had a common god for their ancestor at the sixteenth degree" [Grote, 1869: II, 58-59]; all gentes of this phratry were therefore literally brother gentes. The phratry still appears in Homer as a military unit in the famous passage where Nestor advises Agamemnon: "Marshal the men by tribes and by phratries, so that phratry may assist phratry and tribe may assist tribe."

The phratry has further the right and the duty of prosecuting for bloodguilt incurred against a phrator; hence in earlier times it also had the obligation of blood revenge. Further, it had common shrines and festivals; in fact the elaboration of the whole Greek mythology out of the traditional old Aryan nature cult was essentially conditioned by the phratries and gentes and took place within them. The phratry also had a chief (the *phratriarchos*) and, according to de Coulanges, assemblies which could pass binding resolutions, a tribunal and an administration. Even the later state, while it ignored the gens, left certain public offices in the hands of the phratry.

Several related phratries form a tribe. In Attica there were four tribes, each consisting of three phratries, each phratry numbering thirty gentes. Such a rounded symmetry of groups presupposes conscious, purposeful interference with the naturally developed order. As to how, when, and why this occurred, Greek history is silent; the historical memory of the Greeks only went back to the heroic age.

As the Greeks were crowded together in a relatively small territory, differences of dialect were less developed than in the wide American forests; yet in Greece also it was only tribes of the same main dialect that united in a larger organization, and even Attica, small as it was, had a dialect of its own, which later through its general use as the language of prose became the dominant dialect.

In the Homeric poems we find most of the Greek tribes already united into small nations, within which, however, gentes, phratries, and tribes retained their full independence. They already lived in towns fortified with walls; the population increased with the increase of the herds, the extension of agriculture and the beginnings of handicraft. The differences in wealth thus became more pronounced and with them the aristocratic element within the old primitive democracy. The various small nations waged incessant wars for the possession of the best land and doubtless also for booty; the use of prisoners of war as slaves was already a recognized institution.

The constitution of these tribes and small nations was as follows:

1. The permanent authority was the council (*boulè*), probably composed originally of all the chiefs of the gentes, but later, when their number became too large, of a selection whose choice provided an opportunity of extending and strengthening the aristocratic element. Dionysius actually speaks of the council in the heroic age

as composed of nobles (*kratistoi*). The ultimate decision in important matters rested with the council. Thus in Aeschylus [Seven Against Thebes] the council of Thebes makes what is in the circumstances the vital decision to give Eteocles an honorable burial, but to throw out the corpse of Polynices to be devoured by dogs. When the state was established, this council was merged into the senate.

2. The assembly of the people (*agora*). We saw among the Iroquois how the people, men and women, stood round the council when it was holding its meetings, intervening in an orderly manner in its deliberations and thus influencing its decisions. Among the Homeric Greeks, this *Umstand* [those standing round], to use an old German legal expression, had already developed into a regular assembly of the people, as was also the case among the Germans in primitive times. It was convened by the council to decide important questions; every man had the right to speak. The decision was given by a show of hands (Aeschylus, *The Suppliants*) or by acclamation. The decision of the assembly was supreme and final, for, says Schömann, in *Griechische Altertümer* [Antiquities of Greece] "if the matter was one requiring the cooperation of the people for its execution, Homer does not indicate any means by which the people could be forced to cooperate against their will."

For at this time, when every adult male member of the tribe was a warrior, there was as yet no public power separate from the people which could have been used against the people. Primitive democracy was still in its full strength, and it is in relation to that fact that the power and the position both of the council and of the *basileus* must first be judged.

3. The leader of the army (*basileus*). Marx makes the following comment:

European scholars, born lackeys most of them, make the *basileus* into a monarch in the modern sense. Morgan, the Yankee republican, protests. Very ironically, but truly, he says of the oily-tongued Gladstone and his *Juventus Mundi:* "Mr. Gladstone, who presents to his readers the Grecian chiefs of the heroic age as kings and princes, with the superadded qualities of gentlemen, is forced to admit that 'on the whole we seem to have the custom or law of primogeniture sufficiently but not oversharply defined' " [Morgan, 1963: 255*n*].

Mr. Gladstone will probably agree that such an ambiguous law of primogeniture as may be "sufficiently but not oversharply defined" is just as good as none at all.

In what sense the offices of sachem and chieftain were hereditary among the Iroquois and other Indians we have already seen. All offices were elective, generally within a gens, and to that extent hereditary to the gens. In the course of time, preference when filling vacancies was given to the nearest gentile relation—brother or sister's son—unless there were reasons for passing him over. The fact that among the Greeks under father right the office of *basileus* generally passed to the son or one of the sons only proves that the probabilities were in favor of the sons succeeding to the office by popular election; it is no proof at all of legal hereditary succession without popular election. All that we have here is the first beginnings among the Iroquois and Greeks of distinct noble families within the gentes and, in the case of the Greeks, the first beginnings also of a future hereditary leadership or monarchy. The probability is, therefore, that among the Greeks the *basileus* had either to be elected by the people or at least confirmed in his office by the recognized organs of the people, the council or *agora,* as was the case with the Roman "king" (*rex*).

In the *Iliad* Agamemnon, the ruler of men, does not appear as the supreme king of the Greeks, but as supreme commander of a federal army before a besieged town. It is to this supremacy of command that Odysseus, after disputes had broken out among the Greeks, refers in a famous passage: "Evil is the rule of many; let one be commander," etc. (The favorite line about the scepter is a later addition.)

Odysseus is here not giving a lecture on a form of government, but demanding obedience to the supreme commander in war. Since they are appearing before Troy only as an army, the proceedings in the *agora* secure to the Greeks all necessary democracy. When Achilles speaks of presents—that is, the division of the booty—he always leaves the division, not to Agamemnon or any other *basileus,* but to the "sons of the Achaeans," that is, the people. Such epithets as "descended from Zeus," "nourished by Zeus," prove nothing, for *every* gens is descended from a god, that of the leader of the tribe being already descended from a "superior" god, in this case Zeus. Even those without personal freedom, such as the swineherd Eumaeus and others, are "divine" (*dioi* and *theioi*), and that too in the *Odyssey* which is much later than the *Iliad;* and again in the *Odyssey* the name *Heros* is given to the herald

Mulios as well as to the blind bard Demodocus. Since, in short, council and assembly of the people function together with the *basileus,* the word *basileia,* which Greek writers employ to denote the so-called Homeric kingship (chief command in the army being the principal characteristic of the office), only means—military democracy (Marx).

In addition to his military functions, the *basileus* also held those of priest and judge, the latter not clearly defined, the former exercised in his capacity as supreme representative of the tribe or confederacy of tribes. There is never any mention of civil administrative powers; he seems, however, to be a member of the council *ex officio.* It is therefore quite correct etymologically to translate *basileus* as king since king (*kuning*) is derived from *kuni, künne,* and means head of a gens. But the old Greek *basileus* does not correspond in any way to the present meaning of the word "king." Thucydides expressly refers to the old *basileia* as *patrike,* that is, derived from gentes, and says it had strictly defined and therefore limited functions. And Aristotle says that the *basileia* of the heroic age was a leadership over freemen and that the *basileus* was military leader, judge and high priest; he thus had no governmental power in the later sense.*

Thus in the Greek constitution of the heroic age, we see the old gentile order as still a living force. But we also see the beginnings of its disintegration: father right, with transmission of the property to the children by which accumulation of wealth within the family was favored and the family itself became a power against the gens; reaction of the inequality of wealth on the constitution by the formation of the first rudiments of hereditary nobility and monarchy; slavery, at first only of prisoners of war but already preparing the way for the enslavement of fellow members of the tribe and even of the gens; the old wars between tribe and tribe already

* Like the Greek *basileus,* so also the Aztec military chief has been made out to be a modern prince. The report of the Spaniards, which were at first misinterpretations and exaggerations, and later actual lies, were submitted for the first time to historical criticism by Morgan. He proves that the Mexicans were at the middle stage of barbarism, though more advanced than the New Mexican Pueblo Indians, and that their constitution, so far as it can be recognized in the distorted reports, corresponded to this stage: a confederacy of three tribes which had subjugated a number of other tribes and exacted tribute from them, and which was governed by a federal council and a federal military leader, out of whom the Spaniards made an "emperor."

degenerating into systematic pillage by land and sea for the acquisition of cattle, slaves and treasure, and becoming a regular source of wealth; in short, riches praised and respected as the highest good and the old gentile order misused to justify the violent seizure of riches. Only one thing was wanting: an institution which not only secured the newly acquired riches of individuals against the communistic traditions of the gentile order, which not only sanctified the private property formerly so little valued and declared this sanctification to be the highest purpose of all human society; but, an institution which set the seal of general social recognition on each new method of acquiring property and thus amassing wealth at continually increasing speed; an institution which perpetuated not only this growing cleavage of society into classes but also the right of the possessing class to exploit the non-possessing, and the rule of the former over the latter.

And this institution came. The *state* was invented.

CHAPTER V

THE RISE OF THE ATHENIAN STATE

How THE state developed, how the organs of the gentile constitution were partly transformed in this development, partly pushed aside by the introduction of new organs, and at last superseded entirely by real state authorities while the true "people in arms," organized for its self-defense in its gentes, phratries and tribes, was replaced by an armed "public force" in the service of these state authorities and therefore at their command for use also against the people—this process, at least in its first stages, can be followed nowhere better than in ancient Athens. The changes in form have been outlined by Morgan, but their economic content and cause must largely be added by myself.

In the heroic age the four tribes of the Athenians were still settled in Attica in separate territories; even the twelve phratries composing them seem still to have had distinct seats in the twelve towns of Cecrops. The constitution was that of the heroic age: assembly of the people, council of the people, a *basileus*. As far back as written history goes, we find the land already divided up and privately owned, which is in accordance with the relatively advanced commodity production and the corresponding trade in commodities developed toward the end of the upper stage of barbarism. In addition to grain, wine and oil were produced; to a continually increasing extent, the sea trade in the Aegean was captured from the Phoenicians, and most of it passed into Athenian hands. Through the sale and purchase of land and the progressive division of labor between agriculture and handicraft, trade, and shipping, it was inevitable that the members of the different gentes, phratries, and tribes very soon became intermixed. Into the districts of the phratry and tribe moved inhabitants, who, although fellow countrymen, did not belong to these bodies and were therefore strangers in their own place of domicile. For when times were quiet, each tribe and each phratry administered its own affairs without sending to Athens to consult the council of the people or the *basileus*. But anyone not a member of the phratry or tribe was, of course, excluded from taking any part in this administration, even though living in the district.

The smooth functioning of the organs of the gentile constitution was thus thrown so much out of gear that even in the heroic age remedies had to be found. The constitution ascribed to Theseus was introduced. The principal change which it made was to set up a central authority in Athens—that is, part of the affairs hitherto administered by the tribes independently were declared common affairs and entrusted to the common council sitting in Athens. In taking this step, the Athenians went further than any native people of America had ever done: instead of neighboring tribes forming a simple confederacy, they fused together into one single nation. Hence arose a common Athenian civil law which stood above the legal customs of the tribes and gentes. The Athenian citizen as such acquired definite rights and new protection in law even on territory which was not that of his tribe. The first step had been taken toward undermining the gentile constitution; for this was the first step to the later admission of citizens who did not belong to any tribe in all Attica, but were and remained completely outside the Athenian gentile constitution. By a second measure ascribed to Theseus, the entire people, regardless of gens, phratry or tribe, was divided into three classes: *eupatrides* or nobles, *geomoroi* or farmers, and *demiourgoi* or artisans, and the right to hold office was vested exclusively in the nobility. Apart from the tenure of offices by the nobility, this division remained inoperative, as it did not create any other legal distinctions between the classes. It is, however, important because it reveals the new social elements which had been developing unobserved. It shows that the customary appointment of members of certain families to the offices of the gens had already grown into an almost uncontested right of these families to office; it shows that these families, already powerful through their wealth, were beginning to form groupings outside their gentes as a separate, privileged class, and that the state now taking form sanctioned this presumption. It shows further that the division of labor between peasants and artisans was now firmly enough established in its social importance to challenge the old grouping of gentes and tribes. And, finally, it proclaims the irreconcilable oppo-

sition between gentile society and the state; the first attempt at
forming a state consists in breaking up the gentes by dividing their
members into those with privileges and those with none, and by
further separating the latter into two productive classes and thus
setting them one against the other.

The further political history of Athens up to the time of Solon is
only imperfectly known. The office of *basileus* fell into disuse; the
positions at the head of the state were occupied by archons elected
from the nobility. The power of the nobility continuously increased
until about the year 600 B.C. it became insupportable. And the
principal means for suppressing the common liberty were—money
and usury. The nobility had their chief seat in and around Athens,
whose maritime trade, with occasional piracy still thrown in, enriched them and concentrated in their hands the wealth existing in
the form of money. From here the growing money economy
penetrated like corrosive acid into the old traditional life of the
rural communities founded on natural economy. The gentile constitution is absolutely irreconcilable with money economy; the ruin
of the Attic small farmers coincided with the loosening of the old
gentile bonds which embraced and protected them. The debtor's
bond and the lien on property (for already the Athenians had invented the mortgage also) respected neither gens nor phratry, while
the old gentile constitution for its part knew neither money nor
advances of money nor debts in money. Hence the money rule of
the aristocracy now in full flood of expansion also created a new
customary law to secure the creditor against the debtor and to
sanction the exploitation of the small peasant by the possessor of
money. All the fields of Attica were thick with mortgage columns
bearing inscriptions stating that the land on which they stood was
mortgaged to such and such for so and so much. The fields not so
marked had for the most part already been sold on account of
unpaid mortgages or interest and had passed into the ownership
of the noble usurer. The peasant could count himself lucky if he
was allowed to remain on the land as a tenant and live on *one-sixth*
of the produce of his labor while he paid *five-sixths* to his new
master as rent. And that was not all. If the sale of the land did not
cover the debt or if the debt had been contracted without any
security, the debtor, in order to meet his creditor's claims, had to

sell his children into slavery abroad. Children sold by their father—
such was the first fruit of father right and monogamy! And if the
bloodsucker was still not satisfied, he could sell the debtor himself
as a slave. Thus the pleasant dawn of civilization began for the
Athenian people.

Formerly, when the conditions of the people still corresponded
to the gentile constitution, such an upheaval was impossible; now
it had happened—nobody knew how. Let us go back for a moment
to the Iroquois, amongst whom the situation now confronting the
Athenians, without their own doing so to speak and certainly
against their will, was inconceivable. Their mode of producing the
necessities of life, unvarying from year to year, could never generate
such conflicts as were apparently forced on the Athenians from
without; it could never create an opposition of rich and poor, of
exploiters and exploited. The Iroquois were still very far from controlling nature, but within the limits imposed on them by natural
forces they did control their own production. Apart from bad
harvests in their small gardens, the exhaustion of the stocks of fish
in their lakes and rivers or of the game in their woods, they knew
what results they could expect making their living as they did. The
certain result was a livelihood, plentiful or scanty; but one result
there could never be—social upheavals that no one had ever intended, sundering of the gentile bonds, division of gens and tribe
into two opposing and warring classes. Production was limited in the
extreme, but—the producers controlled their product. That was the
immense advantage of barbarian production which was lost with the
coming of civilization; to reconquer it, but on the basis of the
gigantic control of nature now achieved by man and of the free
association now made possible, will be the task of the next generations.

Not so among the Greeks. The rise of private property in herds
and articles of luxury led to exchange between individuals, to the
transformation of products into *commodities*. And here lie the seeds
of the whole subsequent upheaval. When the producers no longer
directly consumed their product themselves, but let it pass out of
their hands in the act of exchange, they lost control of it. They no
longer knew what became of it; the possibility was there that one
day it would be used against the producer to exploit and oppress

him. For this reason no society can permanently retain the mastery of its own production and the control over the social effects of its process of production unless it abolishes exchange between individuals.

But the Athenians were soon to learn how rapidly the product asserts its mastery over the producer when once exchange between individuals has begun and products have been transformed into commodities. With the coming of commodity production, individuals began to cultivate the soil on their own account, which soon led to individual ownership of land. Money followed, the general commodity with which all others were exchangeable. But when men invented money, they did not think that they were again creating a new social power, the one general power before which the whole of society must bow. And it was this new power, suddenly sprung to life without knowledge or will of its creators, which now in all the brutality of its youth gave the Athenians the first taste of its might.

What was to be done? The old gentile constitution had not only shown itself powerless before the triumphal march of money; it was absolutely incapable of finding any place within its framework for such things as money, creditors, debtors, and forcible collection of debts. But the new social power was there; pious wishes, and yearning for the return of the good old days would not drive money and usury out of the world. Further, a number of minor breaches had also been made in the gentile constitution. All over Attica, and especially in Athens itself, the members of the different gentes and phratries became still more indiscriminately mixed with every generation although even now an Athenian was only allowed to sell land outside his gens, not the house in which he lived. The division of labor between the different branches of production— agriculture, handicrafts (in which there were again innumerable subdivisions), shipping, and so forth—had been carried further with every advance of industry and commerce. The population was now divided according to occupation into fairly permanent groups, each with its new common interests; and since the gens and the phratry made no provision for dealing with them, new offices had to be created. The number of slaves had increased considerably and even at that time must have far exceeded the number of free Athenians. The gentile constitution originally knew nothing of slavery and therefore had no means of keeping these masses of bondsmen in order. Finally, trade had brought to Athens a number of foreigners who settled there on account of the greater facilities of making money; they also could claim no rights or protection under the old constitution; and, though they were received with traditional tolerance, they remained a disturbing and alien body among the people.

In short, the end of the gentile constitution was approaching. Society was outgrowing it more every day; even the worst evils that had grown up under its eyes were beyond its power to check or remove. But in the meantime the state had quietly been developing. The new groups formed by the division of labor, first between town and country, then between the different branches of town labor, had created new organs to look after their interests; official posts of all kinds had been set up. And above everything else the young state needed a power of its own, which in the case of the seafaring Athenians could at first only be a naval power, for the purpose of carrying on occasional small wars and protecting its merchant ships. At some unknown date before Solon, the *naukrariai* were set up, small territorial districts, twelve to each tribe; each *naukraria* had to provide, equip and man a warship and also contribute two horsemen. This institution was a twofold attack on the gentile constitution. In the first place, it created a public force which was now no longer simply identical with the whole body of the armed people; secondly, for the first time it divided the people for public purposes, not by groups of kinship, but *by common place of residence*. We shall see the significance of this.

The gentile constitution being incapable of bringing help to the exploited people, there remained only the growing state. And the state brought them its help in the form of the constitution of Solon, thereby strengthening itself again at the expense of the old constitution. Solon—the manner in which his reform, which belongs to the year 594 B.C., was carried through does not concern us here —opened the series of so-called political revolutions; and he did so with an attack on property. All revolutions hitherto have been revolutions to protect one kind of property against another kind of property. They cannot protect the one without violating the other. In the great French Revolution feudal property was sacrificed to save bourgeois property; in that of Solon, the property of the creditors had to suffer for the benefit of the property of the debtors. The debts were simply declared void. We do not know the exact details, but in his poems Solon boasts of having removed the mortgage columns from the fields and brought back all the people who had fled or been sold abroad on account of debt. This was only possible by open violation of property. And, in fact, from the first to the last, all so-called political revolutions have been made to protect property—of *one* kind; and they have been carried out by confiscating, also called stealing, property—of *another* kind. The plain truth is that for 2,500 years it has been possible to preserve private property only by violating property rights.

But now the need was to protect the free Athenians against the return of such slavery. The first step was the introduction of general measures—for example, the prohibition of debt contracts pledging the person of the debtor. Further, in order to place at least some check on the nobles' ravening hunger for the land of the peasants, a maximum limit was fixed for the amount of land that could be owned by one individual. Then changes were made in the constitution, of which the most important for us are the following:

The council was raised to 400 members, 100 for each tribe; here, therefore, the tribe was still taken as basis. But that was the one and only feature of the new state incorporating anything from the old constitution. For all other purposes Solon divided the citizens into four classes according to their property in land and the amount of its yield: 500, 300 and 150 *medimni* of grain (one *medimnus* equals about 1.16 bushels) were the minimum yields for the first three classes; those who owned less land or none at all were placed in the fourth class. All offices could be filled only from the three upper classes and the highest offices only from the first. The fourth class only had the right to speak and vote in the assembly of the people; but it was in this assembly that all officers were elected. Here they had to render their account; here all laws were made; and here the fourth class formed the majority. The privileges of the aristocracy were partially renewed in the form of privileges of wealth, but the people retained the decisive power. Further, the four classes formed the basis of a new military organization. The first two classes provided the cavalry; the third had to serve as heavy infantry; the fourth served either as light infantry without armor or in the fleet, for which they probably received wages.

A completely new element is thus introduced into the constitution: private ownership. According to the size of their property in land, the rights and duties of the citizens of the state are now assessed, and in the same degree to which the classes based on property gain influence, the old groups of blood relationship lose it; the gentile constitution had suffered a new defeat.

However, the assessment of political rights on a property basis was not an institution indispensable to the existence of the state. In spite of the great part it has played in the constitutional history of states, very many states, and precisely those most highly developed, have not required it. In Athens also its role was only temporary; from the time of Aristides all offices were open to every citizen.

During the next 80 years Athenian society gradually shaped the course along which it developed in the following centuries. Usury on the security of mortgaged land, which had been rampant in the period before Solon, had been curbed, as had also the inordinate concentration of property in land. Commerce and handicrafts, including artistic handicrafts which were being increasingly developed on a large scale by the use of slave labor, became the main occupations. Athenians were growing more enlightened. Instead of exploiting their fellow citizens in the old brutal way, they exploited chiefly the slaves and the non-Athenian customers. Movable property, wealth in the form of money, of slaves and ships continually increased, but it was no longer a mere means to the acquisition of landed property as in the old slow days: it had become an end in itself. On the one hand the old power of the aristocracy now had to contend with successful competition from the new class of rich industrialists and merchants; but, on the other hand, the ground was also cut away from beneath the last remains of the old gentile constitution. The gentes, phratries, and tribes whose members were now scattered over all Attica and thoroughly intermixed had thus become useless as political bodies; numbers of Athenian citizens did not belong to any gens at all; they were immigrants who had indeed acquired rights of citizenship, but had not been adopted into any of the old kinship organizations; in addition, there was the steadily increasing number of foreign immigrants who only had rights of protection.

Meanwhile, the fights went on between parties. The nobility tried to win back their former privileges and for a moment regained the upper hand until the revolution of Cleisthenes (509 B.C.) overthrew them finally, but with them also the last remnants of the gentile constitution.

In his new constitution, Cleisthenes ignored the four old tribes founded on gentes and phratries. In their place appeared a completely new organization on the basis of division of the citizens merely according to their place of residence, such as had been already attempted in the *naukrariai*. Only domicile was now decisive, not membership of a kinship group. Not the people, but the territory was now divided: the inhabitants became a mere political appendage of the territory.

The whole of Attica was divided into 100 communal districts, called "demes," each of which was self-governing. The citizens resident in each deme (*demotes*) elected their president (*demarch*) and treasurer, as well as 30 judges with jurisdiction in minor disputes. They were also given their own temple and patron divinity or hero, whose priests they elected. Supreme power in the deme was vested in the assembly of the *demotes*. As Morgan rightly observes, here is the prototype of the self-governing American township. The modern state in its highest development ends in the same unit with which the rising state in Athens began.

Ten of these units (demes) formed a tribe, which, however, is now known as a local tribe to distinguish it from the old tribe of kinship. The local tribe was not only a self-governing political body, but also a military body; it elected its phylarch, or tribal chief, who commanded the cavalry, the taxiarch commanding the infantry, and the *strategos,* who was in command over all the forces raised in the tribal area. It further provided five warships with their crews and commanders and received as patron deity an Attic hero after whom it was named. Lastly, it elected 50 councillors to the Athenian council.

At the summit was the Athenian state governed by the council composed of the 500 councillors elected by the ten tribes, and in the last instance by the assembly of the people at which every Athenian citizen had the right to attend and to vote; archons and other officials managed the various departments of administration and justice. In Athens there was no supreme official with executive power.

Through this new constitution and the admission to civil rights of a very large number of protected persons, partly immigrants, partly freed slaves, the organs of the gentile constitution were forced out of public affairs; they sank to the level of private associations and religious bodies. But the moral influence of the old gentile period and its traditional ways of thought were still handed down for a long time to come and only died out gradually. We find evidence of this in another state institution.

We saw that an essential characteristic of the state is the existence of a public force differentiated from the mass of the people. At this time, Athens still had only a people's army and a fleet provided directly by the people. Army and fleet gave protection against external enemies and kept in check the slaves, who already formed the great majority of the population. In relation to the citizens, the public power at first existed only in the form of the police force, which is as old as the state itself; for which reason the naive French of the 18th century did not speak of civilized peoples but of policed peoples (*nations policées*). The Athenians then instituted a police force simultaneously with their state, a veritable gendarmerie of bowmen, foot and mounted *Landjäger* [the country's hunters] as they call them in South Germany and Switzerland. But this gendarmerie consisted of *slaves*. The free Athenian considered police duty so degrading that he would rather be arrested by an armed slave than himself have any hand in such despicable work. That was still the old gentile spirit. The state could not exist without police, but the state was still young and could not yet inspire enough moral respect to make honorable an occupation which to the older members of the gens necessarily appeared infamous.

Now complete in its main features, the state was perfectly adapted to the new social conditions of the Athenians as is shown by the rapid growth of wealth, commerce, and industry. The class opposition on which the social and political institutions rested was no longer that of nobility and common people, but of slaves and free men, of protected persons and citizens. At the time of their greatest prosperity, the entire free-citizen population of Athens, women and children included, numbered about 90,000; besides them there were 365,000 slaves of both sexes and 45,000 protected persons—aliens and freedmen. There were therefore at least 18 slaves and more than two protected persons to every adult male citizen. The reason for the large number of slaves was that many of them worked together in manufactories in large rooms under overseers. But with the development of commerce and industry, wealth was accumulated and concentrated in a few hands, and the mass of the free citizens were impoverished. Their only alternatives were to complete against slave labor with their own labor as handicraftsmen, which was considered base and vulgar and also offered very little prospect of success, or to become social scrap. Necessarily, in these circumstances, they did the latter, and as they formed the majority, they thereby brought about the downfall of the whole Athenian state. The downfall of Athens was not caused by democracy as the European lickspittle historians assert to flatter their princes, but by slavery, which banned the labor of free citizens.

The rise of the state among the Athenians is a particularly typical example of the formation of a state; first, the process takes place in a pure form without any interference through use of violent force either from without or from within (the usurpation by Pisistratus left no trace of its short duration); second, it shows a very highly developed form of state, the democratic republic, arising directly out of gentile society; and lastly we are sufficiently acquainted with all the essential details.

CHAPTER VI

THE GENS AND THE STATE IN ROME

ACCORDING TO the legendary account of the foundation of Rome, the first settlement was established by a number of Latin gentes (100, says the legend) who were united in a tribe. These were soon joined by a Sabellian tribe, also said to have numbered 100 gentes, and lastly by a third tribe of mixed elements, again said to have been composed of 100 gentes. The whole account reveals at the first glance that very little was still primitive here except the gens, and that even it was in some cases only an offshoot from a mother gens still existing in its original home. The tribes clearly bear the mark of their artificial composition even though they are generally composed out of related elements and after the pattern of the old tribe, which was not made but grew; it is, however, not an impossibility that the core of each of the three tribes was a genuine old tribe. The intermediate group, the phratry, consisted of ten gentes and was called a *curia;* there were therefore 30 *curiae.*

The Roman gens is recognized to be the same institution as the Greek gens; and since the Greek gens is a further development of the social unit whose original form is found among the American Indians, this of course holds true of the Roman gens also. Here therefore we can be more brief.

The Roman gens, at least in the earliest times of Rome, had the following constitution:

1. Mutual right of inheritance among gentile members; the property remained with the gens. Since father right already prevailed in the Roman gens as in the Greek, descendants in the female line were excluded. According to the Law of the Twelve Tables, the oldest written Roman law known to us, the children, as natural heirs, had the first title to the estate; in default of children, then the agnates (descendants in the *male* line); in default of agnates, the gentiles. In all cases the property remained within the gens. Here we see gentile custom gradually being penetrated by the new legal

provisions springing from increased wealth and monogamy: the original equal right of inheritance of all members of the gens is first restricted in practice to the agnates—probably very early, as already mentioned—finally, to the children and their issue in the male line; in the Twelve Tables this appears, of course, in the reverse order.

2. Possession of a common burial place. On their immigration to Rome from Regilli, the patrician gens of Claudi received a piece of land for their own use and also a common burial place in the town. Even in the time of Augustus, the head of Varus, who had fallen in the battle of the Teutoburg Forest, was brought to Rome and interred in the *gentilitius tumulus* [mound of the gens]; the gens (Quinctilia) therefore still had its own burial mound.

3. Common religious rites. These, the *sacra gentilitia* [sacred celebrations of the gens], are well known.

4. Obligation not to marry within the gens. This seems never to have become written law in Rome, but the custom persisted. Of all the countless Roman married couples whose names have been preserved, there is not one where husband and wife have the same gentile name. The law of inheritance also proves the observance of this rule. The woman loses her agnatic rights on marriage and leaves her gens; neither she nor her children can inherit from her father or his brothers because otherwise the inheritance would be lost to the father's gens. There is no sense in this rule unless a woman may not marry a member of her own gens.

5. Common land. In primitive times the gens had always owned common land ever since the tribal land began to be divided up. Among the Latin tribes, we find the land partly in the possession of the tribe, partly of the gens, and partly of the households, which at that time can hardly have been single families. Romulus is said to have made the first allotments of land to individuals, about two and one-half acres (two *jugera*) to a person. But later we still find land owned by the gentes, to say nothing of the state land, around which the whole internal history of the republic centers.

6. Obligation of mutual protection and help among members of the gens. Only vestiges remain in written history; from the very start the Roman state made its superior power so manifest that the right of protection against injury passed into its hands. When

Appius Claudius was arrested, the whole of his gens, even those who were his personal enemies, put on mourning. At the time of the second Punic War [218-201 B.C.] the gentes joined together to ransom their members who had been taken prisoner; the senate *prohibited* them from doing so.

7. Right to bear the gentile name. This persisted till the time of the emperors; freedmen were allowed to use the gentile name of their former master, but without gentile rights.

8. Right to adopt strangers into the gens. This was done through adoption into a family (as among the Indians), which carried with it acceptance into the gens.

9. The right to elect the chief and to depose him is nowhere mentioned. But since in the earliest days of Rome all offices were filled by election or nomination, from the elected king downward, and since *curiae* also elected their own priests, we may assume the same procedure for the presidents (*principes*) of the gentes—however firmly established the election from one and the same family within the gens may have already become.

Such were the rights of a Roman gens. Apart from the already completed transition to father right, they are the perfect counterpart of the rights and duties in an Iroquois gens; here again "the Iroquois shows through unmistakably" (Marx).

The confusion that still exists today even among our leading historians on the subject of the Roman gens may be illustrated by one example. In his paper on Roman family names in the period of the Republic and of Augustus (*Römische Forschungen,* Berlin, 1864, I, 8-11) Mommsen writes:

The gentile name belongs to all the male members of the gens, excluding, of course, the slaves, but including adopted and protected persons; it belongs also to the women. . . . The tribe [as Mommsen here translates *gens*] is . . . a communal entity, derived from common lineage (real, supposed or even pretended) and united by communal festivities, burial rites and laws of inheritance; to it all personally free individuals, and therefore all women also, may and must belong. But it is difficult to determine what gentile name was borne by married women. So long as the woman may only marry a member of her own gens, this problem does not arise; and there is evidence that for a long period it was more difficult for women to marry outside than inside the gens; for instance, so late as the sixth century [B.C.] the right of *gentis enuptio* [marriage outside the gens] was a personal privilege, conceded as a reward. . . . But when such marriages outside the tribe took place, the wife, in earliest times, must thereby have gone over to her husband's tribe. Nothing is more certain than that the woman, in the old religious marriage, enters completely into the legal and sacramental bonds of her husband's community and leaves her own. Everyone knows that the married woman forfeits the right of inheritance and bequest in relation to members of her own gens but shares rights of inheritance with her husband and children and the members of their gens. And if she is adopted by her husband and taken into his family, how can she remain apart from his gens?

Mommsen therefore maintains that the Roman women who belonged to a gens had originally been permitted to marry only *within* the gens, that the gens had therefore been endogamous, not exogamous. This view, which is in contradiction to all the evidence from other peoples, rests chiefly, if not exclusively, on one much disputed passage from Livy (Book XXXIX, Ch. 19), according to which the senate in the year 568 after the foundation of the city, or 186 B.C., decreed: *"Uti Feceniae Hispallae datio, deminutio, gentis enuptio, tutoris optio item esset quasi ei vir testamento dedisset; utique ei ingenuo nubere liceret, neu quid ei qui eam duxisset ob id fraudi ignominiaeve esset"*—that Fecenia Hispalla shall have the right to dispose of her property, to decrease it, to marry outside the gens, and to choose for herself a guardian exactly as if her (deceased) husband had conferred this right on her by testament; that she may marry a freeman, and that the man who takes her to wife shall not be considered to have committed a wrongful or shameful act thereby.

Without a doubt, Fecenia, a freedwoman, is here granted the right to marry outside the gens. And equally without a doubt the husband possessed the right, according to this passage, to bequeath to his wife by will the right to marry outside the gens after his death. But outside *which* gens?

If the woman had to marry within her gens, as Mommsen assumes, she remained within this gens also after her marriage. But in the first place the endogamous character of the gens which is here asserted is precisely what has to be proved. And, secondly, if the wife had to marry within the gens, then, of course, so had the man, for otherwise he could not get a wife. So we reach the position that the man could bequeath to his wife by will a right which he himself and for himself did not possess; we arrive at a legal absurdity. Mommsen also feels this, and hence makes the assumption: "For a lawful marriage outside the gens, it was probably necessary to have the consent, not only of the chief, but of all members of the gens." That is a very bold assumption in the first place, and, secondly, it contradicts the clear wording of the passage. The senate grants her this right *in the place of her husband;* it grants her expressly neither more nor less than her husband could have granted her, but what it grants her is an *absolute* right, conditional upon no other restriction. Thus it is provided that if she makes use of this right, her new husband also shall not suffer any disability. The senate even directs the present and future consuls and praetors to see to it that no injurious consequences to her follow. Mommsen's assumption therefore seems to be completely inadmissible.

Or assume that the woman married a man from another gens, but herself remained in the gens into which she had been born. Then, according to the above passage, the man would have had the right to allow his wife to marry outside her own gens. That is, he would have had the right to make dispositions in the affairs of a gens to which he did not even belong. The thing is so patently absurd that we need waste no more words on it.

Hence there only remains the assumption that in her first marriage the woman married a man from another gens and thereby immediately entered the gens of her husband, which Mommsen himself actually admits to have been the practice when the woman married outside her gens. Then everything at once becomes clear. Severed from her old gens by her marriage and accepted into the gentile group of her husband, the woman occupies a peculiar position in her new gens. She is, indeed, a member of the gens, but not related by blood. By the mere manner of her acceptance as a gentile member, she is entirely excluded from the prohibition against marrying within the gens, for she has just married into it. Further, she is accepted as one of the married members of the gens, and on her husband's death inherits from his property, the property of a gentile member. What is more natural than that this property should remain within the gens and that she should therefore be obliged to marry a member of her husband's gens and nobody else? And if an exception is to be made, who is so competent to give her the necessary authorization as the man who has bequeathed her this property, her first husband? At the moment when he bequeaths to her a part of his property and at the same time allows her to transfer it into another gens through marriage or in consequence of marriage, this property still belongs to him and he is therefore literally disposing of his own property. As regards the woman herself and her relation to her husband's gens, it was he who brought her into the gens by a free act of will—the marriage. Hence it also seems natural that he should be the proper person to authorize her to leave this gens by a second marriage. In a word, the matter appears simple and natural as soon as we abandon the extraordinary conception of the endogamous Roman gens and regard it, with Morgan, as originally exogamous.

There still remains one last assumption which has also found adherents, and probably the most numerous. On this view, the passage in Livy only means that "freed servants (*libertae*) could not without special permission *e gente enubere* (marry out of the gens) or perform any of the acts, which involving the slightest loss of rights (*capitis deminutio minima*), would have resulted in the *liberta* leaving the gens" (Lange, *Römische Altertümer,* Berlin, 1856, 1, 195, where Huschke is cited in connection with our passage from Livy), If this supposition is correct, the passage then proves nothing at all about the position of free Roman women, and there can be even less question of any obligation resting on them to marry within the gens.

The expression *enuptio gentis* only occurs in this one passage and nowhere else in the whole of Latin literature. The word *enubere,* to marry outside, only occurs three times, also in Livy, and then not in reference to the gens. The fantastic notion that Roman women were only allowed to marry within their gens owes its existence solely to this one passage. But it cannot possibly be maintained. For either the passage refers to special restrictions for freedwomen, in which case it proves nothing about free women (*ingenuae*), or it applies also to free women; and then it proves, on the contrary, that the woman married as a rule outside her gens but on her marriage entered into the gens of her husband, which contradicts Mommsen and supports Morgan.

Almost three centuries after the foundation of Rome, the gentile groups were still so strong that a patrician gens, that of the Fabii, was able to undertake an independent campaign with the permission of the senate against the neighboring town of Veii; 306 Fabii are said to have set out and to have been killed to a man in an ambush; according to the story, only one boy who had remained behind survived to propagate the gens.

As we have said, ten gentes formed a phratry, which among the Romans was called a *curia* and had more important public functions than the Greek phratry. Every *curia* had its own religious rites, shrines and priests; the latter as a body formed one of the Roman priestly colleges. Ten *curiae* formed a tribe, which probably like the rest of the Latin tribes originally had an elected president—military leader and high priest. The three tribes together formed the Roman people, the *populus Romanus*.

Thus no one could belong to the Roman people unless he was a member of a gens and through it of a *curia* and a tribe. The first constitution of the Roman people was as follows: public affairs were managed in the first instance by the senate, which, as Niebuhr first rightly saw, was composed of the presidents of the 300 gentes; it was because they were the elders of the gens that they were called fathers, *patres,* and their body, the senate (council of the elders, from *senex,* old). Here again the custom of electing always from the same family in the gens brought into being the first hereditary nobility. These families called themselves "patricians" and claimed for themselves exclusive right of entry into the senate and tenure of all other offices. The acquiescence of the people in this claim in course of time and its transformation into an actual right, appear in legend as the story that Romulus conferred the patriciate and its privileges on the first senators and their descendants. The senate, like the Athenian *boulè,* made final decisions in many matters and held preparatory discussions on those of greater importance, particularly new laws. With regard to these, the decision rested with the assembly of the people called the *comitia curiata* (assembly of the *curiae*). The people assembled together grouped in *curiae,* each *curia* probably grouped in gentes; each of the 30 *curiae* had one vote in the final decision. The assembly of the *curiae* accepted or rejected all laws, elected all higher officials including the *rex* (so-called king), declared war (the senate, however, concluded peace), and as supreme court, decided on the appeal of the parties concerned all cases involving death sentence on a Roman citizen. Lastly, besides the senate and the assembly of the people, there was the *rex,* who corresponded exactly to the Greek *basileus* and was not at all the almost absolute king which Mommsen made him out to be.* He also was military leader, high priest, and president of certain courts. He had no civil authority whatever, nor any power over the life, liberty, or property of citizens, except such as derived from his disciplinary powers as military leader or his executive powers as president of a court. The office of *rex* was not hereditary; on the contrary, he was first elected by the assembly of the *curiae* probably on the nomination of his predecessor, and then at a second meeting solemnly installed in office. That he could also be deposed is shown by the fate of Tarquinius Superbus.

Like the Greeks of the heroic age, the Romans in the age of the so-called kings lived in a military democracy founded on gentes, phratries, and tribes and developed out of them. Even if the *curiae* and tribes were to a certain extent artificial groups, they were formed after the genuine, primitive models of the society out of which they had arisen and by which they were still surrounded on all sides. Even if the primitive patrician nobility had already gained ground, even if the *reges* were endeavoring gradually to extend their power, it does not change the original, fundamental character of the constitution, and that alone matters.

Meanwhile, Rome and the Roman territory, which had been enlarged by conquest, increased in population partly through immigration, partly through the addition of inhabitants of the subjugated, chiefly Latin, districts. All these new citizens of the state (we leave aside the question of the clients) stood outside the old

* The Latin *rex* is the same as the Celtic-Irish *righ* (tribal chief) and the Gothic *reiks.* That *reiks* signified head of the gens or tribe, as did also originally the German word *Fürst* (meaning "first"—*cf.* English *first* and Danish *förste),* is shown by the fact that already in the fourth century the Goths had a special word for the later "king," the military leader of the whole people: *thiudans.* In Ulfilas' translation of the Bible, Artaxerxes and Herod are never called *reiks,* but *thiudans,* and the empire of Emperor Tiberius is not called *reiki,* but *thiudinassus.* In the name of the Gothic *thiudans* or, as we inaccurately translate, "king," Thiudareik (Theodorich, *i.e.* Dietrich), both titles coalesce.

gentes, *curiae,* and tribes, and therefore formed no part of the *populus Romanus,* the real Roman people. They were personally free, could own property in land, and had to pay taxes and do military service. But they could not hold any office, nor take part in the assembly of the *curiae,* nor share in the allotment of conquered state lands. They formed the class that was excluded from all public rights, the *plebs.* Owing to their continually increasing numbers, their military training and their possession of arms, they became a powerful threat to the old *populus,* which now rigidly barred any addition to its own ranks from outside. Further, landed property seems to have been fairly equally divided between *populus* and *plebs,* while the commercial and industrial wealth, though not as yet much developed, was probably for the most part in the hands of the *plebs.*

The great obscurity which envelops the completely legendary primitive history of Rome—an obscurity considerably deepened by the rationalistically pragmatical interpretations and accounts given of the subject by later authors with legalistic minds—makes it impossible to say anything definite about the time, course, or occasion of the revolution which made an end of the old gentile constitution. All that is certain is that its cause lay in the struggles between *plebs* and *populus.*

The new constitution, which was attributed to the *rex* Servius Tullius and followed the Greek model, particularly that of Solon, created a new assembly of the people in which *populus* and plebeians without distinction were included or excluded according to whether they performed military service or not. The whole male population liable to bear arms was divided on a property basis into six classes. The lower limit in each of the five classes was: (1) 100,000 asses, (2) 75,000 asses, (3) 50,000 asses, (4) 25,000 asses, (5) 11,000 asses, according to Dureau de la Malle, the equivalent to about 14,000, 10,500, 7,000, 3,600, and 1,570 marks respectively. The sixth class, the proletarians, consisted of those with less property than the lowest class and those exempt from military service and taxes. In the new popular assembly of the centuries (*comitia centuriata*), the citizens appeared in military formation arranged by companies in their centuries of 100 men, each century having one vote. Now the first class put 80 centuries in the field, the second 22, the third 20, the fourth 22, the fifth 30, and the sixth also one century for the sake of appearances. In addition, there was the cavalry, drawn from the wealthiest men, with 18 centuries—total, 193; 97 votes were thus required for a clear majority. But the cavalry and the first class alone had together 98 votes and therefore the majority; if they were agreed, they did not ask the others; they made their decision, and it stood.

This new assembly of the centuries now took over all political rights of the former assembly of the *curiae,* with the exception of a few nominal privileges. The *curiae* and the gentes of which they were composed were thus degraded as in Athens to mere private and religious associations and continued to vegetate as such for a long period, while the assembly of the *curiae* soon became completely dormant. In order that the three old tribes of kinship should also be excluded from the state, four local tribes were instituted, each of which inhabited one quarter of the city and possessed a number of political rights.

Thus in Rome also, even before the abolition of the so-called monarchy, the old order of society based on personal ties of blood was destroyed and in its place was set up a new and complete state constitution based on territorial division and difference of wealth. Here the public power consisted of the body of citizens liable to military service, in opposition not only to the slaves but also to those excluded from service in the army and from possession of arms, the so-called proletarians.

The banishment of the last *rex,* Tarquinius Superbus, who usurped real monarchic power, and the replacement of the office of *rex* by two military leaders (consuls) with equal powers (as among the Iroquois) was simply a further development of this new constitution. Within this new constitution, the whole history of the Roman republic runs its course with all the struggles between patricians and plebeians for admission to office and share in the state lands, and the final merging of the patrician nobility in the new class of the great land and money owners, who, gradually swallowing up all the land of the peasants ruined by military service, employed slave labor to cultivate the enormous estates thus formed, depopulated Italy and so threw open the door not only to the emperors but also to their successors, the German barbarians.

CHAPTER VII

THE GENS AMONG CELTS AND GERMANS

SPACE DOES not allow us to consider the gentile institutions still existing in greater or lesser degree of purity among the most various savage and barbarian peoples, nor the traces of these institutions in the ancient history of the civilized peoples of Asia. The institutions or their traces are found everywhere. A few examples will be enough. Before the gens had been recognized, the man who took the greatest pains to misunderstand it, McLennan himself, proved its existence and in the main accurately described it among the Kalmucks, Circassians, Samoyeds and three Indian peoples: the Warali, Magars and Munniporees. Recently it has been discovered and described by M. Kovalevsky among the Pshavs, Shevsurs, Svanets and other Caucasian tribes. Here we will only give some short notes on the occurrence of the gens among Celts and Germans.

The oldest Celtic laws which have been preserved show the gens still fully alive. In Ireland, after being forcibly broken up by the English, it still lives today in the consciousness of the people, as an instinct at any rate. In Scotland it was still in full strength in the middle of the 18th century, and here again it succumbed only to the weapons, laws, and courts of the English.

The old Welsh laws which were recorded in writing several centuries before the English conquest, at the latest in the 11th century, still show common tillage of the soil by whole villages, even if only as an exceptional relic of a once general custom. Each family had five acres for its own cultivation; a piece of land was cultivated collectively as well and the yield shared. In view of the analogy of Ireland and Scotland, it cannot be doubted that these village communities represent gentes or subdivisions of gentes, even though further examination of the Welsh laws, which I cannot undertake for lack of time (my notes date from 1869), should not provide direct proof. But what is directly proved by the Welsh sources and by the Irish is that among the Celts in the 11th century pairing marriage had not by any means been displaced by monogamy.

In Wales a marriage only became indissoluble, or rather it only ceased to be terminable by notification, after seven years had elapsed. If the time was short of seven years by only three nights. husband and wife could separate. They then shared out their property between them; the woman divided and the man chose. The furniture was divided according to fixed and very humorous rules. If it was the man who dissolved the marriage, he had to give the woman back her dowry and some other things; if it was the woman, she received less. Of the children the man took two and the woman one, the middle child. If after the separation the woman took another husband and the first husband came to fetch her back again, she had to follow him even if she had already *one* foot in her new marriage bed. If, on the other hand, the man and woman had been together for seven years, they were husband and wife, even without any previous formal marriage. Chastity of girls before marriage was not at all strictly observed, nor was it demanded; the provisions in this respect are of an extremely frivolous character and not at all in keeping with bourgeois morality. If a woman committed adultery, the husband had the right to beat her (this was one of the three occasions when he was allowed to do so; otherwise he was punished), but not then to demand any other satisfaction since "for the one offense there shall be either atonement or vengeance, but not both" [Ancient Laws and Institutes of Wales, I, 1841, p. 93]. The grounds on which the wife could demand divorce without losing any of her claims in the subsequent settlement were very comprehensive; if the husband had bad breath, it was enough. The money which had to be paid to the chief of the tribe or king to buy off his right of the first night (*gobr merch*, whence the medieval name, *marcheta;* French *marquette*) plays a large part in the code of laws. The women had the right to vote in the assemblies of the people. When we add that the evidence shows similar conditions in Ireland; that there, also, temporary marriages were quite usual and that at the separation very favorable and exactly defined conditions were assured to the woman, including even compensation for her domestic services; that in Ireland there was a "first wife" as well as other wives, and that in the division of an inheritance no distinction was made between children born in wedlock or outside it—we then have a picture of pairing marriage in comparison with which the form of marriage observed in North America appears strict. This is not surprising in the 11th century among a people who even so late as Caesar's time were still living in group marriage.

The existence of the Irish gens (*sept;* the tribe was called *clainne,* clan) is confirmed and described not only by the old legal codes, but also by the English jurists of the 17th century who were sent over to transform the clan lands into domains of the English crown. Until then, the land had been the common property of the clan or gens in so far as the chieftains had not already converted it into their private domains. When a member of the gens died and a household consequently came to an end, the gentile chief (the English jurists called him *caput cognationis*) made a new division of the whole territory among the remaining households. This must have been done, broadly speaking, according to the rules in force in Germany. Forty or 50 years ago village fields were very numerous, and even today a few of these rundales, as they are called, may still be found. The peasants of a rundale, now individual tenants on the soil that had been the common property of the gens till it was seized by the English conquerors, pay rent for their respective piece of land but put all their shares in arable and meadowland together, which they then divide according to position and quality into *Gewanne,* as they are called on the Moselle, each receiving a share in each *Gewann;* moorland and pastureland are used in common. Only 50 years ago new divisions were still made from time to time, sometimes annually. The field-map of such a village looks exactly like that of a German *Gehöferschaft* [peasant community] on the Moselle or in the Hochwald. The gens also lives on in the "fractions." The Irish peasants often divide themselves into parties based apparently on perfectly absurd or meaningless distinctions; to the English they are quite incomprehensible and seem to have no other purpose than the favorite ceremony of two factions hammering one another. They are artificial revivals, modern substitutes for the dispersed gentes, manifesting in their own peculiar manner the persistence of the inherited gentile instinct. In some districts the members of the gens still live pretty much together on the old

territory; in the thirties the great majority of the inhabitants of
County Monaghan still had only four family names, that is, they
were descended from four gentes or clans.*

In Scotland the decay of the gentile organization dates from the
suppression of the rising of 1745. The precise function of the
Scottish clan in this organization still awaits investigation; but that
the clan is a gentile body is beyond doubt. In Walter Scott's novels
the Highland clan lives before our eyes. It is, says Morgan:

. . . an excellent type of the gens in organization and in spirit, and
an extraordinary illustration of the power of the gentile life over its
members. . . . We find in their feuds and blood revenge, in their locali-
zation by gentes, in their use of lands in common, in the fidelity of the
clansman to his chief and of the members of the clan to each other,
the usual and persistent features of gentile society. . . . Descent was
in the male line, the children of the males remaining members of the
clan, while the children of its female members belonged to the clans
of their respective fathers" [1963: 368-69].

But that formerly mother right prevailed in Scotland is proved
by the fact that, according to Bede, in the royal family of the Picts
succession was in the female line. Among the Scots, as among the
Welsh, a relic even of the punaluan family persisted into the Middle
Ages in the form of the right of the first night which the head of the
clan or the king, as last representative of the former community of

* During a few days spent in Ireland [September 1891], I realized afresh
to what an extent the country people still live in the conceptions of the gentile period. The landed proprietor, whose tenant the farmer is, is still regarded
by the latter as a kind of chief of the clan whose duty it is to manage the
land in the interests of all while the farmer pays tribute in the form of rent,
but has a claim upon him for assistance in times of necessity. Similarly,
everyone who is well-off is considered under an obligation to assist his poorer
neighbors when they fall on hard times. Such help is not charity; it is what
the poorer member of the clan is entitled to receive from the wealthier member or the chief. One can understand the complaints of the political economists and jurists about the impossibility of making the Irish peasant grasp the
idea of modern bourgeois property; the Irishman simply cannot get it into
his head that there can be property with rights but no duties. But one can also
understand that when Irishmen with these naive gentile conceptions suddenly
find themselves in one of the big English or American towns among a population with completely different ideas of morality and justice, they easily become completely confused about both morality and justice and lose all their
bearings, with the result that masses of them become demoralized. [*Note to
the Fourth Edition*].

husbands, had the right to exercise with every bride, unless it was compounded for money.

That the Germans were organized in gentes until the time of the migrations is beyond all doubt. They could have occupied the territory between the Danube, Rhine, Vistula, and the northern seas only a few centuries before our era; the Cimbri and Teutons were then still in full migration, and the Suevi did not find any permanent habitation until Caesar's time. Caesar expressly states of them that they had settled in gentes and kindreds (*gentibus cognationibusque*), and in the mouth of a Roman of the Julian gens the word *gentibus* has a definite meaning which cannot be argued away. The same was true of all the Germans; they seem still to have settled by gentes even in the provinces they conquered from the Romans. The code of laws of the Alemanni confirms that the people settled by kindreds (*genealogiae*) in the conquered territory south of the Danube; *genealogia* is used in exactly the same sense as *Markgenossenschaft* or *Dorfgenossenschaft* [mark or village community] later. Kovalevsky has recently put forward the view that these *genealogiae* are the large household communities among which the land was divided and from which the village community only developed later. This would then probably also apply to the *fara,* with which expression the Burgundians and the Lombards—that is, a Gothic and a Herminonian or High German tribe—designated nearly, if not exactly, the same thing as the *genealogia* in the Alemannian code of laws. Whether it is really a gens or a household community must be settled by further research.

The records of language leave us in doubt whether all the Germans had a common expression for gens, and what that expression was. Etymologically, the Gothic *kuni,* Middle High German *künne,* corresponds to the Greek *genos* and the Latin *gens* and is used in the same sense. The fact that the term for woman comes from the same root—Greek *gyne,* Slav *zena,* Gothic *qvino,* Old Norse *kona, kuna*—points back to the time of mother right. Among the Lombards and Burgundians we find, as already mentioned, the term *fara* which Grimm derives from an imaginary root *fisan,* to beget. I should prefer to go back to the more obvious derivation from *faran* (*fahren*), to travel or wander; *fara* would then denote a section of the migrating people which remained permanently together and almost as a matter of course would be composed of relatives. In the several centuries of migration, first to the east and then to the west, the expression came to be transferred to the kinship group itself. There are, further, the Gothic *sibja,* Anglo-Saxon *sib,* Old High German *sippia, sippa, sippe* [kindred]. Old Norse only has the plural *sifjar,* relatives; the singular only occurs as the name of a goddess, *Sif.* Lastly, still another expression occurs in the *Hildebrandslied,* where Hildebrand asks Hadubrand: "Who is thy father among the men of the people . . . or of what kin art thou?" (*eddo huêlîhes cnuosles du sîs*). In as far as there was a common German name for the gens, it was probably the Gothic *kuni* that was used; this is rendered probable, not only by its identity with the corresponding expression in the related languages, but also by the fact that from it is derived the word *kuning, König* (king), which originally denotes the head of a gens or of a tribe. *Sibja, Sippe,* does not seem to call for consideration; at any rate *sifjar* in Old Norse denotes not only blood relations but also relations by marriage; thus it includes the members of at least *two* gentes, and hence *sif* itself cannot have been the term for the gens.

As among the Mexicans and Greeks, so also among the Germans the order of battle, both the cavalry squadrons and the wedge formations of the infantry, was drawn up by gentes. Tacitus' use of the vague expression "by families and kindreds" is to be explained through the fact that in his time the gens in Rome had long ceased to be a living body.

A further passage in Tacitus is decisive. It states that the maternal uncle looks upon his nephew as his own son, and that some even regard the bond of blood between the maternal uncle and the nephew as more sacred and close than that between father and son, so that when hostages are demanded the sister's son is considered a better security than the natural son of the man whom it is desired to bind. Here we have living evidence described as particularly characteristic of the Germans of the matriarchal, and therefore primitive, gens.* If a member of such a gens give his

* The peculiar closeness of the bond between maternal uncle and nephew, which derives from the time of mother right and is found among many peoples, is only recognized by the Greeks in their mythology of the heroic

own son as a pledge of his oath and the son then paid the penalty of death for his father's breach of faith, the father had to answer for that to himself. But if it was a sister's son who was sacrificed, then the most sacred law of the gens was violated. The member of the gens who was nearest of kin to the boy or youth, and more than all others was bound to protect him, was guilty of his death; either he should not have pledged him or he should have kept the agreement. Even if we had no other trace of gentile organization among the Germans, this one passage would suffice.

Still more decisive, because it comes about 800 years later, is a passage from the Old Norse poem of the twilight of the gods and the end of the world, the *Völuspà*. In this "vision of the seeress," into which Christian elements are also interwoven, as Bang and Bugge have now proven, the description of the period of universal degeneration and corruption leading up to the great catastrophe contains the following passage:

> *Broedhr munu berjask*   *ok at bönum verdask,*
> *munu* systrungar   *sifjum spilla.*

"Brothers will make war upon one another and become one another's murderers, *the children of sisters* will break kinship." *Systrungar* means the son of the mother's sister, and that these sisters' sons should betray the blood bond between them is regarded by the poet as an even greater crime than that of fratricide. The force of the climax is in the word *systrungar,* which emphasizes the kinship on the mother's side; if the word had been *syskina-börn,* brothers' or sisters' children, or *syskinasynir,* brothers' or sisters' sons, the second line would not have been a climax to the first but would merely have weakened the effect. Hence even in the time of

---

age. According to Diodorus (IV, 34), Meleager slays the sons of Thestius, the brothers of his mother Althaea. She regards this deed as such an inexpiable crime that she curses the murderer, her own son, and prays for his death. "The gods heard her wishes," the story says, "and put an end to Meleager's life." Also according to Diodorus (IV, 44), the Argonauts land in Thrace under Heracles and there find that Phineus, at the instigation of his new wife, is shamefully maltreating the two sons born to him by his former wife, the Boread Cleopatra, whom he has put away. But among the Argonauts there are also Boreads, brothers of Cleopatra, therefore maternal uncles of the maltreated boys. They at once take up their nephews' cause, free them, and kill their guards.

the Vikings when the *Völuspà* was composed, the memory of mother right had not yet been obliterated in Scandinavia.

In the time of Tacitus, however, mother right had already given way to father right, at least among the Germans with whose customs he was more familiar. The children inherited from the father; if there were no children, the brothers and the uncles on the father's and the mother's side. The fact that the mother's brother was allowed to inherit is connected with the survivals of mother right already mentioned and again proves how new father right still was among the Germans at that time. Traces of mother right are also found until late in the Middle Ages. Apparently even at that time people still did not have any great trust in fatherhood, especially in the case of serfs. When, therefore, a feudal lord demanded from a town the return of a fugitive serf, it was required—for example, in Augsburg, Basle and Kaiserslautern—that the accused person's status as serf should be sworn to by six of his nearest blood relations, and that they should all be relations on the mother's side (Maurer, *Städteverfassung,* I, 381).

Another relic of mother right, which was still only in process of dying out, was the respect of the Germans for the female sex which to the Romans was almost incomprehensible. Young girls of noble family were considered the most binding hostages in treaties with the Germans. The thought that their wives and daughters might be taken captive and carried into slavery was terrible to them and more than anything else fired their courage in battle; they saw in a woman something holy and prophetic and listened to her advice even in the most important matters. Veleda, the priestess of the Bructerians on the River Lippe, was the very soul of the whole Batavian rising in which Civilis, at the head of the Germans and Belgae, shook the foundations of Roman rule in Gaul. In the home, the woman seems to have held undisputed sway, though together with the old people and the children she also had to do all the work while the man hunted, drank, or idled about. That, at least, is what Tacitus says; but as he does not say who tilled the fields and definitely declares that the serfs only paid tribute but did not have to render labor dues, the bulk of the adult men must have had to do what little work the cultivation of the land required.

The form of marriage, as already said, was a pairing marriage which was gradually approaching monogamy. It was not yet strict monogamy, as polygamy was permitted for the leading members of the tribe. In general, strict chastity was required of the girls (in contrast to the Celts), and Tacitus also speaks with special warmth of the sacredness of the marriage tie among the Germans. Adultery by the woman is the only ground for divorce mentioned by him. But there are many gaps here in his report, and it is also only too apparent that he is holding up a mirror of virtue before the dissipated Romans. One thing is certain: if the Germans were such paragons of virtue in their forests, it only required slight contact with the outside world to bring them down to the level of the average man in the rest of Europe. Amidst the Roman world, the last trace of moral austerity disappeared far more rapidly even than the German language. For proof it is enough to read Gregory of Tours. That in the German primeval forests there could be no such voluptuous abandonment to all the refinements of sensuality as in Rome is obvious; the superiority of the Germans to the Roman world in this respect also is sufficiently great, and there is no need to endow them with an ideal continence in things of the flesh, such as has never yet been practiced by an entire nation.

Also derived from the gentile organization is the obligation to inherit the enmities as well as the friendships of the father or the relatives—likewise the *wergeld,* the fine for killing or injuring, in place of blood revenge. The *wergeld,* which only a generation ago was regarded as a specifically German institution, has now been shown to be general among hundreds of peoples as a milder form of the blood revenge originating out of the gentile organization. We find it, for example, among the American Indians, who also regard hospitality as an obligation. Tacitus' description of hospitality as practiced among the Germans (*Germania,* Ch. XXI) is identical almost to the details with that given by Morgan of his Indians.

The endless, burning controversy as to whether the Germans of Tacitus' time had already definitely divided the land or not, and how the relevant passages are to be interpreted, now belongs to the past. No more words need be wasted in this dispute since it has been established that among almost all peoples the cultivated land was tilled collectively by the gens and later by communistic household communities such as were still found by Caesar among the

Suevi, and that after this stage the land was allotted to individual families with periodical repartitions, which are shown to have survived as a local custom in Germany down to our day. If in the 150 years between Caesar and Tacitus the Germans had changed from the collective cultivation of the land expressly attributed by Caesar to the Suevi (they had no divided or private fields whatever, he says) to individual cultivation with annual repartition of the land, that is surely progress enough. The transition from that stage to complete private property in land during such a short period and without any outside interference is a sheer impossibility. What I read in Tacitus is simply what he says in his own dry words: they change (or divide afresh) the cultivated land every year, and there is enough common land left over. It is the stage of agriculture and property relations in regard to the land which exactly corresponds to the gentile constitution of the Germans at that time.

I leave the preceding paragraph unchanged as it stood in the former editions. Meanwhile the question has taken another turn. Since Kovalevsky has shown (see above, 120) that the patriarchal household community was a very common, if not universal, intermediate form between the matriarchal communistic family and the modern isolated family, it is no longer a question of whether property in land is communal or private, which was the point at issue between Maurer and Waitz, but a question of the *form* of the communal property. There is no doubt at all that the Suevi in Caesar's time not only owned the land in common but also cultivated it in common for the common benefit. Whether the economic unit was the gens or the household community or a communistic kinship group intermediate between the two, or whether all three groups occurred according to the conditions of the soil—these questions will be in dispute for a long time to come. Kovalevsky maintains, however, that the conditions described by Tacitus presuppose the existence, not of the mark or village community, but of the household community and that the village community only develops out of the latter much later as a result of the increase in population.

According to this view, the settlements of the Germans in the territory of which they were already in possession at the time of the Romans, and also in the territory which they later took from the

Romans, were not composed of villages but of large household communities which included several generations, cultivated an amount of land proportionate to the number of their members, and had common use with their neighbors of the surrounding waste land. The passage in Tacitus about changing the cultivated land would then have to be taken in an agronomic sense: the community cultivated a different piece of land every year and allowed the land cultivated the previous year to lie fallow or run completely to waste; the population being scanty, there was always enough waste land left over to make any disputes about land unnecessary. Only in the course of centuries when the number of members in the household communities had increased so much that a common economy was no longer possible under the existing conditions of production, did the communities dissolve. The arable lands and meadowlands which had hitherto been common were divided in the manner familiar to us, first temporarily and then permanently among the single households which were now coming into being, while forest, pasture land, and water remained common.

In the case of Russia, this development seems to be a proved historical fact. With regard to Germany and, secondarily, the other Germanic countries, it cannot be denied that in many ways this view provides a better explanation of the sources and an easier solution to difficulties than that held hitherto, which takes the village community back to the time of Tacitus. On the whole, the oldest documents, such as the *Codex Laureshamensis,* can be explained much better in terms of the household community than of the village community. On the other hand, this view raises new difficulties and new questions which have still to be solved. They can only be settled by new investigations; but I cannot deny that in the case also of Germany, Scandinavia and England there is very great probability in favor of the intermediate form of the household community.

While in Caesar's time the Germans had only just taken up or were still looking for settled abodes, in Tacitus' time they already had a full century of settled life behind them; correspondingly, the progress in the production of the necessities of life is unmistakable. They live in log houses; their clothing is still very much that of primitive people of the forests: coarse woolen mantles, skins; for women and notable people underclothing of linen. Their food is milk, meat, wild fruits and, as Pliny adds, oatmeal porridge (still the Celtic national food in Ireland and Scotland). Their wealth consists in cattle and horses, but of inferior breed; the cows are small, poor in build and without horns; the horses are ponies, with very little speed. Money was used rarely and in small amounts; it was exclusively Roman. They did not work gold or silver, nor did they value it. Iron was rare, and at least among the tribes on the Rhine and the Danube seems to have been almost entirely imported, not mined. Runic writing (imitated from the Greek or Latin letters) was a purely secret form of writing used only for religious magic. Human sacrifices were still offered. In short, we here see a people which had just raised itself from the middle to the upper stage of barbarism. But whereas the tribes living immediately on the Roman frontiers were hindered in the development of an independent metal and textile industry by the facility with which Roman products could be imported, such industry undoubtedly did develop in the northeast, on the Baltic. The fragments of weapons found in the Schleswig marshes—long iron sword, coat of mail, silver helmet and so forth, together with Roman coins of the end of the second century—and the German metal objects distributed by the migration show quite a pronounced character of their own, even when they derive from an originally Roman model. Emigration into the civilized Roman world put an end to this native industry everywhere except in England. With what uniformity this industry arose and developed can be seen, for example, in the bronze brooches; those found in Burgundy, Rumania and on the Sea of Azov might have come out of the same workshop as those found in England and Sweden and are just as certainly of Germanic origin.

The constitution also corresponds to the upper stage of barbarism. According to Tacitus, there was generally a council of chiefs (*principes*) which decided minor matters, but prepared more important questions for decision by the assembly of the people. At the lower stage of barbarism, so far as we have knowledge of it, as among the Americans, this assembly of the people still comprises only the members of the gens, not yet of the tribe or of the confederacy of tribes. The chiefs (*principes*) are still sharply distinguished from the military leaders (*duces*) just as they are among the Iroquois. They already subsist partially on gifts of cattle, corn, etc. from the members of the tribe; as in America they are generally elected from the same family. The transition to father right favored, as in Greece and Rome, the gradual transformation of election into hereditary succession and hence the rise of a noble family in each gens. This old so-called tribal nobility disappeared for the most part during the migrations or soon afterward. The military leaders were chosen without regard to their descent, solely according to their ability. They had little power and had to rely on the force of example. Tacitus expressly states that the actual disciplinary authority in the army lay with the priests. The real power was in the hands of the assembly of the people. The king or the chief of the tribe presides; the people decide: "No" by murmurs, "Yes" by acclamation and clash of weapons. The assembly of the people is at the same time an assembly of justice; here complaints are brought forward and decided and sentences of death passed, the only capital crimes being cowardice, treason against the people, and unnatural lust. Also in the gentes and other subdivisions of the tribe, all the members sit in judgment under the presidency of the chief, who as in all the early German courts can only have guided the proceedings and put questions; the actual verdict was always given among Germans everywhere by the whole community.

Confederacies of tribes had grown up since the time of Caesar. Some of them already had kings; the supreme military commander was already aiming at the position of tyrant, as among the Greeks and Romans, and sometimes secured it. But these fortunate usurpers were not by any means absolute rulers; they were, however, already beginning to break the fetters of the gentile constitution. Whereas freed slaves usually occupied a subordinate position since they could not belong to any gens, as favorites of the new kings they often won rank, riches and honors. The same thing happened after the conquest of the Roman Empire by these military leaders, who now became kings of great countries. Among the Franks, slaves and freedmen of the king played a leading part first at the court and then in the state; the new nobility was to a great extent descended from them.

One institution particularly favored the rise of kingship—the retinues. We have already seen among the American Indians how, side by side with the gentile constitution, private associations were formed to carry on wars independently. Among the Germans these private associations had already become permanent. A military leader who had made himself a name gathered around him a band of young men eager for booty whom he pledged to personal loyalty, giving the same pledge to them. The leader provided their keep, gave them gifts, and organized them on a hierarchic basis: a body-guard and a standing troop for smaller expeditions, and a regular corps of officers for operations on a larger scale. Weak as these retinues must have been and as we in fact find them to be later—for example, under Odoacer in Italy—they were nevertheless the beginnings of the decay of the old freedom of the people and showed themselves to be such during and after the migrations. For in the first place they favored the rise of monarchic power. In the second place, as Tacitus already notes, they could only be kept together by continual wars and plundering expeditions. Plunder became an end in itself. If the leader of the retinue found nothing to do in the neighborhood, he set out with his men to other peoples where there was war and the prospect of booty. The German mercenaries who fought in great numbers under the Roman stand-ard even against Germans were partly mobilized through these re-tinues. They already represent the first form of the system of *Landsknechte* [mercenary soldiers], the shame and curse of the Germans. When the Roman Empire had been conquered, these retinues of the kings formed the second main stock, after the unfree and the Roman courtiers, from which the later nobility was drawn.

In general then, the constitution of those German tribes which had combined into peoples was the same as had developed among the Greeks of the heroic age and the Romans of the so-called time of the kings: assembly of the people, council of the chiefs of the gentes, and military leader who is already striving for real monarchic power. It was the highest form of constitution which the gentile order could achieve; it was the model constitution of the upper stage of barbarism. If society passed beyond the limits within which this constitution was adequate, that meant the end of the gentile order; it was broken up and the state took its place.

CHAPTER VIII

THE FORMATION OF THE STATE AMONG THE GERMANS

ACCORDING TO Tacitus, the Germans were a very numerous people. Caesar gives us an approximate idea of the strength of the separate German peoples; he places the number of the Usipetans and the Tencterans who appeared on the left bank of the Rhine at 180,000, women and children included. That is about 100,000 to one people,* already considerably more than, for instance, the total number of the Iroquois in their prime, when, no more than 20,000 strong, they were the terror of the whole country from the Great Lakes to the Ohio and the Potomac. On the map, if we try to group the better known peoples settled near the Rhine according to the evidence of the reports, a single people occupies the space of a Prussian government district—that is, about 10,000 square kilometers or 182 geographical square miles [about 4,000 square miles]. Now the Germania Magna [Greater Germany] of the Romans, which reached as far as the Vistula, had an area of 500,000 square kilometers in round figures. Reckoning the average number of each people at 100,000, the total population of Germania Magna would work out at 5,000,000; a considerable figure for a barbarian group of peoples, but compared with our conditions —ten persons to the square kilometer or about 550 to the geographical square mile—extremely low. But that by no means exhausts the number of the Germans then living. We know that all along the Carpathians and down to the south of the Danube there were German peoples descended from Gothic tribes, such as the Bastarnians, Peucinians and others who were so numerous that

*The number assumed here is confirmed by a statement of Diodorus about the Celts of Gaul: "In Gaul dwell many peoples of varying strength. Among those that are greatest the number is about 200,000 among the smallest, 50,000" (Diodorus Siculus, V, 25)—on an average, therefore, 125,000. It can undoubtedly be assumed that owing to their higher stage of development the single peoples among the Gauls were rather larger than among the Germans.

Pliny classes them together as the fifth main tribe of the Germans. As early as 180 B.C. they make their appearance as mercenaries in the service of the Macedonian King Perseus, and in the first years of Augustus, still advancing, they almost reached Adrianople. If we estimate these at only 1,000,000, the probable total number of the Germans at the beginning of our era must have been at least 6,000,000.

After permanent settlements had been founded in Germany, the population must have grown with increasing rapidity; the advances in industry we mentioned are in themselves proof of this. The objects found in the Schleswig marshes date from the third century, according to the Roman coins discovered with them. At this time, therefore, there was already a developed metal and textile industry on the Baltic, brisk traffic with the Roman Empire and a certain degree of luxury among the more wealthy—all signs of denser population. But also at this time begins the general attack by the Germans along the whole line of the Rhine, the Roman wall and the Danube, from the North Sea to the Black Sea—direct proof of the continual growth and outward thrust of the population. For three centuries the fight went on, during which the whole main body of the Gothic peoples (with the exception of the Scandinavian Goths and the Burgundians) thrust southeast, forming the left wing on the long front of attack; in the center the High Germans (Herminones) pushed forward down the upper Danube; and on the right wing the Ischaevonians, now called Franks, advanced along the Rhine; the Ingaevonians carried out the conquest of Britain. By the end of the fifth century an exhausted and bleeding Roman Empire lay helpless before the invading Germans.

In earlier chapters we were standing at the cradle of ancient Greek and Roman civilization. Now we stand at its grave. Rome had driven the leveling plane of its world rule over all the countries of the Mediterranean basin, and that for centuries. Except when Greek offered resistance, all natural languages had been forced to yield to a debased Latin. There were no more national differences, no more Gauls, Iberians, Ligurians, Noricans; all had become Romans. Roman administration and Roman law had everywhere broken up the old kinship groups and with them the last vestige of local and national independence. The half-baked culture of Rome provided no substitute; it expressed no nationality, only the lack of nationality. The elements of new nations were present everywhere; the Latin dialects of the various provinces were becoming increasingly differentiated; the natural boundaries which once had made Italy, Gaul, Spain, Africa independent territories were still there and still made themselves felt. But the strength was not there to fuse these elements into new nations; there was no longer a sign anywhere of capacity for development or power of resistance, to say nothing of creative energy. The enormous mass of humanity in the whole enormous territory was held together by one bond only—the Roman state; and the Roman state had become in the course of time their worst enemy and oppressor. The provinces had annihilated Rome; Rome itself had become a provincial town like the rest—privileged, but no longer the ruler, no longer the hub of the world empire, not even the seat of the emperors or subemperors who now lived in Constantinople, Treves, Milan. The Roman state had become a huge, complicated machine, exclusively for bleeding its subjects. Taxes, state imposts and tributes of every kind pressed the mass of the people always deeper into poverty; the pressure was intensified until the exactions of governors, tax collectors, and armies made it unbearable. That was what the Roman state had achieved with its world rule. It gave as the justification of its existence that it maintained order within the empire and protected it against the barbarians without. But its order was worse than the worst disorder, and the citizens whom it claimed to protect against the barbarians longed for the barbarians to deliver them.

Social conditions were no less desperate. Already in the last years of the republic the policy of Roman rule had been ruthlessly to exploit the provinces; the empire, far from abolishing this exploitation, had organized it. The more the empire declined, the higher rose the taxes and levies, the more shamelessly the officials robbed and extorted. The Romans had always been too occupied in ruling other nations to become proficient in trade and industry; it was only as usurers that they beat all who came before or after. What commerce had already existed and still survived was now ruined by official extortion; it struggled on only in the eastern, Greek part of the empire, which lies outside the present study.

General improverishment; decline of commerce, handicrafts and art; fall in the population; decay of the towns; relapse of agriculture to a lower level—such was the final result of Roman world rule.

Agriculture, always the decisive branch of production throughout the ancient world, was now more so than ever. In Italy the enormous estates (*latifundia*) which, since the end of the republic, occupied almost the whole country had been exploited in two different ways. They had been used either as pastures, the population being displaced by sheep and cattle which could be tended by a few slaves, or as country estates (*villae*) where large-scale horticulture was carried on with masses of slaves, partly as a luxury for the owner, partly for sale in the town markets. The great grazing farms had kept going and had probably even extended; the country estates and their gardens had been ruined through the impoverishment of their owners and the decay of the towns. The system of *latifundia* run by slave labor no longer paid; but at that time no other form of large-scale agriculture was possible. Small-scale production had again become the only profitable form. One country estate after another was cut up into small lots, which were handed over either to tenants who paid a fixed sum and had hereditary rights or to *partiarii* [sharecroppers], stewards rather than tenants, who received a sixth or even only a ninth of the year's product in return for their labor. For the most part, however, these small lots of land were given out to *coloni* who paid for them a definite yearly amount, were tied to the soil and could be sold together with their plot. True, they were not slaves, but neither were they free; they could not marry free persons, and their marriages with one another were not regarded as full marriages but, like those of slaves, as mere concubinage (*contubernium*). They were the forerunners of the medieval serfs.

The slavery of classical times had outlived itself. Whether employed on the land in large-scale agriculture or in manufacture in the towns, it no longer yielded any satisfactory return—the market for its products was no longer there. But the small-scale agriculture and the small handicraft production to which the enormous production of the empire in its prosperous days was now shrunk had no room for numerous slaves. Only for the domestic and luxury slaves of the wealthy was there still a place in society. But though it was dying out, slavery was still common enough to make all productive labor appear to be work for slaves, unworthy of free Romans— and everybody was a free Roman now. Hence, on the one side, increasing manumissions of the superfluous slaves who were now a burden; on the other hand, a growth in some parts in the numbers of the *coloni* and in other parts of the declassed freemen (like the "poor whites" in the ex-slave states of America). Christianity is completely innocent of the gradual dying out of ancient slavery; it was itself actively involved in the system for centuries under the Roman Empire and never interfered later with slave-trading by Christians—not with the Germans in the north or with the Vene- tians in the Mediterranean or with the later trade in Negroes* Slavery no longer paid; it was for that reason it died out. But in dying it left behind its poisoned sting—the stigma attaching to the productive labor of freemen. This was the blind alley from which the Roman world had no way out: slavery was economically im- possible, the labor of freemen was morally ostracized. The one could be the basic form of social production no longer; the other, not yet. Nothing could help here except a complete revolution.

Things were no better in the provinces. We have most material about Gaul. Here there was still a free small peasantry in addition to *coloni*. In order to be secured against oppression by officials, judges, and usurers, these peasants often placed themselves under the protection, the patronage, of a powerful person; and it was not only individuals who did so, but whole communities, so that in the fourth century the emperors frequently prohibited the practice. But what help was this protection to those who sought it? Their patron made it a condition that they should transfer to him the rights of ownership in their pieces of land in return for which he guaranteed them the use of the land for their lifetime—a trick which the Holy Church took note of and in the ninth and tenth centuries lustily imitated, to the increase of God's glory and its own lands. At this time, it is true, about the year 475, Bishop Salvianus of Marseilles still inveighs indignantly against such theft. He relates that oppres-

---

* According to Bishop Liutprand of Cremona, in the tenth century the chief industry of Verdun—in the Holy German Empire, observe—was the manufacture of eunuchs who were exported at great profit to Spain for the Moorish harems.

sion by Roman officials and great landlords had become so heavy that many "Romans" fled into districts already occupied by the barbarians and that the Roman citizens settled there feared nothing so much as a return to Roman rule. That parents owing to their poverty often sold their children into slavery at this time is proved by a decree prohibiting the practice.

In return for liberating the Romans from their own state, the German barbarians took from them two-thirds of all the land and divided it among themselves. The division was made according to the gentile constitution. The conquerors being relatively few in number, large tracts of land were left undivided, as the property partly of the whole people, partly of the individual tribes and gentes. Within each gens the arable land and meadowland was distributed by lot in equal portions among the individual households. We do not know whether reallotments of the land were repeatedly carried out at this time, but in any event they were soon discontinued in the Roman provinces and the individual lots became alienable private property, *allodium*. Woods and pastures remained undivided for common use; the provisions regulating their common use and the manner in which the divided land was to be cultivated were settled in accordance with ancient custom and by the decision of the whole community. The longer the gens remained settled in its village and the more the Germans and the Romans gradually merged, the more the bond of union lost its character of kinship and became territorial. The gens was lost in the mark community, in which, however, traces of its origin in the kinship of its members are often enough still visible. Thus, at least in those countries where the mark community maintained itself—northern France, England, Germany and Scandinavia—the gentile constitution changed imperceptibly into a local constitution and thus became capable of incorporation into the state. But it nevertheless retained that primitive democratic character which distinguishes the whole gentile constitution, and thus even in its later enforced degeneration and up to the most recent times keeping something of the gentile constitution alive to be a weapon in the hands of the oppressed.

This weakening of the bond of blood in the gens followed from the degeneration of the organs of kinship also in the tribe and in the entire people as a result of their conquests. As we know, rule over subjugated peoples is incompatible with the gentile constitution. Here we can see this on a large scale. The German peoples, now masters of the Roman provinces, had to organize what they had conquered. But they could neither absorb the mass of Romans into the gentile bodies nor govern them through these bodies. At the head of the local Roman governing bodies, many of which continued for the time being to function, had to be placed a substitute for the Roman state, and this substitute could only be another state. The organs of the gentile constitution had to be transformed into state organs, and that very rapidly, for the situation was urgent. But the immediate representative of the conquering people was their military leader. To secure the conquered territory against attack from within and without, it was necessary to strengthen his power. The moment had come to transform the military leadership into kingship: the transformation was made.

Let us take the country of the Franks. Here the victorious Salian people had come into complete possession, not only of the extensive Roman state domains, but also of the very large tracts of land which had not been distributed among the larger and smaller district and mark communities, in particular all the larger forest areas. On his transformation from a plain military chief into the real sovereign of a country, the first thing which the king of the Franks did was to transform this property of the people into crown lands, to steal it from the people and to give it, outright or in fief, to his retainers. This retinue, which originally consisted of his personal following of warriors and of the other lesser military leaders, was presently increased not only by Romans—Romanized Gauls, whose education, knowledge of writing, familiarity with the spoken Romance language of the country and the written Latin language, as well as with the country's laws, soon made them indispensable to him—but also by slaves, serfs and freedmen, who composed his court and from whom he chose his favorites. All these received their portions of the people's land, at first generally in the form of gifts, later of benefices, usually conferred, to begin with, for the king's lifetime. Thus, at the expense of the people the foundation of a new nobility was laid.

And that was not all. The wide extent of the kingdom could not be governed with the means provided by the old gentile constitution; the council of chiefs, even if it had not long since become obsolete, would have been unable to meet, and it was soon displaced by the permanent retinue of the king. The old assembly of the people continued to exist in name, but it also increasingly became a mere assembly of military leaders subordinate to the king and of the new rising nobility. By the incessant civil wars and wars of conquest (the latter were particularly frequent under Charlemagne), the free land-owning peasants, the mass of the Frankish people, were reduced to the same state of exhaustion and penury as the Roman peasants in the last years of the Republic. Though they had originally constituted the whole army and still remained its backbone after the conquest of France, by the beginning of the ninth century they were so impoverished that hardly one man in five could go to the wars. The army of free peasants raised directly by the king was replaced by an army composed of the servitors of the new nobles, including bondsmen, descendants of men who in earlier times had known no master save the king and still earlier no master at all, not even a king. The internal wars under Charlemagne's successors, the weakness of the authority of the crown, and the corresponding excesses of the nobles (including the *gau* counts [county administrators] instituted by Charlemagne, who were now striving to make their office hereditary) had already brought ruin on the Frankish peasantry, and the ruin was finally completed by the invasions of the Norsemen. Fifty years after the death of Charlemagne, the Empire of the Franks lay as defenseless at the feet of the Norsemen as the Roman Empire, 400 years earlier, had lain at the feet of the Franks.

Not only was there the same impotence against enemies from without, but there was almost the same social order or rather disorder within. The free Frankish peasants were in a plight similar to their predecessors, the Roman *coloni*. Plundered and ruined by wars, they had been forced to put themselves under the protection of the new nobles or of the Church, the crown being too weak to protect them. But they had to pay dearly for it. Like the Gallic peasants earlier, they had to transfer their rights of property in land to their protecting lord and received the land back from him in tenancies of various and changing forms, but always only in return for services and dues. Once in this position of dependence, they gradually lost their personal freedom also; after a few generations most of them were already serfs. How rapid was the disappearance of the free peasantry is shown by Irminon's records of the monastic possessions of the Abbey of Saint-Germain-des-Prés, at that time near, now in, Paris. On the huge holdings of this Abbey, which were scattered in the surrounding country, there lived in Charlemagne's time 2,788 households whose members were almost without exception Franks with German names. They included 2,080 *coloni,* 35 *liti* [semi-free peasants], 220 slaves, and only eight freehold tenants! The godless practice, as Salvianus had called it, by which the protecting lord had the peasant's land transferred to himself as his own property and only gave it back to the peasant for use during life, was now commonly employed by the Church against the peasants. The forced services now imposed with increasing frequency had had their prototype as much in the Roman *angariae,* compulsory labor for the state, as in the services provided by members of the German mark for bridge and road making and other common purposes. To all appearances, therefore, after 400 years the mass of the people were back again where they had started.

But that only proved two things: first, that the social stratification and the distribution of property in the declining Roman Empire completely correspond to the level of agricultural and industrial production at that time and had therefore been inevitable; secondly, that this level of production had neither risen nor fallen significantly during the following four centuries and had therefore with equal necessity again produced the same distribution of property and the same classes in the population. In the last centuries of the Roman Empire, the town had lost its former supremacy over the country, and in the first centuries of German rule it had not regained it. This implies a low level of development both in agriculture and industry. This general situation necessarily produces big ruling landowners and a dependent small peasantry. How impossible it was to graft onto such a society either the Roman system of *latifundia* worked by slave labor or the newer large-scale agriculture worked by forced services is proved by Charlemagne's experiments with the famous imperial country estates (*villae*). These experiments were gigantic in scope, but they left scarcely a trace. They were continued only by the monasteries, and only for them were they fruitful. But the monasteries were abnormal social bodies, founded on celibacy; they could produce exceptional results, but for that very reason necessarily continued to be exceptional themselves.

And yet progress was made during these 400 years. Though at the end we find almost the same main classes as at the beginning, the human beings who formed these classes were different. Ancient slavery had gone, and so had the pauper freemen who despised work as only fit for slaves. Between the Roman *colonus* and the new bondsman had stood the free Frankish peasant. The "useless memories and aimless strife" of decadent Roman culture were dead and buried. The social classes of the ninth century had been formed, not in the rottenness of a decaying civilization, but in the birth pangs of a new civilization. Compared with their Roman predecessors, the new breed, whether masters or servants, was a breed of men. The relation of powerful landowners and subject peasants which had meant for the ancient world the final ruin from which there was no escape was for them the starting point of a new development. And further, however unproductive these four centuries appear, *one* great product they did leave—the modern nationalities, the new forms and structures through which Western European humanity was to make coming history. The Germans had, in fact, given Europe new life, and therefore the breakup of the states in the Germanic period ended, not in subjugation by the Norsemen and Saracens, but in the further development of the system of benefices and protection into feudalism, and in such an enormous increase of the population that scarcely two centuries later the severe bloodletting of the Crusades was borne without injury.

But what was the mysterious magic by which the Germans breathed new life into a dying Europe? Was it some miraculous power innate in the Germanic race, such as our chauvinist historians romance about? Not a bit of it. The Germans, especially at that time, were a highly gifted Aryan tribe and in the full vigor of development. It was not, however, their specific national qualities which rejuvenated Europe, but simply—their barbarism, their gentile constitution.

Their individual ability and courage, their sense of freedom, their democratic instinct which in everything of public concern felt itself concerned; in a word all the qualities which had been lost to the Romans and were alone capable of forming new states and making new nationalities grow out of the slime of the Roman world—what else were they than the characteristics of the barbarian of the upper stage, fruits of his gentile constitution?

If they recast the ancient form of monogamy, moderated the supremacy of the man in the family, and gave the woman a higher position than the classical world had ever known, what made them capable of doing so if not their barbarism, their gentile customs, their living heritage from the time of mother right?

If in at least three of the most important countries, Germany, northern France and England, they carried over into the feudal state a genuine piece of gentile constitution in the form of mark communities, thus giving the oppressed class, the peasants, even under the harshest medieval serfdom a local center of solidarity and a means of resistance such as neither the slaves of classical times nor the modern proletariat found ready to their hand—to what was this due, if not to their barbarism, their purely barbarian method of settlement in kinship groups?

Lastly, they were able to develop and make universal the milder form of servitude they had practiced in their own country, which even in the Roman Empire increasingly displaced slavery; a form of servitude which, as Fourier first stressed, gives to the bondsmen the means of their gradual liberation as a *class* (*"fournit aux cultivateurs des moyens d'affranchissement collectif et progressif"*); a form of servitude which thus stands high above slavery, where the only possibility is the immediate release without any transitional stage of individual slaves (abolition of slavery by successful rebellion is unknown to antiquity), whereas the medieval serfs gradually won their liberation as a class. And to what do we owe this if not to their barbarism, thanks to which they had not yet reached the stage of fully developed slavery, neither the labor slavery of the classical world nor the domestic slavery of the Orient?

All the vigorous and creative life which the Germans infused into the Roman world was barbarism. Only barbarians are able to rejuvenate a world in the throes of collapsing civilization. And precisely the highest stage of barbarism, to which and in which the Germans worked their way upward before the migrations, was the most favorable for this process. That explains everything.

CHAPTER IX

BARBARISM AND CIVILIZATION

WE HAVE now traced the dissolution of the gentile constitution in the three great instances of the Greeks, the Romans, and the Germans. In conclusion, let us examine the general economic conditions which already undermined the gentile organization of society at the upper stage of barbarism and with the coming of civilization over-threw it completely. Here we shall need Marx's *Capital* as much as Morgan's book.

Arising in the middle stage of savagery, further developed during its upper stage, the gens reaches its most flourishing period, so far as our sources enable us to judge, during the lower stage of bar-barism. We begin therefore with this stage.

Here—the American Indians must serve as our example—we find the gentile constitution fully formed. The tribe is now grouped in several gentes, generally two. With the increase in population, each of these original gentes splits up into several daughter gentes, their mother gens now appearing as the phratry. The tribe itself breaks up into several tribes, in each of which we find again, for the most part, the old gentes. The related tribes, at least in some cases, are united in a confederacy. This simple organization suffices completely for the social conditions out of which it sprang. It is nothing more than the grouping natural to those conditions, and it is capable of settling all conflicts that can arise within a society so organized. War settles external conflicts; it may end with the an-nihilation of the tribe but never with its subjugation. It is the great-ness but also the limitation of the gentile constitution that it has no place for ruler and ruled. Within the tribe there is as yet no differ-ence between rights and duties; the question whether participation in public affairs, in blood revenge or atonement, is a right or a duty does not exist for the Indian; it would seem to him just as absurd as the question whether it was a right or a duty to sleep, eat, or hunt. A division of the tribe or of the gens into different classes was equally impossible. And that brings us to the examination of the economic basis of these conditions.

The population is extremely sparse; it is dense only at the tribe's place of settlement, around which lie in a wide circle first the hunting grounds and then the protective belt of neutral forest which separates the tribe from others. The division of labor is purely primitive, between the sexes only. The man fights in the wars, goes hunting and fishing, procures the raw materials of food and the tools necessary for doing so. The woman looks after the house and the preparation of food and clothing, cooks, weaves, sews. They are each master in their own sphere: the man in the forest, the woman in the house. Each is owner of the instruments which he or she makes and uses: the man of the weapons, the hunting and fishing implements; the woman of the household gear. The housekeeping is communal among several and often many families.*
What is made and used in common is common property—the house, the garden, the long boat. Here therefore, and here alone, there still exists in actual fact that "property created by the owner's labor" which in civilized society is an ideal fiction of the jurists and economists, the last lying legal pretense by which modern capitalist property still bolsters itself up.

But humanity did not everywhere remain at this stage. In Asia they found animals which could be tamed and, when once tamed, bred. The wild buffalo cow had to be hunted; the tame buffalo cow gave a calf yearly and milk as well. A number of the most advanced tribes—the Aryans, Semites, perhaps already also the Turanians— now made their chief work first the taming of cattle, later their breeding and tending only. Pastoral tribes separated themselves from the mass of the rest of the barbarians—*the first great social division of labor*. The pastoral tribes produced not only more necessities of life than the other barbarians, but different ones. They possessed the advantage over them of having not only milk, milk products and greater supplies of meat, but also skins, wool, goat hair, and spun and woven fabrics, which became more common as

* Especially on the northwest coast of America—*see* Bancroft. Among the Haidahs on Queen Charlotte Islands there are households with as many as 700 persons under one roof. Among the Nootkas whole tribes used to live under one roof.

the amount of raw material increased. Thus for the first time regular exchange became possible. At the earlier stages only occasional exchanges can take place; particular skill in the making of weapons and tools may lead to a temporary division of labor. Thus in many places undoubted remains of workshops for the making of stone tools have been found dating from the later Stone Age. The artists who here perfected their skill probably worked for the whole community, as each special handicraftsman still does in the gentile communities in India. In no case could exchange arise at this stage except within the tribe itself, and then only as an exceptional event. But now, with the differentiation of pastoral tribes, we find all the conditions ripe for exchange between branches of different tribes and its development into a regular established institution. Originally tribe exchanged with tribe through the respective chiefs of the gentes; but as the herds began to pass into private ownership, exchange between individuals became more common and, finally, the only form. Now the chief article which the pastoral tribes exchanged with their neighbors was cattle; cattle became the commodity by which all other commodities were valued and which was everywhere willingly taken in exchange for them—in short, cattle acquired a money function and already at this stage did the work of money. With such necessity and speed, even at the very beginning of commodity exchange, did the need for a money commodity develop.[28]

Horticulture, probably unknown to Asiatic barbarians of the lower stage, was being practiced by them in the middle stage at the latest, as the forerunner of agriculture. In the climate of the Turanian plateau, pastoral life is impossible without supplies of fodder for the long and severe winter. Here, therefore, it was essential that land should be put under grass and corn cultivated. The same is

28. Trade was more common among hunter-gatherers than this suggests. Although often for luxury items (amber found its way from the North Sea to the Mediterranean in Paleolithic times), it was also for foodstuffs (such as forest products for seacoast products) and important materials (such as flint). This is not to contradict the point that it was a long time before it became significant enough to involve an established division of labor. The possible role of trade between wild-grass gatherers and potential herdsmen in the highlands of Iraq and Iran in the encouragement of plant cultivation is discussed by Kent V. Flannery in "The Ecology of Early Food Production in Mesopotamia," *Science,* Vol. 147, March 12, 1965.

true of the steppes north of the Black Sea. But when once corn had been grown for the cattle, it also soon became food for men. The cultivated land still remained tribal property; at first it was allotted to the gens, later by the gens to the household communities and finally to individuals for use. The users may have had certain rights of possession, but nothing more.

Of the industrial achievements of this stage, two are particularly important. The first is the loom, the second the smelting of metal ores and the working of metals. Copper and tin, and their alloy, bronze, were by far the most important. Bronze provided serviceable tools and weapons though it could not displace stone tools; only iron could do that, and the method of obtaining iron was not yet understood. Gold and silver were beginning to be used for ornament and decoration and must already have acquired a high value as compared with copper and bronze.

The increase of production in all branches—cattle raising, agriculture, domestic handicrafts—gave human labor power the capacity to produce a larger product than was necessary for its maintenance. At the same time it increased the daily amount of work to be done by each member of the gens, household community or single family. It was now desirable to bring in new labor forces. War provided them; prisoners of war were turned into slaves. With its increase of the productivity of labor and therefore of wealth, and its extension of the field of production, the first great social division of labor was bound, in the general historical conditions prevailing, to bring slavery in its train. From the first great social division of labor arose the first great cleavage of society into two classes: masters and slaves, exploiters and exploited.

As to how and when the herds passed out of the common possession of the tribe or the gens into the ownership of individual heads of families, we know nothing at present. But in the main it must have occurred during this stage. With the herds and the other new riches, a revolution came over the family. To procure the necessities of life had always been the business of the man; he produced and owned the means of doing so.[29] The herds were the new means of producing these necessities; the taming of the animals in the first

29. The word "always" is puzzling, since women were responsible for most of the plant cultivation, and men for hunting, in the early stages of agricultural society.

instance and their later tending were the man's work. To him, therefore, belonged the cattle and to him the commodities and the
slaves received in exchange for cattle. All the surplus which the
acquisition of the necessities of life now yielded fell to the man;
the woman shared in its enjoyment, but had no part in its ownership. The "savage" warrior and hunter had been content to take
second place in the house, after the woman; the "gentler" shepherd,
in the arrogance of his wealth, pushed himself forward into the first
place and the woman down into the second. And she could not
complain. The division of labor within the family had regulated the
division of property between the man and the woman. That division
of labor had remained the same; and yet it now turned the previous
domestic relation upside down simply because the division of labor
outside the family had changed. The same cause which had ensured to the woman her previous supremacy in the house—that
her activity was confined to domestic labor—this same cause now
ensured the man's supremacy in the house. The domestic labor of
the woman no longer counted beside the acquisition of the necessities of life by the man; the latter was everything, the former an
unimportant extra. We can already see from this that to emancipate
woman and make her the equal of the man is and remains an
impossibility so long as the woman is shut out from social productive labor and restricted to private domestic labor. The emancipation of woman will only be possible when woman can take part in
production on a large, social scale, and domestic work no longer
claims anything but an insignificant amount of her time. And only
now has that become possible through modern large-scale industry,
which does not merely permit the employment of female labor
over a wide range, but positively demands it, while it also tends
toward ending private domestic labor by changing it more and
more into a public industry.

The man now being actually supreme in the house, the last
barrier to his absolute supremacy had fallen. This autocracy was
confirmed and perpetuated by the overthrow of mother right, the
introduction of father right, and the gradual transition of the pairing
marriage into monogamy. But this tore a breach in the old gentile
order; the single family became a power, and its rise was a menace
to the gens.

The next step leads us to the upper stage of barbarism, the period when all civilized peoples have their heroic age: the age of the iron sword, but also of the iron plowshare and ax. Iron was now at the service of man, the last and most important of all the raw materials which played a historically revolutionary role—until the potato. Iron brought about the tillage of large areas, the clearing of wide tracts of virgin forest; iron gave to the handicraftsman tools so hard and sharp that no stone, no other known metal, could resist them. All this came gradually; the first iron was often even softer than bronze. Hence stone weapons only disappeared slowly; not merely in the *Hildebrandslied,* but even as late as the battle of Hastings in 1066, stone axes were still used for fighting. But progress could not now be stopped; it went forward with fewer checks and greater speed. The town, with its houses of stone or brick encircled by stone walls, towers and ramparts, became the central seat of the tribe or the confederacy of tribes—an enormous architectural advance, but also a sign of growing danger and need for protection. Wealth increased rapidly, but as the wealth of individuals. The products of weaving, metalwork and the other handicrafts, which were becoming more and more differentiated, displayed growing variety and skill. In addition to corn, leguminous plants and fruits, agriculture now provided wine and oil, the preparation of which had been learned. Such manifold activities were no longer within the scope of one and the same individual; the *second great division of labor* took place—handicraft separated from agriculture. The continuous increase of production and simultaneously of the productivity of labor heightened the value of human labor power. Slavery, which during the preceding period was still in its beginnings and sporadic, now becomes an essential constituent part of the social system; slaves no longer merely help with production—they are driven by dozens to work in the fields and the workshops. With the splitting up of production into the two great main branches, agriculture and handicrafts, arises production directly for exchange, commodity production; with it came commerce, not only in the interior and on the tribal boundaries, but also already overseas. All this, however, was still very undeveloped; the precious metals were beginning to be the predominant and general money commodity, but still uncoined, exchanging simply by their naked weight.

The distinction of rich and poor appears beside that of freemen and slaves—with the new division of labor, a new cleavage of society into classes. The inequalities of property among the individual heads of families break up the old communal household communities wherever they had still managed to survive, and with them the common cultivation of the soil by and for these communities. The cultivated land is allotted for use to single families, at first temporarily, later permanently. The transition to full private property is gradually accomplished, parallel with the transition of the pairing marriage into monogamy. The single family is becoming the economic unit of society.

The denser population necessitates closer consolidation both for internal and external action. The confederacy of related tribes becomes everywhere a necessity, and soon also their fusion involving the fusion of the separate tribal territories into one territory of the nation. The military leader of the people—*rex, basileus, thiudans*—becomes an indispensable, permanent official. The assembly of the people takes form wherever it did not already exist. Military leader, council, assembly of the people are the organs of gentile society developed into military democracy— military, since war and organization for war have now become regular functions of national life. Their neighbors' wealth excites the greed of peoples who already see in the acquisition of wealth one of the main aims of life. They are barbarians; they think it easier and in fact more honorable to get riches by pillage than by work. War, formerly waged only in revenge for injuries or to extend territory that had grown too small, is now waged simply for plunder and becomes a regular industry. Not without reason the bristling battlements stand menacingly about the new fortified towns; in the moat at their foot yawns the grave of the gentile constitution, and already they rear their towers into civilization. Similarly in the interior, the wars of plunder increase the power of the supreme military leader and the subordinate commanders; the customary election of their successors from the same families is gradually transformed, especially after the introduction of father right, into a right of hereditary succession, first tolerated, then claimed, finally usurped; the foundation of the hereditary monarchy and the hereditary nobility is laid. Thus the organs of the gentile constitution gradually tear themselves loose from their roots in the people, in gens, phratry, tribe, and the whole gentile constitution changes into its opposite: from an organization of tribes for the free ordering of their own affairs it becomes an organization for the plundering and oppression of their neighbors; and correspondingly its organs change from instruments of the will of the people into independent organs for the domination and oppression of the people. That, however, would never have been possible if the greed for riches had not split the members of the gens into rich and poor, if "the property differences within one and the same gens had not transformed its unity of interest into antagonism between its members" (Marx), if the extension of slavery had not already begun to make working for a living seem fit only for slaves and more dishonorable than pillage.

We have now reached the threshold of civilization. Civilization opens with a new advance in the division of labor. At the lowest stage of barbarism men produced only directly for their own needs; any acts of exchange were isolated occurrences, the object of exchange merely some fortuitous surplus. In the middle stage of barbarism we already find among the pastoral peoples a possession in the form of cattle which, once the herd has attained a certain size, regularly produces a surplus over and above the tribe's own requirements, leading to a division of labor between pastoral peoples and backward tribes without herds, and hence to the existence of two different levels of production side by side with one another and to the conditions necessary for regular exchange. The upper stage of barbarism brings us the further division of labor between agriculture and handicrafts, hence the production of a continually increasing portion of the products of labor directly for exchange, so that exchange between individual producers assumes the importance of a vital social function. Civilization consolidates and intensifies all these existing divisions of labor, particularly by sharpening the opposition between town and country (the town may economically dominate the country, as in antiquity, or the country the town, as in the middle ages), and it adds a third division of labor peculiar to itself and of decisive importance. It creates a class which no longer concerns itself with production, but only

with the exchange of the products—the *merchants*. Hitherto whenever classes had begun to form, it had always been exclusively in
the field of production; the persons engaged in production were
separated into those who directed and those who executed or else
into large-scale and small-scale producers. Now for the first time a
class appears which, without in any way participating in production,
captures the direction of production as a whole and economically
subjugates the producers; which makes itself into an indispensable
middleman between any two producers and exploits them both.
Under the pretext that they save the producers the trouble and risk
of exchange, extend the sale of their products to distant markets
and are therefore the most useful class of the population, a class
of parasites comes into being, genuine social sycophants, who,
as a reward for their actually very insignificant services, skim all
the cream off production at home and abroad, rapidly amass enormous wealth and a corresponding social influence, and for that
reason receive under civilization ever higher honors and ever greater
control of production until at last they also bring forth a product
of their own—the periodical trade crises.

At our stage of development, however, the young merchants
had not even begun to dream of the great destiny awaiting them.
But they were growing and making themselves indispensable, which
was quite sufficient. And with the formation of the merchant class
came also the development of *metallic money,* the minted coin, a
new instrument for the domination of the non-producer over the
producer and his production. The commodity of commodities had
been discovered, that which holds all other commodities hidden in
itself, the magic power which can change at will into everything
desirable and desired. The man who had it ruled the world of
production, and who had more of it than anybody else?—the
merchant. The worship of money was safe in his hands. He took
good care to make it clear that, in face of money, all commodities
and hence all producers of commodities must prostrate themselves
in adoration in the dust. He proved practically that all other forms
of wealth fade into mere semblance beside this incarnation of
wealth as such. Never again has the power of money shown itself
in such primitive brutality and violence as during these days of
its youth. After commodities had begun to sell for money, loans

and advances in money came also, and with them interest and usury. No legislation of later times so utterly and ruthlessly delivers over the debtor to the usurious creditor as the legislation of ancient Athens and ancient Rome—and in both cities it rose spontaneously as customary law without any compulsion other than the economic.

Alongside wealth in commodities and slaves, alongside wealth in money, there now appeared wealth in land also. The individuals' rights of possession in the pieces of land originally allotted to them by gens or tribe had now become so established that the land was their hereditary property. Recently they had striven above all to secure their freedom against the rights of the gentile community over these lands since these rights had become for them a fetter. They got rid of the fetter—but soon afterward of their new landed property also. Full, free ownership of the land meant not only power, uncurtailed and unlimited, to possess the land; it meant also the power to alienate it. As long as the land belonged to the gens, no such power could exist. But when the new landed proprietor shook off once and for all the fetters laid upon him by the prior right of gens and tribe, he also cut the ties which had hitherto inseparably attached him to the land. Money, invented at the same time as private property in land, showed him what that meant. Land could now become a commodity; it could be sold and pledged. Scarcely had private property in land been introduced than the mortgage was already invented (*see* Athens). As hetaerism and prostitution dog the heels of monogamy, so from now onward mortgage dogs the heels of private land ownership. You asked for full, free alienable ownership of the land and now you have got it—*"tu l'as voulu, Georges Dandin."*

With trade expansion, money and usury, private property in land and mortgages, the concentration and centralization of wealth in the hands of a small class rapidly advanced, accompanied by an increasing improverishment of the masses and an increasing mass of impoverishment. The new aristocracy of wealth, in so far as it had not been identical from the outset with the old hereditary aristocracy, pushed it permanently into the background (in Athens, in Rome, among the Germans). And simultaneous with this division of the citizens into classes according to wealth, there was an

enormous increase, particularly in Greece, in the number of slaves*
whose forced labor was the foundation on which the superstructure
of the entire society was reared.

Let us now see what had become of the gentile constitution in
this social upheaval. Confronted by the new forces in whose growth
it had had no share, the gentile constitution was helpless. The
necessary condition for its existence was that the members of a
gens or at least of a tribe were settled together in the same territory
and were its sole inhabitants. That had long ceased to be the case.
Every territory now had a heterogeneous population belonging to
the most varied gentes and tribes; everywhere slaves, protected
persons and aliens lived side by side with citizens. The settled conditions of life which had only been achieved toward the end of the
middle stage of barbarism were broken up by the repeated shifting
and changing of residence under the pressure of trade, alteration of
occupation and changes in the ownership of the land. The members
of the gentile bodies could no longer meet to look after their common concerns; only unimportant matters, like the religious festivals,
were still perfunctorily attended to. In addition to the needs and
interests with which the gentile bodies were intended and fitted to
deal, the upheaval in productive relations and the resulting change
in the social structure had given rise to new needs and interests
which were not only alien to the old gentile order, but ran directly
counter to it at every point. The interests of the groups of handicraftsmen which had arisen with the division of labor, the special
needs of the town as opposed to the country, called for new
organs. But each of these groups was composed of people of the
most diverse gentes, phratries, and tribes, and even included aliens.
Such organs had therefore to be formed outside the gentile constitution, alongside of it, and hence in opposition to it. And this
conflict of interests was at work within every gentile body, appearing in its most extreme form in the association of rich and
poor, usurers and debtors, in the same gens and the same tribe.
Further, there was the new mass of population outside the gentile
bodies, which, as in Rome, was able to become a power in the land

* For the number of slaves in Athens, *see* above, 181. In Corinth at
the height of its power, the number of slaves was 460,000, in Aegina, 470,000
—in both cases, ten times the population of free citizens.

and at the same time was too numerous to be gradually absorbed into the kinship groups and tribes. In relation to this mass, the gentile bodies stood opposed as closed, privileged corporations; the primitive natural democracy had changed into a malign aristocracy. Lastly, the gentile constitution had grown out of a society which knew no internal contradictions, and it was only adapted to such a society. It possessed no means of coercion except public opinion. But here was a society which by all its economic conditions of life had been forced to split itself into freemen and slaves, into the exploiting rich and the exploited poor; a society which not only could never again reconcile these contradictions, but was compelled always to intensify them. Such a society could only exist either in the continuous open fight of these classes against one another or else under the rule of a third power, which, apparently standing above the warring classes, suppressed their open conflict and allowed the class struggle to be fought out at most in the economic field, in so-called legal form. The gentile constitution was finished. It had been shattered by the division of labor and its result, the cleavage of society into classes. It was replaced by the *state*.

The three main forms in which the state arises on the ruins of the gentile constitution have been examined in detail above. Athens provides the purest, classic form; here the state springs directly and mainly out of the class oppositions which develop within gentile society itself. In Rome, gentile society becomes a closed aristocracy in the midst of the numerous *plebs* who stand outside it and have duties but no rights; the victory of *plebs* breaks up the old constitution based on kinship and erects on its ruins the state, into which both the gentile aristocracy and the *plebs* are soon completely absorbed. Lastly, in the case of the German conquerors of the Roman Empire, the state springs directly out of the conquest of large foreign territories which the gentile constitution provides no means of governing. But because this conquest involves neither a serious struggle with the original population nor a more advanced division of labor; because conquerors and conquered are almost on the same level of economic development, and the economic basis of society remains therefore as before—for these reasons the gentile constitution is able to survive for many centuries in the altered, territorial form of the mark constitution and even for a time to rejuvenate itself in a feebler shape in the later noble and patrician families, and indeed in peasant families, as in Ditmarschen.*

The state is therefore by no means a power imposed on society from without; just as little is it "the reality of the moral idea," "the image and the reality of reason," as Hegel maintains. Rather, it is a product of society at a particular stage of development; it is the admission that this society has involved itself in insoluble self-contradiction and is cleft into irreconcilable antagonisms which it is powerless to exorcise. But in order that these antagonisms, classes with conflicting economic interests, shall not consume themselves and society in fruitless struggle, a power, apparently standing above society, has become necessary to moderate the conflict and keep it within the bounds of "order"; and this power, arisen out of society but placing itself above it and increasingly alienating itself from it, is the state.

In contrast to the old gentile organization, the state is distinguished firstly by the grouping of its members *on a territorial basis*. The old gentile bodies, formed and held together by ties of blood had, as we have seen, become inadequate largely because they presupposed that the gentile members were bound to one particular locality, whereas this had long ago ceased to be the case. The territory was still there, but the people had become mobile. The territorial division was therefore taken as the starting point and the system introduced by which citizens exercised their public rights and duties where they took up residence, without regard to gens or tribe. This organization of the citizens of the state according to domicile is common to all states. To us, therefore, this organization seems natural; but, as we have seen, hard and protracted struggles were necessary before it was able in Athens and Rome to displace the old organization founded on kinship.

The second distinguishing characteristic is the institution of a *public force* which is no longer immediately identical with the

---

* The first historian who had at any rate an approximate conception of the nature of the gens was Niebuhr, and for this he had to thank his acquaintance with the Ditmarschen families, though he was overhasty in transferring their characteristics to the gens.

people's own organization of themselves as an armed power. This special public force is needed because a self-acting armed organization of the people has become impossible since their cleavage into classes. The slaves also belong to the population; as against the 365,000 slaves, the 90,000 Athenian citizens constitute only a privileged class. The people's army of the Athenian democracy confronted the slaves as an aristocratic public force and kept them in check; but to keep the citizens in check as well, a police force was needed as described above. This public force exists in every state; it consists not merely of armed men but also of material appendages, prisons and coercive institutions of all kinds, of which gentile society knew nothing. It may be very insignificant, practically negligible, in societies with still undeveloped class antagonisms and living in remote areas, as at times and in places in the United States of America. But it becomes stronger in proportion as the class antagonisms within the state become sharper and as adjoining states grow larger and more populous. It is enough to look at Europe today, where class struggle and rivalry in conquest have brought the public power to a pitch that it threatens to devour the whole of society and even the state itself.

In order to maintain this public power, contributions from the citizens are necessary—*taxes*. These were completely unknown to gentile society. We know more than enough about them today. With advancing civilization, even taxes are not sufficient; the state draws drafts on the future, contracts loans—*state debts*. Our old Europe can tell a tale about these, too.

In possession of the public power and the right of taxation, the officials now present themselves as organs of society standing *above* society. The free, willing respect accorded to the organs of the gentile constitution is not enough for them, even if they could have it. Representatives of a power which estranges them from society, they have to be given prestige by means of special decrees which invest them with a peculiar sanctity and inviolability. The lowest police officer of the civilized state has more "authority" than all the organs of gentile society put together; but the mightiest prince and the greatest statesman or general of civilization might envy the humblest of the gentile chiefs, the unforced and unquestioned respect accorded to him. For the one stands in the midst of society; the other is forced to pose as something outside and above it.

As the state arose from the need to keep class antagonisms in check, but also arose in the thick of the fight between the classes, it is normally the state of the most powerful, economically dominant class, which by its means becomes also the politically dominant class and so acquires new means of holding down and exploiting the oppressed class. The ancient state was, above all, the state of the slave owners for holding down the slaves, just as the feudal state was the organ of the nobility for holding down the peasant serfs and bondsmen, and the modern representative state is an instrument for exploiting wage labor by capital. Exceptional periods, however, occur when the warring classes are so nearly equal in forces that the state power, as apparent mediator, acquires for the moment a certain independence in relation to both. This applies to the absolute monarchy of the 11th and 18th centuries, which balanced the nobility and the bourgeoisie against one another, and to the Bonapartism of the First and particularly of the Second French Empire, which played off the proletariat against the bourgeoisie and the bourgeoisie against the proletariat. The latest achievement in this line, in which ruler and ruled look equally comic, is the new German Empire of the Bismarckian nation; here the capitalists and the workers are balanced against one another and both of them fleeced for the benefit of the decayed Prussian cabbage Junkers.

Further, in most historical states the rights conceded to citizens are graded on a property basis whereby it is directly admitted that the state is an organization for the protection of the possessing class against the non-possessing class. This is already the case in the Athenian and Roman property classes; similarly in the medieval feudal state in which the extent of political power was determined by the extent of land-ownership; similarly, also, in the electoral qualifications in modern parliamentary states. This political recognition of property differences is, however, by no means essential. On the contrary, it marks a low stage in the development of the state. The highest form of the state, the democratic republic, which in our modern social conditions becomes more and more an unavoidable necessity and is the form of state in which alone the last decisive battle between proletariat and bourgeoisie can be fought out—the democratic republic no longer officially recognizes differences of property. Wealth here employs its power indirectly, but all the more surely. It does this in two ways: by plain corruption of officials, of which America is the classic example; and by an alliance between the government and the stock exchange, which is effected all the more easily the higher the state debt mounts and the more the joint-stock companies concentrate in their hands not only transport but also production itself, and themselves have their own center in the stock exchange. In addition to America, the latest French republic illustrates this strikingly, and honest little Switzerland has also given a creditable performance in this field. But that a democratic republic is not essential to this brotherly bond between government and stock exchange is proved not only by England but also by the new German Empire, where it is difficult to say who scored most by the introduction of universal suffrage, Bismarck or the Bleichröder bank. And lastly the possessing class rules directly by means of universal suffrage. As long as the oppressed class—in our case, therefore, the proletariat—is not yet ripe for its self-liberation, so long will it in its majority recognize the existing order of society as the only possible one and remain politically the tail of the capitalist class, its extreme left wing. But in the measure in which it matures toward its self-emancipation, in the same measure it constitutes itself as its own party and votes for its own representatives, not those of the capitalists. Universal suffrage is thus the gauge of the maturity of the working class. It cannot and never will be anything more in the modern state; but that is enough. On the day when the thermometer of universal suffrage shows boiling point among the workers, they as well as the capitalists will know where they stand.

The state, therefore, has not existed from all eternity. There have been societies which have managed without it, which had no notion of the state or state power. At a definite stage of economic development, which necessarily involved the cleavage of society into classes, the state became a necessity because of this cleavage. We are now rapidly approaching a stage in the development of production at which the existence of these classes has not only ceased to be a necessity but becomes a positive hindrance to production. They will fall as inevitably as they once arose. The state inevitably falls with them. The society which organizes production anew on the basis of free and equal association of the producers will put the whole state machinery where it will then belong—into the museum of antiquities, next to the spinning wheel and the bronze ax.

Civilization is, therefore, according to the above analysis, the stage of development in society at which the division of labor, the exchange between individuals arising from it, and the commodity production which combines them both come to their full growth and revolutionizes the whole of previous society.

At all earlier stages of society, production was essentially collective, just as consumption proceeded by direct distribution of the products within larger or smaller communistic communities. This collective production was very limited; but inherent in it was the producers' control over their process of production and their product. They knew what became of their product: they consumed it; it did not leave their hands. And so long as production remains on this basis, it cannot grow above the heads of the producers nor raise up incorporeal alien powers against them, as in civilization is always and inevitably the case.

But the division of labor slowly insinuates itself into this process of production. It undermines the collectivity of production and appropriation, elevates appropriation by individuals into the general rule, and thus creates exchange between individuals—how it does so, we have examined above. Gradually commodity production becomes the dominating form.

With commodity production, production no longer for use by the producers but for exchange, the products necessarily change hands. In exchanging his product, the producer surrenders it; he no longer knows what becomes of it. When money, and with money the merchant, steps in as intermediary between the producers, the process of exchange becomes still more complicated, the final fate of the products still more uncertain. The merchants are numerous, and none of them knows what the other is doing. The commodities already pass not only from hand to hand; they also pass from market to market; the producers have lost control over the total production within their own spheres, and the merchants have not gained it. Products and production become subjects of chance.

But chance is only the one pole of a relation whose other pole is named "necessity." In the world of nature where chance also seems to rule, we have long since demonstrated in each separate field the inner necessity and law asserting itself in this chance. But what is true of the natural world is true also of society. The more a social activity, a series of social processes, becomes too powerful for men's consicious control and grows above their heads, and the more it appears a matter of pure chance, then all the more surely within this chance the laws peculiar to it and inherent in it assert themselves as if by natural necessity. Such laws also govern the chances of commodity production and exchange. To the individuals producing or exchanging, they appear as alien, at first often unrecognized, powers, whose nature must first be laboriously investigated and established. These economic laws of commodity production are modified with the various stages of this form of production; but in general the whole period of civilization is dominated by them. And still to this day the product rules the producer; still to this day the total production of society is regulated, not by a jointly devised plan, but by blind laws which manifest themselves with elemental violence in the final instance in the storms of the periodical trade crises.

We saw above how at a fairly early stage in the development of production, human labor power obtains the capacity of producing a considerably greater product than is required for the maintenance of the producers, and how this stage of development was in the main the same as that in which division of labor and exchange between individuals arises. It was not long then before the great "truth" was discovered that man also can be a commodity, that human energy can be exchanged and put to use by making a man into a slave. Hardly had men begun to exchange than already they themselves were being exchanged. The active became the passive, whether the men liked it or not.

With slavery, which attained its fullest development under civilization, came the first great cleavage of society into an exploiting and an exploited class. This cleavage persisted during the whole civilized period. Slavery is the first form of exploitation, the form peculiar to the ancient world; it is succeeded by serfdom in the middle ages and wage labor in the more recent period. These are the three great forms of servitude characteristic of the three great epochs of civilization; open, and in recent times disguised, slavery always accompanies them.

The stage of commodity production with which civilization begins is distinguished economically by the introduction of (1) metal money and with it money capital, interest and usury, (2) merchants as the class of intermediaries between the producers, (3) private ownership of land and the mortgage system, (4) slave labor as the dominant form of production. The form of family corresponding to civilization and coming to definite supremacy with it is monogamy, the domination of the man over the woman and the single family as the economic unit of society. The central link in civilized society is the state, which in all typical periods is without exception the state of the ruling class and in all cases continues to be essentially a machine for holding down the oppressed, exploited class. Also characteristic of civilization is the establishment of a permanent opposition between town and country as the basis of the whole social division of labor; and further, the introduction of wills whereby the owner of property is still able to dispose over it even when he is dead. This institution, which is a direct affront to the old gentile constitution, was unknown in Athens until the time of Solon; in Rome it was introduced early, though we do not know the date;* among the Germans it was the clerics who introduced it in order that there might be nothing to stop the pious German from leaving his legacy to the Church.

With this as its basic constitution, civilization achieved things of which gentile society was not even remotely capable. But it achieved them by setting in motion the lowest instincts and passions in man and developing them at the expense of all his other abilities. From its first day to this, sheer greed was the driving spirit of civilization; wealth and again wealth and once more wealth, wealth, not of society but of the single scurvy individual—here was its one and final aim. If at the same time the progressive development of science

---

* The second part of Lassalle's *Das System der erworbenen Rechte (System of Acquired Rights)* turns chiefly on the proposition that the Roman testament is as old as Rome itself, that there was never in Roman history "a time when there were no testaments," and that, on the contrary, the testament originated in pre-Roman times out of the cult of the dead. Lassalle, as a faithful Hegelian of the old school, derives the provisions of Roman law not from the social relations of the Romans but from the "speculative concept" of the human will, and so arrives at this totally unhistorical conclusion. This is not to be wondered at in a book which comes to the conclusion, on the ground of the same speculative concept, that the transfer of property was a purely secondary matter in Roman inheritance. Lassalle not only believes in the illusions of the Roman jurists, particularly of the earlier periods; he outdoes them.

and a repeated flowering of supreme art dropped into its lap, it was only because without them modern wealth could not have completely realized its achievements.

Since civilization is founded on the exploitation of one class by another class, its whole development proceeds in a constant contradiction. Every step forward in production is at the same time a step backward in the position of the oppressed class, that is, of the great majority. Whatever benefits some necessarily injures the others; every fresh emancipation of one class is necessarily a new oppression for another class. The most striking proof of this is provided by the introduction of machinery, the effects of which are now known to the whole world. And if among the barbarians, as we saw, the distinction between rights and duties could hardly be drawn, civilization makes the difference and antagonism between them clear even to the dullest intelligence by giving one class practically all the rights and the other class practically all the duties.

But that should not be; what is good for the ruling class must also be good for the whole of society with which the ruling class identifies itself. Therefore the more civilization advances, the more it is compelled to cover the evils it necessarily creates with the cloak of love and charity, to palliate them or to deny them—in short, to introduce a conventional hypocrisy which was unknown to earlier forms of society and even to the first stages of civilization, and which culminates in the pronouncement: the exploitation of the oppressed class is carried on by the exploiting class simply and solely in the interests of the exploited class itself; and if the exploited class cannot see it and even grows rebellious, that is the basest ingratitude to its benefactors, the exploiters.*

And now, in conclusion, Morgan's judgment of civilization:

Since the advent of civilization, the outgrowth of property has been so immense, its forms so diversified, its uses so expanding and its

---

* I originally intended to place the brilliant criticism of civilization which is found scattered through the work of Charles Fourier beside that of Morgan and my own. Unfortunately, I have not the time. I will only observe that Fourier already regards monogamy and private property in land as the chief characteristics of civilization, and that he calls civilization a war of the rich against the poor. We also find already in his work the profound recognition that in all societies which are imperfect and split into antagonisms single families (les familles incohérentes) are the economic units.

management so intelligent in the interests of its owners, that it has become, on the part of the people, *an unmanageable power. The human mind stands bewildered in the presence of its own creation.* The time will come, nevertheless, when human intelligence will rise to the mastery over property, and define the relations of the state to the property it protects, as well as the obligations and the limits of the rights of its owners. The interests of society are paramount to individual interests, and the two must be brought into just and harmonious relations. A mere property career is not the final destiny of mankind, if progress is to be the law of the future as it has been of the past. The time which has passed away since civilization began is but a fragment of the past duration of man's existence; and but a fragment of the ages yet to come. The dissolution of society bids fair to become the termination of a career of which property is the end and aim; because such a career contains the elements of self-destruction. Democracy in government, brotherhood in society, equality in rights and privileges, and universal education, foreshadow the next higher plane of society to which experience, intelligence and knowledge are steadily tending. *It will be a revival, in a higher form, of the liberty, equality and fraternity of the ancient gentes* [1963: 561-562; Engels' italics].

A RECENTLY DISCOVERED CASE OF GROUP MARRIAGE [30]

SINCE IT has recently become fashionable among certain rationalistic ethnographers to deny the existence of group marriage, the following report is of interest; I translate it from the *Russkiye Vyedomosti,* Moscow, October 14, 1892 (Old Style). Not only group marriage, i.e., the right of mutual sexual intercourse between a number of men and a number of women, is expressly affirmed to be in full force, but a form of group marriage which closely follows the punaluan marriage of the Hawaiians, the most developed and classic phase of group marriage. While the typical punaluan family consists of a number of brothers (own and collateral) who are married to a number of own and collateral sisters, we here find on the island of Sakhalin that a man is married to all the wives of his brothers and to all the sisters of his wife, which means, seen from the woman's side, that his wife may freely practice sexual intercourse with the brothers of her husband and the husbands of her sisters. It therefore differs from the typical form of punaluan marriage only in the fact that the brothers of the husband and the husbands of the sisters are not necessarily the same persons.

It should further be observed that this report again confirms what I said in *The Origin of the Family,* 4th edition: [31] group marriage does not look at all like what our brother-obsessed philistine imagines; the partners in group marriage do not lead in public the same kind of lascivious life as he practices in secret, but that this form of marriage, at least in the instances still known to occur today, differs in practice from a loose pairing marriage or from polygamy only in the fact that custom permits sexual intercourse in a number of cases where otherwise it would be severely punished.

30. This article by Engels was published in *Die Neue Zeit* in 1892 (XI, No. 12, Band 2, 373-75).
31. See p. 109 of this volume.

That the actual exercise of these rights is gradually dying out only proves that this form of marriage is itself destined to die out, which is further confirmed by its infrequency.

The whole description, moreover, is interesting because it again demonstrates the similarity, even the identity in their main characteristics, of the social institutions of primitive peoples at approximately the same stage of development. Most of what the report states about these Mongoloids on the island of Sakhalin also holds for the Dravidian tribes of India, the South Sea Islanders at the time of their discovery, and the American Indians. The report runs:

"At the session of October 10 (Old Style; October 22, New Style) of the Anthropological Section of the Society of the Friends of Natural Science, N. A. Yanchuk read an interesting communication from Mr. [Lev J.] Sternberg on the Gilyaks, a little-studied tribe on the island of Sakhalin, who are at the cultural level of savagery. The Gilyaks are acquainted neither with agriculture nor with pottery; they procure their food chiefly by hunting and fishing; they warm water in wooden vessels by throwing in heated stones, etc. Of particular interest are their institutions relating to the family and to the gens. The Gilyak addresses as father, not only his own natural father, but also all the brothers of his father; all the wives of these brothers, as well as all the sisters of his mother, he addresses as his mothers; the children of all these 'fathers' and 'mothers' he addresses as his brothers and sisters. This system of address also exists, as is well known, among the Iroquois and other Indian tribes of North America, as also among some tribes of India. But whereas in these cases it has long since ceased to correspond to the actual conditions, among the Gilyaks it serves to designate *a state still valid today*. To this day *every Gilyak has the rights of a husband in regard to the wives of his brothers and to the sisters of his wife;* at any rate, the exercise of these rights is not regarded as impermissible. These survivals of group marriage on the basis of the gens are reminiscent of the well-known punaluan marriage which still existed in the Sandwich Islands in the first half of this century. Family and gens relations of this type form the basis of the whole gentile order and social constitution of the Gilyaks.

"The gens of a Gilyak consists of all—nearer and more remote,

real and nominal—brothers of his father, of their fathers and
mothers (?), of the children of his brothers, and of his own
children. One can readily understand that a gens so constituted may
comprise an enormous number of people. Life within the gens proceeds according to the following principles. Marriage within the
gens is unconditionally prohibited. When a Gilyak dies, his wife
passes by decision of the gens to one of his brothers, own or
nominal. The gens provides for the maintenance of all of its members who are unable to work. 'We have no poor,' said a Gilyak to
the writer. 'Whoever is in need, is fed by the *khal* [gens].' The
members of the gens are further united by common sacrificial ceremonies and festivals, a common burial place, etc.

"The gens guarantees the life and security of its members against
attacks by non-gentiles; the means of repression used is blood
revenge, though under Russian rule the practice has very much
declined. Women are completely excepted from gentile blood
revenge. In some very rare cases the gens adopts members of other
gentes. It is a general rule that the property of a deceased member
may not pass out of the gens; in this respect the famous provision
of the Twelve Tables holds literally among the Gilyaks: *si suos
heredes non habet, gentiles familiam habento*—if he has no heirs
of his own, the members of the gens shall inherit. No important
event takes place in the life of a Gilyak without participation by
the gens. Not very long ago, about one or two generations, the
oldest gentile member was the head of the community, the *starosta*
of the gens; today the functions of the chief elder of the gens are
restricted almost solely to presiding over religious ceremonies. The
gentes are often dispersed among widely distant places, but even
when separated the members of a gens still remember one another
and continue to give one another hospitality, and to provide mutual
assistance and protection, etc. Except under the most extreme
necessity, the Gilyak never leaves the fellow members of his gens
or the graves of his gens. Gentile society has impressed a very
definite stamp on the whole mental life of the Gilyaks, on their
character, their customs and institutions. The habit of common
discussion and decision on all matters, the necessity of continually
taking an active part in all questions affecting the members of the
gens, the solidarity of blood revenge, the fact of being compelled
and accustomed to live together with ten or more like himself in

great tents (*yurtas*), and, in short, to be always with other people—all this has given the Gilyak a sociable and open character. The Gilyak is extraordinarily hospitable; he loves to entertain guests and to come himself as a guest. This admirable habit of hospitality is especially prominent in times of distress. In a bad year, when a Gilyak has nothing for himself or for his dogs to eat, he does not stretch out his hand for alms, but confidently seeks hospitality, and is fed, often for a considerable time.

"Among the Gilyaks of Sakhalin crimes from motives of personal gain practically never occur. The Gilyak keeps his valuables in a storehouse, which is never locked. He has such a keen sense of shame that if he is convicted of a disgraceful act, he immediately goes into the forest and hangs himself. Murder is very rare, and is hardly ever committed except in anger, never from intentions of gain. In his dealings with other people, the Gilyak shows himself honest, reliable, and conscientious.

"Despite their long subjection to the Manchurians, now become Chinese, and despite the corrupting influence of the settlement of the Amur district, the Gilyaks still preserve in their moral character many of the virtues of a primitive tribe. But the fate awaiting their social order cannot be averted. One or two more generations, and the Gilyaks on the mainland will have been completely Russianized, and together with the benefits of culture they will also acquire its defects. The Gilyaks on the island of Sakhalin, being more or less remote from the centers of Russian settlement, have some prospect of preserving their way of life unspoiled rather longer. But among them, too, the influence of their Russian neighbors is beginning to make itself felt. The Gilyaks come into the villages to trade, they go to Nikolaievsk to look for work; and every Gilyak who returns from such work to his home brings with him the same atmosphere which the Russian worker takes back from the town into his village. And at the same time, working in the town, with its chances and changes of fortune, destroys more and more that primitive equality which is such a prominent feature of the artlessly simple economic life of these peoples.

"Mr. Sternberg's article, which also contains information about their religious views and customs and their legal institutions, will appear unabridged in the *Etnografitcheskoye Obozrenie* (*Ethnographical Review*)."

APPENDIX

THE PART PLAYED BY LABOR IN THE TRANSITION FROM APE TO MAN

by Frederick Engels

EDITOR'S INTRODUCTION

THE CONCEPT that Engels apparently intended to develop in this unfinished essay[1] is most pertinent today: the complete interdependence of human social relations and human relations to nature. His argument runs that central to both is labor, the "basic prime condition for all human existence." It was through labor that humanity created itself as a skillful, large-brained, language-using animal, and through labor that it created an elaborate cultural superstructure. The very impressiveness of mankind's mental achievements, however, has obscured the fundamental significance of labor. Furthermore, the separation of planning for labor from the labor itself, a development of complex society, contributed to the rise of an idealistic world outlook, one that explains people's actions "as arising out of thoughts instead of their needs."

This idealistic viewpoint, Engels continues, has made it difficult for people to comprehend how labor has transformed their physical selves, their natural surroundings, and their own society. However, through overcoming idealism and through the enormous advances being made in the natural sciences, we are increasingly in a position to apprehend the far-reaching natural and social effects of our actions. Centrally important is the fact that humanity has allowed labor to become transferred from production for use to production for profit, regardless of the consequences for itself or for the earth. People cannot, however, stand apart from nature and "rule over" it; they can only learn and apply its laws correctly. It is when Engels embarks on an elaboration of the destructiveness to nature as a result of man's profit-making course and the necessity for revolutionizing society in order to arrest its pernicious effects that, tantalizingly, he breaks off.

The body of the essay as it stands, then, deals with human

---

1. Written in 1876, this essay was originally planned as an introduction to a more extensive work under the title of "Three Main Forms of Enslavement." The project was never completed, and the essay breaks off in the middle of a sentence.

physical evolution, for which Engels projects a sequence of related processes. When the gregarious tree-dwelling animal described by Darwin took to the ground and began to assume erect posture, its hands were freed from locomotion. It could then—painfully and slowly—embark on the use of tools to assist in obtaining food. This use of tools distinguished its activity from the foraging of the other primates; it constituted *labor,* "planned" action directed toward the *mastery* of nature. It led to the need for communication, hence the emergence of language. It also led to the refinement of the hand and enlargement of the brain which together made possible the making of better tools, as well as clothing and shelter. This, plus the extension of the diet to include meat, enabled our ancestor to move into all climates; full-fledged humans had emerged. Engels speaks of *society* (*gesellschaft*) as now appearing although the term today is used for simpler as well as more complex social forms. In any case, mankind was now prepared to create more adequate and diversified industries, to domesticate animals and plants, and to develop art and science, and political and religious life.

As is to be expected, some details of Engels' outline are incorrect; some today seem bizarre, such as that peoples exist who have physically degenerated (252); that new chemical substances from an increasingly varied diet were "premises" for the transition to man (256); or the possibility that any major continental changes could have occurred recently enough to affect human evolution. On the whole, however, Engels' statement has a remarkably contemporary ring, and for anything comparable, we have to turn to recent work. For example, Washburn writes in an article on "Tools and Human Evolution":

. . . it appears that man-apes—creatures able to run but not yet walk on two legs, and with brains no larger than those of apes now living— had already learned to make and to use tools. It follows that the structure of modern man must be the result of the change in the terms of natural selection that came with the tool-using way of life. . . . It was the success of the simplest tools that started the whole trend of human evolution. . . . Tools, hunting, fire, complex social life, speech, the human way and the brain evolved together to produce ancient man of the genus Homo about half a million years ago. Then the brain evolved under the pressures of more complex social life until the species Homo sapiens appeared perhaps as recently as 50,000 years ago.[2]

Engels criticizes Darwin's followers for being so caught up in idealistic modes of thinking as not to perceive the centrality of labor—as expressed in tool-making—in human evolution. Darwin himself was more concerned to prove man's kinship to the higher primates than to define basic differences, and to demonstrate the basis for human development in such things as their sociability, curiosity, and display of emotion. In the extremely productive, but very pragmatic, scientific atmosphere of ensuing years, attention was focused not so much on the processes through which man emerged as on ascertaining the major morphological steps in human evolution, or, in popular terms, on discovering "missing links." Successive discoveries of very early skeletal and skull fragments were first assigned to separate genera, but recently, with their increasing numbers and need for synthesis, they have been grouped into what are widely accepted as four definable evolutionary stages:

1. *Australopithecus,* discovered by Leakey in East Africa, evolved prior to and during the long early Pleistocene (the "Ice Age"). Although very small-brained, he has been found in juxtaposition with stone tools that could have been made by no other candidate that has yet appeared. It was the final acceptance of his humanity that led to statements such as Washburn's above, stressing that tool-making preceded human brain size, and not vice versa. In fact, the period during which small-brained men used crude tools with little change turns out to be extremely long. It was more than two million years before circumstances impelled and/or the evolution of the brain enabled a new advance in the refinement and specialization of tools.[3]

2. Sherwood L. Washburn, "Tools and Human Evolution," *Scientific American,* September 1960 *(Scientific American* Offprint No. 601). For further discussion of man's evolution see the chapters by Washburn and Irven DeVore, by G. F. Debetz, and by Kenneth P. Oakley in Sherwood L. Washburn, ed., *Social Life of Early Man,* Chicago, Aldine Publishing Company, 1961.

3. Jane B. Lancaster, "On the Evolution of Tool-Using Behavior," *American Anthropoligist,* Vol. 70, No. 1, 1968.

2. *Homo erectus* of the Lower Pleistocene, including "Java man" (*Pithecanthropus erectus*), "China man" (*Sinanthropus pekinensis*) and various other finds that are now accepted as more closely related than they were originally thought to be.

3. *Homo neanderthalensis*, of the Middle Pleistocene. Beetle-browed and stooped, but very close to modern humans, Neanderthal man is the "cave man" of cartoon fame to whom all manner of doubtful behaviors have been imputed by the mass media.

4. *Homo sapiens*, who entered the scene some 50,000 years ago during the end of the Ice Age. His close kinship to his predecessor is sometimes expressed by considering them separate sub-species. hence *Homo sapiens neanderthalensis* and *Homo sapiens sapiens*.

While there is still considerable interest in filling in more details of what is a very sketchy picture, physical anthropology, in keeping with the mid-20th century concern with processes, has largely turned its attention in both laboratory and field to the interpretation of evolutionary steps and mechanisms. Extremely fruitful has been the extrapolation of suppositions about early human behavior based on observations of man's living primate relatives, on archaeological materials, and on ethnographic data pertaining to the demography, economy, and social forms among hunter-gatherers. In particular the data verify the cooperativeness of early man, and contradict the cliché—so common in casual talk, political rhetoric, and science itself—that becoming "civilized" has been a process of overcoming our brutish "animal" nature. This theme, that allocates our contemporary problems not to the nature of our social structure but to imputed "instinctual" causes, has recently been widely popularized by Robert Ardrey's argument that war and competition are based on the predatory instincts of our "killer ape" ancestor.[4] The fact is that the adoption of hunting must have enormously strengthened human cooperative activity.

When one does not know interrelated developments in precise sequential detail, it is extremely difficult to describe them in other than teleological phrasings that confuse outcomes with causes. We do not know what combination of circumstances committed randomly tool-using apes to dependence upon tools. but the func-

4. Robert Ardrey, *African Genesis*, New York, Dell Publishing Co., 1963.

tional interrelation of ultimate outcomes is clear. In addition to and along with an expanded brain and the emergence of language was the prolongation of infancy. This was in turn related to a number of other developments: the need for tighter band organization and a home base to support and protect the young, and the concomitant need for regularized intergroup relations for the finding of mates. (The prolongation of infancy would reduce the number of available mates in a group of a small enough size to maintain itself within a given territory; hence the practice of out-marriage and all its further consequences in relation to incest taboos and the like would have occurred early in human evolution.) The carrying of food to the home base must early have led to the development of containers, which, unlike stone tools, leave no record of their existence. And in this context, the sexual division of labor, with men turning to hunting, would strengthen cooperative effort. Washburn and Lancaster write, "hunting and butchering large animals put a maximum premium on cooperation among males, a behavior that is at an absolute minimum among the nonhuman primates. . . . It is important to stress . . . that human hunting is a set of ways of life. It involves divisions of labor between male and female, sharing according to custom, cooperation among males, planning, knowledge of many species and large areas, and technical skill."[5] This, then, is the heritage of the "killer ape."

—E.B.L.

5. Sherwood L. Washburn and C. S. Lancaster, "The Evolution of Hunting," in Richard B. Lee and Irven DeVore, eds., *Man the Hunter,* Chicago, Aldine Publishing Company, 1968.

THE PART PLAYED BY LABOR IN THE TRANSITION FROM APE TO MAN

LABOR IS the source of all wealth, the political economists assert. And it really is the source—next to nature, which supplies it with the material that it converts into wealth. But it is even infinitely more than this. It is the prime basic condition for all human existence, and this to such an extent that, in a sense, we have to say that labor created man himself.

Many hundreds of thousands of years ago, during an epoch, not yet definitely determinable, of that period of the earth's history known to geologists as the Tertiary period, most likely toward the end of it, a particularly highly-developed race of anthropoid apes lived somewhere in the tropical zone—probably on a great continent that has now sunk to the bottom of the Indian Ocean. Darwin has given us an approximate description of these ancestors of ours. They were completely covered with hair, they had beards and pointed ears, and they lived in bands in the trees.

Climbing assigns different functions to the hands and the feet, and when their mode of life involved locomotion on level ground, these apes gradually got out of the habit of using their hands [in walking] and adopted a more and more erect posture. This was *the decisive step in the transition from ape to man.*

All extant anthropoid apes can stand erect and move about on their feet alone, but only in case of urgent need and in a very clumsy way. Their natural gait is in a half-erect posture and includes the use of the hands. The majority rest the knuckles of the fist on the ground and, with legs drawn up, swing the body through their long arms, much as a cripple moves on crutches. In general, all the transition stages from walking on all fours to walking on two legs are still to be observed among the apes today. The latter gait, however, has never become more than a makeshift for any of them.

It stands to reason that if erect gait among our hairy ancestors became first the rule and then, in time, a necessity, other diverse functions must, in the meantime, have devolved upon the hands. Already among the apes there is some difference in the way the hands and the feet are employed. In climbing, as mentioned above, the hands and feet have different uses. The hands are used mainly for gathering and holding food in the same way as the forepaws of the lower mammals are used. Many apes use their hands to build themselves nests in the trees or even to construct roofs between the branches to protect themselves against the weather, as the chimpanzee, for example, does. With their hands they grasp sticks to defend themselves against enemies, and with their hands they bombard their enemies with fruits and stones. In captivity they use their hands for a number of simple operations copied from human beings. It is in this that one sees the great gulf between the undeveloped hand of even the most man-like apes and the human hand that has been highly perfected by hundreds of thousands of years of labor. The number and general arrangement of the bones and muscles are the same in both, but the hand of the lowest savage can perform hundreds of operations that no simian hand can imitate—no simian hand has ever fashioned even the crudest stone knife.

The first operations for which our ancestors gradually learned to adapt their hands during the many thousands of years of transition from ape to man could have been only very simple ones. The lowest savages, even those in whom regression to a more animal-like condition with a simultaneous physical degeneration can be assumed, are nevertheless far superior to these transitional beings. Before the first flint could be fashioned into a knife by human hands, a period of time probably elapsed in comparison with which the historical period known to us appears insignificant. But the decisive step had been taken, *the hand had become free* and could henceforth attain ever greater dexterity; the greater flexibility thus acquired was inherited and increased from generation to generation.

Thus the hand is not only the organ of labor, *it is also the product of labor*. Labor, adaptation to ever new operations, the inheritance of muscles, ligaments, and, over longer periods of time, bones that had undergone special development and the ever renewed employment of this inherited finesse in new, more and more complicated operations, have given the human hand the high degree of perfection required to conjure into being the pictures of a Raphael, the statues of a Thorwaldsen, the music of a Paganini.

But the hand did not exist alone, it was only one member of an integral, highly complex organism. And what benefited the hand, benefited also the whole body it served; and this in two ways.

In the first place, the body benefited from the law of correlation of growth, as Darwin called it. This law states that the specialized forms of separate parts of an organic being are always bound up with certain forms of other parts that apparently have no connection with them. Thus all animals that have red blood cells without cell nuclei, and in which the head is attached to the first vertebra by means of a double articulation (condyles), also without exception possess lacteal glands for suckling their young. Similarly, cloven hoofs in mammals are regularly associated with the possession of a multiple stomach for rumination. Changes in certain forms involve changes in the form of other parts of the body, although we cannot explain the connection. Perfectly white cats with blue eyes are always, or almost always, deaf. The gradually increasing perfection of the human hand, and the commensurate adaptation of the feet for erect gait, have undoubtedly, by virtue of such correlation, reacted on other parts of the organism. However, this action has not as yet been sufficiently investigated for us to be able to do more here than to state the fact in general terms.

Much more important is the direct, demonstrable influence of the development of the hand on the rest of the organism. It has already been noted that our simian ancestors were gregarious; it is obviously impossible to seek the derivation of man, the most social of all animals, from non-gregarious immediate ancestors. Mastery over nature began with the development of the hand, with labor, and widened man's horizon at every new advance. He was continually discovering new, hitherto unknown, properties in natural objects. On the other hand, the development of labor necessarily helped to bring the members of society closer together by increasing cases of mutual support and joint activity, and by making clear the advantage of this joint activity to each individual. In short, men in the making arrived at the point where *they had something to say* to each other. Necessity created the organ; the undeveloped larynx of the ape was slowly but surely transformed by modulation to produce constantly more developed modulation, and the organs of the mouth gradually learned to pronounce one articulate sound after another.[1]

Comparison with animals proves that this explanation of the origin of language from and in the process of labor is the only correct one. The little that even the most highly developed animals need to communicate to each other does not require articulate speech. In a state of nature, no animal feels handicapped by its inability to speak or to understand human speech. It is quite different when it has been tamed by man. The dog and the horse, by association with man, have developed such a good ear for articulate speech that they easily learn to understand any language within their range of concept. Moreover they have acquired the capacity for feelings such as affection for man, gratitude, etc., which were previously foreign to them. Anyone who has had much to do with such animals will hardly be able to escape the conviction that in many cases they *now* feel their inability to speak as a defect, although, unfortunately, it is one that can no longer be remedied because their vocal organs are too specialized in a definite direction. However, where vocal organs exist, within certain limits even this inability disappears. The buccal organs of birds are as different from those of man as they can be, yet birds are the only animals that can learn to speak; and it is the bird with the most hideous voice, the parrot, that speaks best of all. Let no one object that the parrot does not understand what it says. It is true that for the sheer pleasure of talking and associating with human beings, the parrot will chatter for hours at a stretch, continually repeating its whole vocabulary. But within the limits of its range of concepts it can also learn to understand what it is saying. Teach a parrot swear words in such a way that it gets an

---

1. Actually pronunciation is not the main problem; instead, it is the intellectual feat of symbolization basic to language. Animals communicate in many ways, but their communication is limited to reactions to the immediate situation—to warnings of danger, sexual invitations, challenges, and the like. Language involves being able to detach the communication from the immediate situation, through assigning to arbitrary clusters of sounds specific meanings to do not only with objects, acts, and feelings, but also with things and events of the past and the future, both possible and impossible.

idea of their meaning (one of the great amusements of sailors returning from the tropics); tease it and you will soon discover that it knows how to use its swear words just as correctly as a Berlin costermonger. The same is true of begging for titbits.

First labor, after it and then with it, speech—these were the two most essential stimuli under the influence of which the brain of the ape gradually changed into that of man, which for all its similarity is far larger and more perfect. Hand in hand with the development of the brain went the development of its most immediate instruments—the senses. Just as the gradual development of speech is inevitably accompanied by a corresponding refinement of the organ of hearing, so the development of the brain as a whole is accompanied by a refinement of all the senses. The eagle sees much farther than man, but the human eye discerns considerably more in things than does the eye of the eagle. The dog has a far keener sense of smell than man, but it does not distinguish a hundredth part of the odors that for man are definite signs denoting different things. And the sense of touch, which the ape hardly possesses in its crudest form, has been developed only side by side with the development of the human hand itself, through the medium of labor.

The reaction on labor and speech of the development of the brain and its attendant senses, of the increasing clarity of consciousness, power of abstraction and of judgement, gave both labor and speech an ever renewed impulse to further development. This development did not reach its conclusion when man finally became distinct from the ape, but on the whole made further powerful progress, its degree and direction varying among different peoples and at different times, and here and there even being interrupted by local or temporary regression. This further development has been strongly urged forward, on the one hand, and guided along more definite directions, on the other, by a new element which came into play with the appearance of fully fledged man, namely, *society*.

Hundreds of thousands of years—of no greater significance in the history of the earth than one second in the life of man*—

* A leading authority in this respect, Sir William Thompson, has calculated that *little more than a hundred million years* could have elapsed since the time when the earth had cooled sufficiently for plants and animals to be able to live on it.

certainly elapsed before human society arose out of a troupe of tree-climbing monkeys. Yet it did finally appear. And what do we find once more as the characteristic difference between the troupe of monkeys and human society? *Labor.* The ape herd was satisfied to browse over the feeding area determined for it by geographical conditions or the resistance of neighboring herds; it undertook migrations and struggles to win new feeding grounds, but it was incapable of extracting from them more than they offered in their natural state, except that it unconsciously fertilized the soil with its own excrement. As soon as all possible feeding grounds were occupied, there could be no further increase in the ape population; the number of animals could at best remain stationary. But all animals waste a great deal of food, and, in addition, destroy in the germ the next generation of the food supply. Unlike the hunter, the wolf does not spare the doe which would provide it with the young the next year; the goats in Greece, that eat away the young bushes before they grow to maturity, have eaten bare all the mountains of the country. This "predatory economy" of animals plays an important part in the gradual transformation of species by forcing them to adapt themselves to other than the usual food, thanks to which their blood acquires a different chemical composition and the whole physical constitution gradually alters, while species that have remained unadapted die out. There is no doubt that this predatory economy contributed powerfully to the transition of our ancestors from ape to man. In a race of apes that far surpassed all others in intelligence and adaptability, this predatory economy must have led to a continual increase in the number of plants used for food and to the consumption of more and more edible parts of food plants. In short, food became more and more varied, as did also the substances entering the body with it, substances that were the chemical premises for the transition to man. But all that was not yet labor in the proper sense of the word. Labor begins with the making of tools. And what are the most ancient tools that we find—the most ancient judging by the heirlooms of prehistoric man that have been discovered, and by the mode of life of the earliest historical peoples and of the rawest of contemporary savages? They are hunting and fishing implements, the former at the same time serving as weapons. But hunting and

fishing presuppose the transition from an exclusively vegetable diet
to the concomitant use of meat, and this is another important step
in the process of transition from ape to man. A *meat diet* contained
in an almost ready state the most essential ingredients required by
the organism for its metabolism. By shortening the time required
for digestion, it also shortened the other vegetative bodily processes that correspond to those of plant life, and thus gained further
time, material and desire for the active manifestation of animal
life proper. And the farther man in the making moved from the
vegetable kingdom the higher he rose above the animal. Just as
becoming accustomed to a vegetable diet side by side with meat
converted wild cats and dogs into the servants of man, so also
adaptation to a meat diet, side by side with a vegetable diet, greatly
contributed toward giving bodily strength and independence to man
in the making. The meat diet, however, had its greatest effect on
the brain, which now received a far richer flow of the materials
necessary for its nourishment and development, and which, therefore, could develop more rapidly and perfectly from generation to
generation. With all due respect to the vegetarians, man did not
come into existence without a meat diet, and if the latter, among
all peoples known to us, has led to cannibalism at some time or
other (the forefathers of the Berliners, the Weletabians or Wilzians,
used to eat their parents as late as the tenth century), that is of no
consequence to us today.

The meat diet led to two new advances of decisive importance—
the harnessing of fire and the domestication of animals.[2] The first
still further shortened the digestive process, as it provided the
mouth with food already, as it were, half digested; the second made
meat more copious by opening up a new, more regular source of
supply in addition to hunting, and moreover provided, in milk

2. An infelicitous juxtaposition, since the harnessing of fire occurred so
early in human evolution and the domestication of animals so late. As for
the addition of meat to the diet, its greatest significance (apart from the fact
of hunting itself) probably lay in its high caloric value relative to unprocessed
vegetable foods and its greater efficiency, therefore, as food; that protein
deficiency has adverse effects on *Homo sapiens* does not mean our vegetarian
ancestors needed meat. On cannibalism, the practice of eating dead parents
(or dead children) as part of funeral ritual is a custom that recurs in cultures
scattered around the world.

and its products, a new article of food at least as valuable as meat in its composition. Thus both these advances were, in themselves, new means for the emancipation of man. It would lead us too far afield to dwell here in detail on their indirect effects notwithstanding the great importance they have had for the development of man and society.

Just as man learned to consume everything edible, he also learned to live in any climate. He spread over the whole of the habitable world, being the only animal fully able to do so of its own accord. The other animals that have become accustomed to all climates—domestic animals and vermin—did not become so independently, but only in the wake of man. And the transition from the uniformly hot climate of the original home of man to colder regions, where the year was divided into summer and winter, created new requirements—shelter and clothing as protection against cold and damp, and hence new spheres of labor, new forms of activity, which further and further separated man from the animal.

By the combined functioning of hands, speech organs and brain, not only in each individual but also in society, men became capable of executing more and more complicated operations, and were able to set themselves, and achieve, higher and higher aims. The work of each generation itself became different, more perfect and more diversified. Agriculture was added to hunting and cattle raising; then came spinning, weaving, metalworking, pottery and navigation. Along with trade and industry, art and science finally appeared. Tribes developed into nations and states. Law and politics arose, and with them that fantastic reflection of human things in the human mind—religion. In the face of all these images, which appeared in the first place to be products of the mind and seemed to dominate human societies, the more modest productions of the working hand retreated into the background, the more so since the mind that planned the labor was able, at a very early stage in the development of society (for example, already in the primitive family), to have the labor that had been planned carried out by other hands than its own. All merit for the swift advance of civilization was ascribed to the mind, to the development and activity of the brain. Men became accustomed to explain their actions as arising out of thoughts instead of their needs (which in any case are reflected and perceived in the mind); and so in the course of time there emerged that idealistic world outlook which, especially since the fall of the world of antiquity, has dominated men's minds. It still rules them to such a degree that even the most materialistic natural scientists of the Darwinian school are still unable to form any clear idea of the origin of man, because under this ideological influence they do not recognize the part that has been played therein by labor.

Animals, as has already been pointed out, change the environment by their activities in the same way, even if not to the same extent, as man does, and these changes, as we have seen, in turn react upon and change those who made them. In nature nothing takes place in isolation. Everything affects and is affected by every other thing, and it is mostly because this manifold motion and interaction is forgotten that our natural scientists are prevented from gaining a clear insight into the simplest things. We have seen how goats have prevented the regeneration of forests in Greece; on the island of St. Helena, goats and pigs brought by the first arrivals have succeeded in exterminating its old vegetation almost completely, and so have prepared the ground for the spreading of plants brought by later sailors and colonists. But animals exert a lasting effect on their environment unintentionally and, as far as the animals themselves are concerned, accidentally. The further removed men are from animals, however, the more their effect on nature assumes the character of premeditated, planned action directed toward definite preconceived ends. The animal destroys the vegetation of a locality without realizing what it is doing. Man destroys it in order to sow field crops on the soil thus released, or to plant trees or vines which he knows will yield many times the amount planted. He transfers useful plants and domestic animals from one country to another and thus changes the flora and fauna of whole continents. More than this. Through artificial breeding both plants and animals are so changed by the hand of man that they become unrecognizable. The wild plants from which our grain varieties originated are still being sought in vain. There is still some dispute about the wild animals from which our very different breeds of dogs or our equally numerous breeds of horses are descended.

Of course, it would not occur to us to dispute the ability of animals to act in a planned, premeditated fashion. On the contrary, a planned mode of action exists in embryo wherever protoplasm, living albumen, exists and reacts, that is, carries out definite, even if extremely simple, movements as a result of definite external stimuli. Such reaction takes place even where there is yet no cell at all, far less a nerve cell. There is something of the planned action in the way insect-eating plants capture their prey, although they do it quite unconsciously. In animals the capacity for conscious, planned action is proportional to the development of the nervous system, and among mammals it attains a fairly high level. While fox hunting in England, one can daily observe how unerringly the fox makes use of its excellent knowledge of the locality in order to elude its pursuers, and how well it knows and turns to account all favorable features of the ground that cause the scent to be lost. Among our domestic animals, more highly developed thanks to association with man, one can constantly observe acts of cunning on exactly the same level as those of children. For, just as the developmental history of the human embryo in the mother's womb is only an abbreviated repetition of the history, extending over millions of years, of the bodily evolution of our animal ancestors, starting from the worm, so the mental development of the human child is only a still more abbreviated repetition of the intellectual development of these same ancestors, at least of the later ones. But all the planned action of all animals has never succeeded in impressing the stamp of their will upon the earth. That was left for man.

In short, the animal merely *uses* its environment, and brings about changes in it simply by his presence; man by his changes makes it serve his ends, *masters* it. This is the final, essential distinction between man and other animals, and once again it is labor that brings about this distinction.

Let us not, however, flatter ourselves overmuch on account of our human victories over nature. For each such victory nature takes its revenge on us. Each victory, it is true, in the first place brings about the results we expected, but in the second and third places it has quite different, unforeseen effects which only too often cancel the first. The people who, in Mesopotamia, Greece, Asia Minor and elsewhere, destroyed the forests to obtain cultivable land, never dreamed that by removing along with the forests the collecting centers and reservoirs of moisture they were laying the basis for the present forlorn state of those countries. When the Italians of the Alps used up the pine forests on the southern slopes, so carefully cherished on the northern slopes, they had no inkling that by doing so they were cutting at the roots of the dairy industry in their region; they had still less inkling that they were thereby depriving their mountain springs of water for the greater part of the year, and making it possible for them to pour still more furious torrents on the plains during the rainy seasons. Those who spread the potato in Europe were not aware that with these farinaceous tubers they were at the same time spreading scrofula.[3] Thus at every step we are reminded that we by no means rule over nature like a conqueror over a foreign people. like someone standing outside nature—but that we, with flesh, blood and brain, belong to nature, and exist in its midst, and that all our mastery of it consists in the fact that we have the advantage over all other creatures of being able to learn its laws and apply them correctly.

And, in fact, with every day that passes we are acquiring a better understanding of these laws and getting to perceive both the more immediate and the more remote consequences of our interference with the traditional course of nature. In particular, after the mighty advances made by the natural sciences in the present century, we are more than ever in a position to realize and hence to control even the more remote natural consequences of at least our day-to-day production activities. But the more this progresses the more will men not only feel but also know their oneness with nature, and the more impossible will become the senseless and unnatural idea of a contrast between mind and matter, man and nature, soul and body, such as arose after the decline of classical antiquity in Europe and obtained its highest elaboration of Christianity.

It required the labor of thousands of years for us to learn a little of how to calculate the more remote *natural* effects of our actions in the field of production, but it has been still more dif-

3. Scrofula, once thought to be spread by potatoes, is associated with the poverty and malnourishment of people subsisting almost entirely on them.

ficult in regard to the more remote *social* effects of these actions. We mentioned the potato and the resulting spread of scrofula. But what is scrofula compared to the effect which the reduction of the workers to a potato diet had on the living conditions of the masses of the people in whole countries, or compared to the famine the potato blight brought to Ireland in 1847, which consigned to the grave a million Irishmen, nourished solely or almost exclusively on potatoes, and forced the emigration overseas of two million more? When the Arabs learned to distil spirits, it never entered their heads that by so doing they were creating one of the chief weapons for the annihilation of the aborigines of the then still undiscovered American continent. And when afterward Columbus discovered this America, he did not know that by doing so he was laying the basis for the Negro slave trade and giving a new lease of life to slavery, which in Europe had long ago been done away with. The men who in the 17th and 18th centuries labored to create the steam engine had no idea that they were preparing the instrument which more than any other was to revolutionize social relations throughout the world. Especially in Europe, by concentrating wealth in the hands of a minority and dispossessing the huge majority, this instrument was destined at first to give social and political domination to the bourgeoisie, but later, to give rise to a class struggle between bourgeoisie and proletariat which can end only in the overthrow of the bourgeoisie and the abolition of all class antagonisms. But in this sphere, too, by long and often cruel experience and by collecting and analyzing historical material, we are gradually learning to get a clear view of the indirect, more remote, social effects of our production activity, and so are afforded an opportunity to control and regulate these effects as well.

This regulation, however, requires something more than mere knowledge. It requires a complete revolution in our hitherto existing mode of production, and simultaneously a revolution in our whole contemporary social order.

All hitherto existing modes of production have aimed merely at achieving the most immediately and directly useful effect of labor. The further consequences, which appear only later and become effective through gradual repetition and accumulation, were

THE PART PLAYED BY LABOR

totally neglected. The original common ownership of land corresponded, on the one hand, to a level of development of human beings in which their horizon was restricted in general to what lay immediately available, and presupposed, on the other hand, a certain superfluity of land that would allow some latitude for correcting the possible bad results of this primeval type of economy. When this surplus land was exhausted, common ownership also declined. All higher forms of production, however, led to the division of the population into different classes and thereby to the antagonism of ruling and oppressed classes. Thus the interests of the ruling class became the driving factor of production, since production was no longer restricted to providing the barest means of subsistence for the oppressed people. This has been put into effect most completely in the capitalist mode of production prevailing today in Western Europe. The individual capitalists, who dominate production and exchange, are able to concern themselves only with the most immediate useful effect of their actions. Indeed, even this useful effect—inasmuch as it is a question of the usefulness of the article that is produced or exchanged—retreats far into the background, and the sole incentive becomes the profit to be made on selling.

Classical political economy, the social science of the bourgeoisie, examines mainly only effects of human actions in the fields of production and exchange that are actually intended. This fully corresponds to the social organization of which it is the theoretical expression. As individual capitalists are engaged in production and exchange for the sake of the immediate profit, only the nearest, most immediate results must first be taken into account. As long as the individual manufacturer or merchant sells a manufactured or purchased commodity with the usual coveted profit, he is satisfied and does not concern himself with what afterwards becomes of the commodity and its purchasers. The same thing applies to the natural effects of the same actions. What cared the Spanish planters in Cuba, who burned down forests on the slopes of the mountains and obtained from the ashes sufficient fertilizer for *one* generation of very highly profitable coffee trees—what cared they that the heavy tropical rainfall afterward washed away the unprotected upper stratum of the soil, leaving behind only bare rock! In relation to nature, as to society, the present mode of production is predominantly concerned only about the immediate, the most tangible result; and then surprise is expressed that the more remote effects of actions directed to this end turn out to be quite different, are mostly quite the opposite in character; that the harmony of supply and demand is transformed into the very reverse opposite, as shown by the course of each ten years' industrial cycle—even Germany has had a little preliminary experience of it in the "crash" [economic crisis of 1873]; that private ownership based on one's own labor must of necessity develop into the expropriation of the workers, while all wealth becomes more and more concentrated in the hands of non-workers; that [here the manuscript breaks off].

GLOSSARY OF SOME CONTEMPORARY TERMS
AND CONCORDANCE WITH ENGELS' USAGE

BRIDE-PRICE: Food, cloth, cattle, or other goods given by kinsmen of the bridegroom to the family of the bride, referred to by Engels as "gift payments" (112).

CROSS-COUSINS: Children of siblings of the opposite sex, i.e., child of one's mother's brother or one's father's sister. Children of siblings of the same sex are called parallel cousins. When descent is "unilineal," or counted on one side only, and marriage is "exogamous," or outside of the kin group, cross-cousins are outside of one's clan and are very commonly preferred marriage partners. Hence Engels' discussion, 105, 109.

ENDOGAMY: Marriage within the defined group—lineage, clan, village, etc. Castes are by definition endogamous; classes tend to be so.

EXOGAMY: Marriage outside the defined group. Clans and lineages are typically exogamous.

GENS: A group of actual and fictive kinsmen related through one parental line only. The term most commonly used today is "clan." Matrilineal lines trace relationship through the mother, patrilineal through the father. Bilateral clans are presumably transitional. All clan members are theoretically descendants of a common ancestor. Sections of the clan that can directly trace their relationships are usually referred to as lineages. Another term for a unilineal descent group, though not in common use, is "sib."

HAWAIIAN SYSTEM: A form of kin terminology in which siblings and cousins of the same sex are all referred to by the same term. The system is common in the Pacific Islands and in the Americas, although with variants in the terms used for aunts and uncles. The study of kinship terminologies and their many variations has become highly specialized with regard to typology;

more needs to be done, however, on the changes that take place within them under the impact of colonialism.

MATRILOCALITY: Residence of a newly married couple with the parents of the woman, by contrast with patrilocality, or residence with the parents of the man. Temporary matrilocality is often followed by patrilocality. Residence may also be "neolocal."

MOIETY: A division of a society into two groups, generaly unilineal and exogamous. A moiety may subsume several clans.

MOTHER RIGHT: Descent reckoned through the mother, now referred to as "matrilineality." "Patrilineal" descent is reckoned through the father. Our descent system is "bilateral." The notion of "matriarchy," or rule by women, as accompanying matrilineal descent is specifically contradicted by Engels. He writes: "To denote this exclusive recognition of descent through the mother and the relations of inheritance which in time resulted from it, he [Bachofen] uses the term 'mother right,' which for the sake of brevity I retain. The term is, however, ill-chosen, since at this stage of society [primitive communism] there cannot yet be any talk of 'right' in the legal sense" (106).

POLYGAMY, POLYGYNY, POLYANDRY: Forms of plural marriage. Polygamy is the inclusive term, although it may often be used to denote "polygyny" or plural wives. Polyandry refers to plural husbands.

PRIMITIVE: The term for peoples living in a hunting and gathering, or horticultural, economy is awkward due to its negative connotations in popular use. I retain it somewhat reluctantly for the sake of simplicity and clarity. Suffice it to say, as Engels' book documents so thoroughly, primitive peoples are more "civilized" than more "advanced" societies if the term is used to denote humanistic interpersonal relations.

TRIBE: The term generally used for groups who share a common language and culture, but who do not constitute historically evolved "nations." The term has been too loosely used, however. It has been applied alike to societies which are no more than a loose aggregate of autonomous villages and to societies where there is a relatively centralized administrative and judicial apparatus. In many cases the development of formal tribal chieftainship has taken place as part of the struggle against colonial domination. The history of many North American Indian peoples exemplifies a transition from a more informal, to a "tribal," and then "national" organization and orientation.

BIBLIOGRAPHY

Aberle, David *et al.*
1963
"The Incest Taboo and the Mating Patterns of Animals." *American Anthropologist,* Vol. 65.

Adams, Robert M.
1960
"Early Civilizations, Subsistence, and Environment." In Carl H. Kraeling and Robert M. Adams, eds., *City Invincible.* Chicago: University of Chicago Press.

1966
The Evolution of Urban Society. Chicago: Aldine Publishing Co.

Armstrong, Robert G.
1950
State Formation in Negro Africa. Unpublished doctoral dissertation. University of Chicago.

Averkieva, Iu. P.
1962
"Problems of Property in Contemporary American Ethnography." *Soviet Anthropology and Archeology,* Vol. 1, No. 1. New York: International Arts and Sciences Press.

1964
"Relationship Between Gens and Neighborhood Communities Among North American Indians." *Proceedings of the 7th International Congress of the Anthropological and Ethnological Sciences,* Moscow, Vol. IV.

Barnouw, Victor
1961
"Chippewa Social Atomism." *American Anthropologist,* Vol. 63.

Bohannan, Paul
1963
Social Antropology. New York: Holt, Rinehart and Winston.

1964
Africa and Africans. Garden City, N.Y.: The Natural History Press.

Briffault, Robert
1931
The Mothers, The Matriarchal Theory of Social Origins. New York: The Macmillan Company.

Carneiro, Robert L.
1962
"Scale Analysis as an Instrument for the Study of Cultural Evolution." *Southwestern Journal of Anthropology,* Vol. 18, No. 2.

1968
"Ascertaining, Testing, and Interpreting Sequences of Cultural Development." *Southwestern Journal of Anthropology,* Vol. 24, No. 4.

1970
"A Theory of the Origin of the State." *Science,* Vol. 169, August 21.

Childe, V. Gordon
1939
Man Makes Himself. New York: Oxford University Press.

1944
"Archaeological Ages as Technological Stages." *The Journal of the Royal Anthropological Institute of Great Britain and Ireland,* Vol. 74.

1965
What Happened in History. London: Penguin Books.

Danilova, L. V.
1966
"A Discussion of an Important Problem." *Soviet Studies in History,* Vol. IV, No. 4. New York: International Arts and Sciences Press.

Davidson, Basil
1959
Lost Cities of Africa. Boston: Little, Brown & Co.

Dole, Gertrude and
Carneiro, Robert
1960
Eds., *Essays in the Science of Culture.* New York: Thomas Y. Crowell and Co.

Engels, Frederick
1935
Ludwig Feuerbach. New York: International Publishers.

1939
Herr Eugen Dühring's Revolution in Science. New York: International Publishers.

Finley, Moses I.
1964
"Between Slavery and Freedom." *Comparative Studies in Society and History,* Vol. 6.

Fried, Morton H.
1960
"On the Evolution of Social Stratification and the State." In S. Diamond, ed., *Culture in History.* New York: Columbia University Press.

1967
The Evolution of Political Society. New York: Random House.

Godelier, Maurice
1965
"The Concept of the Asian Mode of Production and the Marxist Model of Social Development." *Soviet Anthropology and Archeology,* Vol. IV, No. 2. New York: International Arts and Sciences Press.

Goodale, Jane C.
1971
Tiwi Wives, A Study of the Women of Melville Island, North Australia. Seattle: University of Washington Press.

Grote, George
1869
A History of Greece, 12 vols., first published London, 1846-56. References are to 1869 edition.

Hamamsy, Laila Shukry
1957
"The Role of Women in a Changing Navajo Society." *American Anthropologist,* Vol. 59.

Harris, Marvin
1959
"The Economy Has No Surplus?" *American Anthropologist,* Vol. 61.

1964 — *Patterns of Race in the Americas.* New York: Walker and Company.

1965 — "The Myth of the Sacred Cow." In Anthony Leeds & Andrew P. Vayda, eds., *Man, Culture, and Animals.* Publication No. 78 of the American Association of the Advancement of Science, Washington, D.C.

1968a — *The Rise of Anthropological Theory, A History of Theories of Culture.* New York: Thomas Y. Crowell Co.

1968b — "The Rise of Anthropological Theory, Author's Précis." *Current Anthropology,* Vol. IX.

1971 — *Culture, Man, and Nature.* New York: Thomas Y. Crowell Company.

Hickerson, Harold
1962 — *The Southwestern Chippewa: An Ethnohistorical Study.* Memoir 92, The American Anthropological Association.

1967 — "Some Implications of the Theory of Particularity, or 'Atomism,' of Northwestern Algonkians." *Current Anthropology,* Vol. VIII, No. 4.

Hobhouse, L. T., Wheeler, G. and Ginsberg, M.
1965 — *The Material Conditions and Social Institutions of the Simpler Peoples.* London: Routledge and Kegan Paul.

Hogbin, Ian
1970 — *The Island of Menstruating Men.* San Francisco: Chandler Publishing Co.

Hughes, Charles Campbell
1958 — "Anomie, the Ammassalik, and the Standardization of Error." *Southwestern Journal of Anthropology,* Vol. 14, No. 4.

Jenness, Diamond
1935 — *The Ojibwa Indians of Parry Island, Their Social and Religious Life.* National Museum of Canada Bulletin, Vol. 78, Anthropological Series No. 17.

1937 — *The Sekeni Indians of British Columbia.* National Museum of Canada Bulletin, Vol. 84, Anthropological Series No. 20.

Kaberry, Phyllis M.
1939 — *Aboriginal Woman, Sacred and Profane.* London: Routledge and Sons, Ltd.

Kardiner, Abram
1939 — Ed., *The Individual and His Society.* New York: Columbia University Press.

Kardiner, Abram, Linton, Ralph, *et al.*
1945 — *The Psychological Frontiers of Society.* New York: Columbia University Press.

Klein, A. Norman
1969
Introduction to W. E. B. Du Bois, *The Suppression of the African Slave Trade to the United States of America—1638-1870.* New York: Schocken Books.

Krader, Lawrence
1968
Formation of the State. Foundations of Modern Anthropology Series, Englewood Cliffs, N.J.: Prentice-Hall.

Lantis, Margaret
1960
Eskimo Childhood and Interpersonal Relationships, Nunivak Biographies and Genealogies. Seattle: University of Washington Press.

Leacock, Eleanor
1954
The Montagnais "Hunting Territory" and the Fur Trade. Memoir 78, The American Anthropological Association.

1955
"Matrilocality in a Simple Hunting Economy (Montagnais-Naskapi)." *Southwestern Journal of Anthropology,* Vol. 11, No. 1.

1958a
Introduction to "Social Stratification and Evolutionary Theory: A Symposium." *Ethnohistory,* Vol. 5, No. 3.

1958b
"Status Among the Montagnais-Naskapi of Labrador." *Ethnohistory,* Vol. 5, No. 3.

1964
"North American Indian Society and Psychology in Historical Perspective." *Proceedings of the 7th International Congress of the Anthropological and Ethnological Sciences,* Moscow.

1969
"The Montagnais-Naskapi Band." Band Societies, ed. David Damas, *National Museums of Canada Contributions to Anthropology,* Bulletin 228, Ottawa.

1971
Ed., *The Culture of Poverty: A Critique.* New York: Simon & Schuster.

Leacock, Eleanor and
Lurie, Nancy
1971
Eds., *North American Indians in Historical Perspective.* New York: Random House.

Lee, Richard B. and
DeVore, Irven
1968
Eds., *Man the Hunter.* Chicago: Aldine Publishing Co.

Lentsman, Ia. A.
1966
"A Contribution to the Discussion of the Asiatic Mode of Production." *Soviet Studies in History,* Vol. IV, No. 4. New York: International Arts and Sciences Press.

Lévy, Jean-Philippe
1964
The Economic Life of the Ancient World. Trans. by John G. Biram. Chicago: University of Chicago Press.

Linton, Ralph
1926

Ethnology of Polynesia and Micronesia. Field Museum of Natural History, Department of Anthropology Guide, Part 6.

Lowie, Robert H.
1929

The Origin of the State. New York: Harcourt.

1939

The History of Ethnological Theory. New York: Farrar & Rinehart.

1946

"Evolution in Cultural Anthropology: A Reply to Leslie White." *American Anthropologist.* Vol. 48.

Malinowski, Bronislaw
1926

Crime and Custom in Savage Society. New York: Harcourt Brace.

Mandel, Ernest
1968

Marxist Economic Theory, Vol. I. New York: Monthly Review Press.

Martin, Kay M.
1969

"South American Foragers: A Case Study in Cultural Devolution." *American Anthropologist,* Vol. 71.

Marx, Karl
1967

Capital, Vol. I. New York: International Publishers.

1965

Pre-Capitalist Economic Formations, ed. by Eric J. Hobsbawm. New York: International Publishers.

Marx, Karl and
Engels, Frederick
1970

The German Ideology. New York: International Publishers.

Mason, Otis Tufton
1898

Woman's Share in Primitive Culture. New York: D. Appleton and Co.

Mead, Margaret
1937

Ed., *Cooperation and Competition Among Primitive Peoples.* New York: McGraw-Hill.

1950

Sex and Temperament in Three Primitive Societies. New York: New American Library.

1955

Male and Female, a Study of the Sexes in a Changing World. New York: New American Library.

Mintz, Sidney W.
1971

"Men, Women, and Trade." *Comparative Studies in History and Society,* Vol. 13, No. 3.

Morgan, Lewis Henry
1876

"Montezuma's Dinner." *North American Review,* Vol. 122. (Reprint A-251 in Bobbs-Merrill Reprint Series in the Social Sciences.)

1963

Ancient Society, ed. by Eleanor Burke Leacock. New York: World Publishing Company

Murra, John V.   *The Economic Organization of the Inca State.*
1956   Unpublished doctoral dissertation. University
                             of Chicago.

1962   "Cloth and its Function in the Inca State."
                             American Anthropologist, Vol. 64.

1967   "On Inca Political Structure." In Ronald
                             Cohen and John Middleton, eds., *Compara-
                             tive Political Systems,* Garden City, N.Y.:
                             Natural History Press.

Murdock, George Peter   "Correlations of Matrilineal and Patrilineal
1937   Institutions." In G. P. Murdock, ed., *Studies
                             in the Science of Society.* New Haven: Yale
                             University Press.

1949   *Social Structure.* New York: The Macmillan
                             Company.

Naroll, Raoul   "What Have We Learned from Cross-Cultural
                             Surveys?" *American Anthropologist,* Vol. 72.

Parsons, Talcott   *Essays on Sociological Theory.* Glencoe, Il-
1954   linois: The Free Press.

Polanyi, Karl,   *Trade and Market in the Early Empires.*
Arensberg, Conrad M. and   Glencoe, Illinois: The Free Press.
Pearson, Harry W.
1957

Resek, Carl   *Lewis Henry Morgan: American Scholar.* Chi-
1960   cago: University of Chicago Press.

Rörig, Fritz   *The Medieval Town.* Berkeley: University of
1967   California Press.

Sahlins, Marshall   *Social Stratification in Polynesia.* Seattle:
1958   University of Washington Press.

1968   *Tribesmen.* Foundations of Modern Anthro-
                             pology Series, Englewood Cliffs, N.J.: Pren-
                             tice-Hall.

Sahlins, Marshall and   *Evolution and Culture.* Ann Arbor: University
Service, Elman   of Michigan Press.
1960

Schneider, David and   Eds., *Matrilineal Kinship.* Berkeley: Univer-
Gough, Kathleen   sity of California Press.
1961

Semenov, Iu. I   "Group Marriage, Its Nature and Role in
1964   the Evolution of a Family and Marital Rela-
                             tions." *Proceedings of the 7th International
                             Congress of Anthropological and Ethnolog-
                             ical Sciences,* Moscow, Vol. IV.

1965   "The Doctrine of Morgan, Marxism and Contemporary Ethnography." *Soviet Anthropology and Archeology,* Vol. IV, No. 2. New York: International Arts and Sciences Press.

Service, Elman R.
1962   *Primitive Social Organization: An Evolutionary Perspective.* New York: Random House.

1963   *Profiles in Ethnology.* New York: Harper and Brothers.

1966   *The Hunters.* Englewood Cliffs, N.J.: Prentice-Hall.

Slater, Marian Kreiselman
1959   "Ecological Factors in the Origin of Incest." *American Anthropologist,* Vol. 61.

Soviet Studies in History
1966   Vol. IV, No. 4. New York: International Arts and Sciences Press.

Speck, Frank G.
1926   "Land Ownership among Hunting Peoples in Primitive America and the World's Marginal Areas." *Twenty-Second International Congress of Americanists,* Vol. 2.

Speck, Frank G. and Eiseley, Loren
1939   "The Significance of the Hunting Territory Systems of the Algonkian in Social Theory." *American Anthropologist,* Vol. 41.

1942   "Montagnais-Naskapi Bands and Family Hunting Districts of the Central and Southern Labrador Peninsula." *Proceedings of the American Philosophical Society,* Vol. 85.

Steward, Julian H.
1941   "Determinism in Primitive Society?" *Scientific Monthly,* Vol. 53.

1955   *Theory of Culture Change.* Urbana: University of Illinois Press.

Tax, Sol
1960   Ed., *Evolution After Darwin, Vol. II (The Evolution of Man).* Chicago: University of Chicago Press.

Thomas, Elizabeth Marshall
1959   *The Harmless People.* New York: Alfred A. Knopf.

Thompson, George
1949   *Studies in Ancient Greek Society, Vol. I (The Prehistoric Aegean).* New York: International Publishers.

1955   *Studies in Ancient Greek Society, Vol. II (The First Philosophers).* London: Lawrence & Wishart.

Thwaites, R. G.
1906   Ed., *The Jesuit Relations and Allied Documents.* 71 vols. Cleveland: The Burrows Brothers Co.

Turnbull, Colin
1968
The Forest People. New York: Simon & Schuster.

Washburn, Sherwood L.
1960
"Tools and Human Evolution." *Scientific-American,* September. Scientific American Offprint No. 601.

1961
Ed., *Social Life of Early Man,* Chicago: Aldine Publishing Co.

Washburne, Heluiz Chandler
1959
Land of the Good Shadows, the Life Story of Anauta, an Eskimo Woman. New York: Alfred A. Knopf.

White, Leslie A.
1945
"Diffusion vs. Evolution: An Anti-Evolutionist Fallacy." *American Anthropologist,* Vol. 47.

1947
"Evolutionism in Cultural Anthropology: A Rejoinder." *American Anthropologist,* Vol. 49.

1949
The Science of Culture. New York: Farrar, Straus & Company.

1959
The Evolution of Culture. New York: McGraw-Hill.

Whiting, John,
Child, W. M. and I. L.
1953
Child Training and Personality: A Cross-Cultural Study. New Haven: Yale University Press.

Wittfogel, Karl
1957
Oriental Despotism: A Comparative Study of Total Power. New Haven: Yale University Press.

Wolf, Eric R.
1959
Sons of the Shaking Earth. Chicago: University of Chicago Press.

NAME INDEX

Adams, Robert L., 52*ff*

Aeschylus (525-456 B.C.), "the father of Greek tragedy," 76, 126, 167

Agassiz, J. Louis R. (1807-73), French-American naturalist, 115

Alexander the Great (356-23 B.C.), 123

Ammianus, Marcellinus (330-400), historian of Rome, 133, 155

Anacreaon (VI century B.C.), Greek lyrical poet, 140

Anaxandridas (VII-VI centuries B.C.), king of ancient Sparta, 126

Appius Claudius (V century B.C.), Roman statesman, reputed to be author of the oldest Roman code of laws known as the Twelve Tables, 184

Ardrey, Robert, 248

Aristides (535-467 B.C.), Greek statesman and military leader, 178

Ariston (VII-VI centuries B.C.), king of ancient Sparta, 126

Aristophanes (450-335 B.C.), Greek writer of comedies, 127

Aristotle (384-22 B.C.), Greek philosopher, 169

Augustus (63 B.C.-14 A.D.), first Roman emperor, 183, 207

Averkieva, Iu. P., Soviet ethnologist, 20*n*, 29*n*, 32*n*

Bachofen, Johann J. (1815-87), Swiss jurist, historian and archeologist, 74*ff*, 84, 97*n*, 105*n*, 106, 113, 115*ff*, 120, 144

Bancroft, Hubert H. (1832-1918), ethnologist, 100, 14*f*, 218*n*

Bang, K. D. (1822-98), Norwegian historian of literature, 198

Becker, Wilhelm A. (1796-1846), German archeologist, 163

Bede the Venerable (674-735), English theologian, 195

Benedict, Ruth F. (1887-1948), American anthropologist, 22

Bismarck, Otto von (1815-98), chancellor of Germany, 127, 232*f*

Bleichröder, Gerson (1822-93), head of a Berlin bank of that name, 232

Boas, Franz (1858-1942), American anthropologist, 12, 16

Bohannan, Paul, American anthropologist, 48*n*

Briffault, Robert, 37

Bugge, Sophus (1833-1907), Norwegian philologist, 198

Caesar, Julius (100-44 B.C.), 82, 92, 105, 153, 194, 196, 200*ff*, 206

Carneiro, Robert L., American anthropologist, 50*n*, 59*n*

Charlemagne (742-814), king of the Franks, Roman emperor and founder of the "Holy Empire of the German Nation," 213*ff*

Childe, V. Gordon, British archeologist, 17, 54

Civilis, Julius (I century A.D.), leader of the rebellion of the Batavians and other Germanic tribes against Roman rule in 68 A.D., 199

Cleisthenes (VI century B.C.), Athenian statesman, 179

Comte, Auguste (1798-1857), French sociologist, 8

Condorcet, Marquis de (1743-94), French historian, 8

Cooley, Horton, American social-psychologist, 22

Cunow, Heinrich (1862-1936), German ethnologist, 123

Cuvier, Georges, Baron de (1769-1832), French natural scientist, 96

Danilova, L. V., Soviet ethnologist, 53

Darwin, Charles R. (1809-82), 10, 83, 246*f*

Demosthenes (384-22 B.C.), Greek statesman and orator, 162

Dicaearchus (IV century B.C.), Greek historian and geographer, 163

Diodorus, Siculus (I century B.C.), Greek historian, author of the 40-volume "Historical Library," 198n, 206

Dionysium (I century B.C.), Greek writer of Roman history, 166f

Dureau de la Malle, Adolphe (1777-1857), French economist and historian, 190

Durkheim, Emile (1858-1917), French sociologist, 22

Espinas, Alfred V. (1844-1922), French biologist and sociologist, 98f

Euripides (480-06 B.C.), writer of Greek tragedies, 127

Ferdinand the Catholic (1452-1516), king of Castile and Aragon, 116

Fison, Lorimer (1832-1907), author (with Alfred W. Howitt) of *Group Marriage among the Australian Aborigines,* 107, 109

Fourier, Charles (1772-1837), French utopian Socialist, 84, 135, 216, 236n

Freeman, Edward A. (1823-92), English historian, 72

Freud, Sigmund (1856-1939), Austrian psychiatrist, founder of psychoanalysis, 22

Fried, Morton H., American anthropologist, 20, 48, 50

Fustel de Coulanges, Numa Denis (1830-89), French historian, 166

Gaius (II century A.D.), Roman jurist, 121

Giraud-Teulon, Alexis, Franco-Swiss historian, 82, 85, 98f, 125

Gladstone, William E. (1809-98), 167

Godelier, Maurice, French anthropologist, 53

Goethe, Johann Wolfgang, von (1749-1832), 102n

Goodale, Jane C., 38

Gregory of Tours (539-94), bishop, theologian and historian, 200

Grimm, Jakob (1785-1863), German philologist, 196

Grote, George (1794-1871), English historian, 162ff

Harris, Marvin, American anthropologist, 18n, 61ff

Hegel, Georg W. F. (1770-1831), 229

Herod, King of Judea (37 B.C.-4 A.D.), 189

Herodotus (484-25 B.C.), ancient Greek historian, 105, 127

Heusler, Andreas (1834-1921), Swiss jurist, 123

Hickerson, Harold, 20n

Hobhouse, L. T., 35n

Hogbin, Ian, 40

Homer (IX century B.C.), reputed author of the *Iliad* and the *Odyssey,* 92, 126, 165, 167, 169

Howitt, Alfred W. (1830-1908), see Lorimer Fison, 109

Hughes, Charles C., 23

Huschke, Georg P. E. (1830-1909), German writer on the history of law, 187

Irminon (IX century), Frankish Benedictine monk, 214

Jenness, Diamond, Canadian anthropologist, 19

Kaberry, Phyllis M., 37

Kaye, John W. (1814-76), English ethnologist, 106

Klemm, Gustave, 8

Kovalevsky, Maxim (1851-1916), Russian ethnographist and sociologist, 120f, 122, 192, 196, 201f

Krader, Lawrence, 48n

Lancaster, Jane B., 247n

Landes, Ruth, 24

Lange, Ludwig (1825-85), German philologist and historian, 187

Lantis, Margaret, 38

Latham, Robert Gordon (1812-1888), English philologist and ethnographist, 79

0rk?

Sugenheim, Samuel (1811-77), German historian, 116

Tacitus (55-120), Roman historian, 72, 82, 92, 155, 197*ff*

Tarquinius Superbus (reigned 534-10 B.C.), seventh king of Rome. After he was deposed, Rome became a republic, 189, 191

Theocritus (III century B.C.), Greek poet, 140

Thucydides (471-01 B.C.), Greek historian, author of *The Peloponnesian War*, 169

Thwaites, R. G., 38

Tiberius (42 B.C.-37 A.D.), emperor of Rome, 189n

Tylor, Edward B. (1832-1917), English anthropologist and ethnologist, 75

Ulfilas (310-83), first bishop of the Goths, invented the Gothic alphabet and translated the Bible into Gothic, 189n

Varus, P. Quinctilius (died IX century A.D.), Roman consul in Germany, 183

Vico, Giovanni B. (1668-1744), Italian philosopher and jurist, 8

Wachsmuth, Ernst, W. G. (1784-1886), German historian, 127

Waitz, Georg (1813-86), German historian, 201

Washburn, Sherwood L., 246*f*

Washburne, Heluiz C., 38

Watson, John F. (1827-92), English ethnologist, 106

Westermarck, Edward A. (1862-1939), Finnish anthropologist, 98, 101, 114

White, Leslie, American anthropologist, 17

Wittfogel, Karl, 54n

Wolfram, von Eschenbach (1170-1220), German poet, 133

Wright, Ashur (1803-75), a missionary among the Iroquois, a collaborator with Morgan, 113

Yanchuk, Nikolai (1859-1921), Russian ethnographer, 239

Zurita, Alonso de (1500-64), Spanish historian, one of the first explorers of ancient Mexico, 123

SUBJECT INDEX

Adaptation, functional, 10
Adoption, 118, 150, 163, 184
Adultery, 111*f*, 125*f*, 129*f*, 131, 133*f*, 138, 140, 193, 200
Africa, 21, 95, 159
Agriculture, 12*f*, 93, 258; among the Athenians, 175; in Roman Empire, 209; separation of handicraft from, 222, 224, 227
Algonkians, 23*f*, 58
Alphabet, 13, 92
American Indians, and gens, 9, 19*ff*, 25, 217*f*; and mother right and father right, 119*f*; and treatment of prisoners, 118; confederation of, 156; council and military organization of, 155; gentile organization of, 151*ff*, 162; offices and religion of, 154; system of consanguinity among, 94*f*, 104*ff*, 111*ff*; *see also* Iroquois
Ancestor, gentile, 148, 164, 165
Animal mating and societies, 97*ff*
Anthropoid apes, 98, 100
Anthropology, Boasian school of, 18; English school of, 74, 80, 83*f*, 147
Arapesh, 27
Archaelogy, 16*f*, 29, 58, 66
Archons, 163, 180
Aristocracy, at beginning of civilization, 226*ff*; during barbarism, 223; gentile, 168*f*; in Athenian state, 169, 171*ff*, 178*f*; German, 204*f*, 212*f*; Roman, 189
Aryans and Semites, 91, 118, 122, 218
Asian mode of production, *see* Oriental mode of production
Assemblies, German, 203, 212*f*; Greek, 166*ff*, 171, 177, 180; Iroquois, 151, 155; Roman, 188*ff*; Welsh, 193
Australian oborigine, 11, 21, 30, 38, 57
Aztecs, 11, 51

Barbarism, 10, 13, 17*n*, 89*ff*

Basileus, 163, 167*ff*, 169*n*, 189, 223
Black people, 45
Blood revenge, 150, 159, 165, 195, 200, 240
Bonapartism, 231
Britons, 82, 105
Burial, 151*f*, 162, 183

Cannibalism, 88, 91, 257
Capital, 71, 161*n*, 217
Capital punishment, 159, 204
Capitalist class, 137, 231*f*
Capitalist production, 138, 142, 144*f*
Capitalist property, 218
Cattle-raising, 89*ff*, 117*f*, 209, 219, 224, 258
Celts, family communities, 123; gens, 192*ff*
Chiefs, American Indian, 113, 148, 151; Gentile, 151; German, 204*f*; Greek, 158, 163, 166; Irish, 194; Scottish, 195; *see also Basileus;* Rex; Sachems
Children, care of, 106; custody of, 112, 192; sale of, 173, 211
China, 53
Christianity, 209*f*
Church patronage, 210, 213, 235
Civil War, 45
Civilization, 10, 52*ff*, 92*f*, 174; Arabic, 9; and class antagonisms, 234*ff*; and monogamy, 125, 128, 235; and prostitution, 130; rise of, 160*f*, 224*ff*, 233*ff*
Clan, 113, 194, 195
Classes, among the Greeks, 170, 176*ff*; and gentile constitution, 227; and marriage, 144; and the state, 228*ff*; in Rome, 189*ff*; rise of, 72, 220; struggle between, 129, 131, 229*f*, 234*f*
Classifactory system; *see* Consanguinity; Family; Gens
Code Napoleon, 125, 130

derivation of word, 147, 196; German, 196*ff*, 201, 212, 215; Gilyak, 239; Greek, 162*ff*, 175*f*; Irish, 194; Iroquois, 147*ff*; misunderstanding of, 163*f*; origin of, 103, 106*ff*, 147*f*, 150; Roman, 182*ff*; Scotland, 195

Geographical factors, 89*ff*

German gens, 196*ff*; state, 206*ff*

German Ideology, The, 10, 129*n*

Germanic migrations, 196

Gilyaks, 239*ff*

Greek gens, 162*ff*; family and position of women in, 125*ff*; marriage in, 127*f*

Group marriage, among American Indians, 106; among Britons, 105; and men, 116, 137*f*; and pairing marriage, 30, 110*f*; and polyandry, 125; Australian, 106*ff*; Gilyaks and, 239*ff*; Hawaiian and, 81, 107

Handicrafts, and rise of Athenian state, 175, 178; in Greek gens, 166; in India, 218; in Roman Empire, 209; separation from agriculture, 222*f*, 227

Hawaii, punaluan family in, 26, 103*ff*; system of consanguinity in, 95*ff*, 103*f*

Herd, the, 98*ff*

Hetaerism, Bachofen's use of term, 75, 97*n*, 116; Morgan's use of, 129

Hetairai, 127*f*

Historicism, 16

Holy Roman Empire, 210*n*

Horticulture, 25, 30, 90*f*, 209, 219

Hospitality, 200 240*f*

House-building, 89*f*

Household communities, 124, 196, 200*ff*, 223

Housekeeping, 43, 113, 137, 139, 218

Hunting, 12, 88, 118, 218

Idealism, 63*f*, 245

Illegitimacy, 116, 193

Inca, 51, 55

Incest, 100, 102*n*, 104, 107; *see also* Inbreeding; Marriage prohibitions, Natural selection

Industry; *see* Commerce; Production

Infanticide, 79

Inheritance, among Germans, 204; among Irish, 195; among Iroquois, 149*f*; among Romans, 121, 182*f*, 186*f*; and father right, 119*ff*; and freedom of choice in marriage, 127*ff*; and mother right, 106; in Greek gens, 162

Ireland, 123, 192, 195*n*

Irish gens, 194

Iron, 92, 203, 220, 222

Iroquois, confederation of, 8, 11, 34, 47*f*, 156*ff*, 160*f*; gens, 147*ff*; system of consanguinity among, 94*ff*, 111

Jealousy, 99*ff*

Jus primae noctis, 116, 193, 195

Kings and kingship, 168*f*, 189*n*, 197, 203*f*, 212*f*, 223; *see also Basileus;* Rex Kinship; *see* Consanguinity

Kinship and residence, 72, 176, 180, 191, 212, 227, 229

Labor, compulsory, 214*f*

Labor power, 118, 222, 234

Land ownership, and the rise of civilization, 226, 235; during barbarism, 222*f*, 226; in Athenian state, 173*f*, 177*f*; in German gens, 200*f*; in German state, 211*f*, 214; in Irish gens, 194; in Roman gens, 189*ff*; *see also* Command land; Latifundia

Language, 87, 156, 207, 246, 254

Latifundia, 209*f*, 214

Latin dialects, 207

Law, 135*ff*, 143*f*, 173, 192*ff*, 235*n*; comparative, 85, 120*ff*, 136

Literature, 133*ff*

Love, and abolition of capitalism, 144*ff*; and proletariat, 135, 139, 144; and rise of monogamy, 112, 126, 132*ff*; in antiquity, 139*f*; middle ages, 140; modern, 142*ff*

Machinery, 236

Mark community, 123*f*, 158, 196, 211, 216, 229; *see also* Village community

Marriage, and property, 142; bourgeois, 134*f*, 142*ff*; by capture, 78, 110, 112; by purchase, 112, 116,